CHINA BOUND

HEILONGJIANG
(HEILUNGKIANG)

Harbin
(Harbin)

Urumqi
(Urumchi)

JILIN
(KIRIN)

XINJIANG
(SINKIANG)

LIAONING   Shenyang
(LIAONING)   (Shenyang; Mukden)

GANSU
(KANSU)

NEI MONGGOL
(INNER MONGOLIA)

NINGXIA
(NINGSIA)

Bejing (Peking)

HEBEI   Tianjin (Tientsin)
(HOPEH)

QINGHAI
(TSINGHAI)

Lanzhou
(Lanchow)

SHANXI
(SHANSI)

Jinan
(Tsinan) Qingdao (Tsingtao)

SHANDONG (SHANTUNG)

Xi'an
(Sian)

XIZANG
(TIBET)

Lhasa
(Lhasa)

SHAANXI
(SHENSI)

HENAN
(HONAN)

JIANGSU
(KIANGSU)

Nanjing (Nanking)

SICHUAN
(SZECHWAN)

HUBEI
(HUPEH)

ANHUI
(ANHWEI)

SHANGHAI (SHANGHAI)

Chengdu (Ch'eng-tu)

Wuhan
(Wu-han)

Hangzhou (Hangchow)

Chongqing
(Chungking)

ZHEJIANG
(CHEKIANG)

JIANGXI
(KIANGSI)

GUIZHOU
(KWEICHOW)

HUNAN
(HUNAN)

FUJIAN
(FUKIEN)

Fuzhou
(Foochow)

Kunming
(K'un-ming)

YUNNAN
(YUNNAN)

GUANGXI
(KWANGSI)

GUANGDONG
(KWANGTUNG)

TAIWAN

Nanning
(Nan-ning)

Guangzhou
(Canton)

(HAINAN)

Size of China compared
to the continental United States

CHINA BOUND

A Guide to Academic Life

and Work in the PRC

Revised

Anne F. Thurston
with
Karen Turner-Gottschang and Linda A. Reed

for the Committee on Scholarly Communication with China

American Council of Learned Societies
National Academy of Sciences
Social Science Research Council

NATIONAL ACADEMY PRESS
Washington, D.C. 1994

NATIONAL ACADEMY PRESS • 2101 Constitution Avenue, NW • Washington, DC 20418

NOTICE: The project that is the subject of this publication was sponsored by the Committee on Scholarly Communication with China (formerly the Committee on Scholarly Communication with the People's Republic of China). It is a revised edition of *China Bound: A Guide to Academic Life and Work in the PRC*, published in 1987.

The Committee on Scholarly Communication with China (CSCC) is jointly sponsored by the American Council of Learned Societies, the National Academy of Sciences, and the Social Science Research Council.

Since the normalization of diplomatic relations between the United States and China in 1979, the CSCC has developed programs with the Chinese Academy of Sciences, the Chinese Academy of Social Sciences, and the State Education Commission, in addition to those with the China Association for Science and Technology, with whom the CSCC began exchanges in 1972. Current activities include a program for American graduate students and postdoctoral scholars to carry out long-term study or research in affiliation with Chinese universities and research institutes; a fellowship program for Chinese scholars to conduct research in the United States; and field development and training programs in archaeology, economics, international relations, law, library science, and sociology.

This publication was supported by grants from the National Science Foundation and the Andrew W. Mellon Foundation.

The accuracy of the information presented and the views expressed in this publication are the responsibility of the authors and not the sponsoring organizations.

Library of Congress Cataloging-in-Publication Data

Thurston, Anne F.
    China bound : a guide to academic life and work in the PRC /
revised by Anne F. Thurston ; with Karen Turner-Gottschang and Linda
A. Reed.
      p. cm.
    "For the Committee on Scholarly Communication with China."
    Includes bibliographical references and index.
    ISBN 0-309-04932-6
    1. Foreign study—China. 2. American students—China.
3. Teachers, Foreign—China. 4. China—Description and travel.
I. Turner-Gottschang, Karen. II. Reed, Linda A. III. Committee on
Scholarly Communication with the People's Republic of China (U.S.)
IV. Title.
LB2376.3.C6T48   1994
370.19'6—dc20   94-736
                                                 CIP

The calligraphy appearing in the text was kindly prepared by Fu Shen, Curator of Chinese Art, Freer Gallery of Art of the Smithsonian Institution, Washington, D.C. The cover photograph is by Bernard Van Leer.

Acknowledgments

The author wishes to thank the following individuals for reading and commenting on this manuscript:

Mark Bender, Ohio State University
Mary Bullock, Woodrow Wilson International Center for Scholars
Joan Carey, Committee on Scholarly Communication with China
Keith Clemenger, Committee on Scholarly Communication with China
Richard Connor, Texas A&M University
Deborah Davis, Yale University
James Feinerman, Committee on Scholarly Communication with China
Robert Geyer, Committee on Scholarly Communication with China
James Hargett, State University of New York at Albany
Alice Hogan, National Science Foundation
Mary Beth Kennedy, ICF Incorporated
Scott Kennedy, The Brookings Institution
Megan Klose, Committee on Scholarly Communication with China
Beryl Leach, The World Bank
John Olsen, University of Arizona
Leo Orleans, Library of Congress
Tony Reese, Yale-China Association
Scott Rozelle, Stanford University
David Shambaugh, University of London
Audrey Spiro, independent scholar
Karen Turner-Gottschang, Holy Cross College
Cameron Wake, University of New Hampshire
Andrew Walder, Harvard University
Haynie Wheeler, Yale-China Association
Meng Yang, Embassy of the People's Republic of China, Washington, D.C.

ACKNOWLEDGMENTS

The author also wishes to thank Mary Ernst of the Council on International Exchange of Scholars and William Shine at the United States Information Agency for providing information and reports from Fulbright lecturers.

This publication was supported with funding from the U.S. National Science Foundation and the Andrew W. Mellon Foundation.

Preface

China Bound is a guidebook for American students, teachers, and researchers who plan to live and work in China. Its purpose is to help make the experience there as rich and rewarding as possible.

The book introduces some of the available research and teaching opportunities and study programs. It explains the structure of China's academic institutions and relates the experiences of other Americans who have worked within them. It discusses the range of opportunities and suggests relevant strategies for archival and field research and collaborative projects in scientific laboratories. It provides advice ranging from preparation for departure to daily life in China—from bringing and setting up a computer to handling a medical emergency and how to stay healthy and fit. *China Bound* will be most useful to those who are going for the first time, but "old China hands" should find much of practical value as well.

Americans' fascination with China is as old as the United States, and the "opening up" that began in 1979 has provided hundreds of thousands of Americans with the opportunity to experience China first-hand. Thousands of U.S. scholars, students, and teachers have resided in China, and their opportunity to learn about China from the inside has been unique. As many have returned to relate those experiences or publish their research results, our understanding of China has increased.

Harold Isaacs, writing between 1949 and 1979, when only a handful of Americans were able to visit, noted a curious ambivalence in the American fascination with China—admiration coupled with fear, the China of Marco Polo contradicted by the China of Genghis Khan, the world's oldest civilization ruled by emperors with a capacity for cruelty. "In the long history of our associations with China, these two sets of images rise and fall, move in and out of the center of people's minds over time, never wholly displacing each other, always coexisting, each ready to emerge at the fresh call of circumstance," he wrote.

The cycle of ambivalence that Isaacs describes has already been repeated in the years since the economic reforms of the 1980s encouraged more outsiders to live and work in China. The thrill of being able to live and work in China again was followed by horror over the Tiananmen Square tragedy of June 1989; the attraction we have for the Chinese people has been coupled with frustration over the Chinese bureaucracy; our excitement at the speed of China's economic development has been accompanied by distress over growing corruption; our hope for China's modernization has carried with it a deep concern that too much of the past is being destroyed.

Isaacs also discovered that those who liked China most were those who knew it best. And what Americans liked best, in addition to China's rich history and culture, were the Chinese people. This is true today as well. After a brief hiatus in the wake of Tiananmen, American researchers, students, and teachers have returned to China to live, work, and learn. Americans going today, like those who have gone before, are likely to find their work—whether teaching, studying, or conducting research—to be deeply satisfying—indeed, among the richest and most rewarding of their lives. Many will have made lifelong Chinese friends—colleagues and research collaborators, fellow students, fellow teachers, or students taught, or the person met by chance encounter on a train. They will have been witnesses to a remarkable period in China's own history.

China Bound was first published in 1981 shortly after academic exchanges were renewed; it was rewritten in 1987 by Linda Reed and Karen Turner-Gottschang. But China continues to change and, by 1992, many people who knew how valuable earlier editions of *China Bound* had been concluded that the time had come for another update. Kathlin Smith at the Committee on Scholarly Communication with China has guided the endeavor from its inception—securing funding, providing background materials, and supervising the preparation of the manuscript with unfailing good humor and efficiency. She has been assisted by three hardworking interns: Dan Ewing, from the Johns Hopkins University; S. Quinn Hanzel, from Georgetown University; and Richard Michael Victorio, also from Georgetown University. The book could not have been done without their contributions and assistance. My thanks to them all.

This newly revised edition reflects not only changes in China but also the increasingly diverse experiences of American students, teachers, and researchers who have lived there. Both the preface and the section on research are completely new. In making these revisions, I have spoken to dozens of Americans who have lived in China as researchers, students, and teachers, and I have read numerous reports that researchers have written for the Committee on Scholarly Communication with China (CSCC) as well as reports from many professors in the Fulbright program. The CSCC's *China Exchange News* has provided a wealth of information. In December 1992, I visited China and met with researchers, teachers, and students. I also have conducted research in China and lived for five years in Beijing. And I drew on many personal accounts in making these revisions. Although most people are not thanked by name, I would like to express my appreciation to everyone with whom I have spoken and whose accounts I have read, while noting, with apologies, that there is little way to do them justice here. Each individual's experience in China is unique, and the picture that emerges is one of great diversity. This guidebook attempts to reflect that diversity. At the same time, it also attempts to distill from many different experiences a core of advice for anyone planning to study, teach, or conduct research in China. The people consulted for this revision shared their experiences with the hope that others could benefit from them.

ANNE F. THURSTON

November 1993

Contents

1. Research, Study, and Teaching in China / 1

Research Fellowships and Grants / 1
  Social Sciences and Humanities / 2
  Sciences / 2
  Dissertation Research / 3
Study / 3
  U.S. University-Sponsored Programs / 4
  Applying to Chinese Universities / 4
  Hopkins-Nanjing Center / 4
Teaching / 5
  U.S.-Sponsored Programs / 5
  Chinese-Sponsored Opportunities / 6
Spouses / 7

2. Preparing for the Trip / 8

Leaving the United States / 9
  Passports and Visas / 9
  Inviting Relatives to China / 12
  Health Preparations / 12
  Medical Insurance / 16
  Medications and Toiletries / 17
  Money, Banking, and Credit Cards / 18
  Customs Regulations / 20
  Baggage and Shipping / 23
  Income Taxes / 24

Suggested Reading / 24
Preparing for Daily Life / 24
Clothing / 26
Food and Cooking Supplies / 29
Electrical Appliances / 30
Office Equipment / 31
Radios and Tape Recorders / 35
Cameras and Film / 35
Bicycles / 37
I.D. Photos / 37
Reading Material / 37
Games / 38
Gifts / 38
Preparing for Professional Life / 39
Researchers / 40
Teachers / 42

3. Settling In / 46

Arriving in China / 46
The Tenor of Life in China / 48
The Work Unit / 48
The Foreign Affairs Office / 51
The Quality of Life / 53
Personal Relationships / 57
Friendship / 57
Guanxi / 58
Reciprocity / 60
Ritual / 60
Legality and Ethics / 65
The Foreign Community / 68
Housing / 69
Student Dormitories / 72
Campus Apartments / 74
Hotels / 75
Arrangements for Accompanying Spouses and Children / 77
The Academic Calendar / 81

4. Research / 83

The Research Climate / 83
Laying the Groundwork for Research / 85
Implementing Your Plan / 85
The Importance of Your Host Unit / 85
The Research Proposal / 89

Fees / 91
Finalizing a Plan / 91
Archival Research / 92
Research Affiliation / 93
Use of Collections / 94
Fees / 95
Library Rules / 96
Library Hours / 97
Fieldwork / 97
Costs / 100
Placement in the Field / 102
The Research Team / 102
The Research Site / 105
Equipment and Supplies / 107
Survey Research / 109
Laboratory Research / 110
Short-term Academic Visits / 112
Preparations / 113
Academic Conferences / 114

5. Teaching / 115

The Bureaucratic Structure / 117
Workloads / 119
Students / 120
English Language Ability / 121
Class Participation / 122
Students' Prior Background / 123
Homework and Workloads / 123
The Class Monitor and Group Pressure / 123
Student-Teacher Relationships / 124
Plagiarism and "Cheating" / 124
Working Conditions / 124
Professional Relationships / 125
Social Relationships / 126
Chinese Language Lessons / 128
General Adjustment Advice / 128

6. Study / 130

American-Sponsored Programs / 130
Chinese-Language Institutes / 132
Attending a Chinese University / 133
Student Life / 134
Classes / 136

7. Services Available / 138

The U.S. Embassy and Consulates / 138
Postal Services / 140
Currency and Banking / 142
Electronic Mail, Fax, and Telex Facilities / 143
The Telephone / 144
Medical Care / 145
Urban Transportation / 147
Recreation and Entertainment / 148
Internal Travel / 149

8. Leaving China / 153

Glossary of Chinese Terms / 155

Appendixes

A. Funding for Graduate and Postdoctoral Research in China / 159
B. Language Study Programs in the People's Republic of China / 173
C. Colleges and Universities Accepting Direct Application from Foreign Students / 177
D. General Guidelines for Direct Application to a Chinese College or University as a Self-Sponsored Student and Excerpts from "Regulations Concerning the Admission of Foreign Students in Chinese Schools (1986)" / 184
E. Visa Application for Foreigners Wishing to Study in China / 194
F. The People's Republic of China Visa Application Form / 195
G. Physical Examination Record for Foreigners / 196
H. Organizations Sponsoring English Teachers in China / 198
I. Application for Teaching Positions in China / 201
J. Sample Contract for Teachers / 205
K. American Express Emergency Check Cashing Locations / 211
L. Approximate Costs of Hotel Rooms, Food, Internal Travel, Services, Clothing, and Medical Care, Fall 1993 / 214
M. Selected Reading List and References / 220
N. Trial Procedures for Foreign Organizations and Individuals to Use Chinese Archives / 225
O. Packing it in: Preparing for Fieldwork in the PRC / 227
P. Student Advisory Resource Centers and General Reference Holdings / 233
Q. Protocol Between the Government of the United States of America and the Government of the People's Republic of China for Cooperation in Educational Exchanges / 239

Index / 243

CHINA BOUND

1. Research, Study, and Teaching in China

Diverse opportunities exist for U.S. students, scholars, and teachers who want to live and work in China. Programs abound for undergraduates, recent college graduates with a strong sense of adventure and minimal training in the Chinese language, well-published senior scholars of Chinese history, field scientists with no previous experience in China, and established professors who want to spend a year teaching abroad. Locales open to foreigners wishing to study, teach, and conduct research are also diverse, from the sophisticated, increasingly Western-influenced cities of Beijing, Shanghai, and Guangzhou (Canton) to inland cities, the remote Tibetan Plateau, or a village in one of China's ethnic minority regions.

This chapter discusses relevant programs and offers advice for accompanying spouses or friends. Subsequent chapters explain how to prepare for life in China, how to set up there, what services are available, and even how to leave. Chapters on research, study, and teaching relate the experiences of others who have already been to China, offering advice on what to expect and how to reach your goals. Supplemental sources are noted throughout the book, and their citations may be found in References, Appendix M.

Below are suggestions for learning more about the programs available to Americans.

RESEARCH FELLOWSHIPS AND GRANTS

Research fellowships are available from U.S. sources for postdoctoral and established scholars in the sciences, social sciences, and humanities as well as for advanced graduate students in the social sciences and humanities. Fewer advanced graduate students in scientific disciplines conduct research in China, although several have done so. Chapter 4 examines the types of research being done in China today—archival, scientific, and fieldwork—and gives advice about arranging for and carrying out research projects.

SOCIAL SCIENCES AND HUMANITIES   The Committee on Scholarly Communication with China (CSCC), formerly the Committee on Scholarly Communication with the People's Republic of China (CSCPRC), has much experience placing American social scientists and humanists in China. Its competitive National Program for Advanced Study and Research in China is still the preferred route for many scholars. Because it operates an office in Beijing to facilitate the work of the people it funds, scholars in the program receive not only financial support but help in placement as well. Further information about the research program for scholars may be obtained from:

Committee on Scholarly Communication with China
1055 Thomas Jefferson Street, NW
Suite 2013
Washington, DC 20007

The Henry Luce Foundation sponsors a United States-China Cooperative Research Program "to encourage sustained joint research by American and Chinese scholars on significant topics in the humanities and social sciences that will lead to an improved understanding of China." Cooperative projects normally involve two or more collaborators on both the Chinese and American sides, working together over a three-year period. Further information about the research program for scholars may be obtained from:

U.S.-China Cooperative Research Program
The Henry Luce Foundation, Inc.
111 West 50th Street
Room 3710
New York, NY 10020

In addition, most organizations funding social scientists and humanists will provide grants for research in China if you are able to make your own arrangements for placement. These include the National Endowment for the Humanities and the Joint Committee on Chinese Studies, sponsored by the American Council of Learned Societies and the Social Science Research Council. For a full description of possible funding sources and their addresses, see Appendix A.

SCIENCES   The U.S. National Science Foundation (NSF) continues to be a major source of funding for scientific research in China through its East Asia and Pacific Program and its diverse scientific programs, and it encourages collaborative research with Chinese scientists. The foundation encourages prospective applicants to contact program officers of the Division of International Programs directly at 703-306-1704. For application forms, contact the Forms and Publications unit at:

National Science Foundation
4201 Wilson Blvd.
Arlington, VA 22230
Internet: pubs@nsf.gov
Telephone: 703-306-1130

The National Geographic Society, Earthwatch, the World Wildlife Fund, and the Smithsonian Institution are other sources of research funding. A description of their programs and list of their addresses and telephone numbers appear in Appendix A. More than 30 governmental institutions in the United States have signed protocols with counterpart Chinese institutions, and a few of them also provide funding for nongovernment employees. Some applied scientists have received funding from private corporations with practical research interests in China.

DISSERTATION RESEARCH   There are several routes for students wishing to pursue dissertation research in the social sciences and humanities. Support for such research is offered by the graduate component of the National Program for Advanced Study and Research in China administered by the Committee on Scholarly Communication with China. Some universities and foundations also provide graduate student fellowships for research in China.

Few students in the natural sciences, however, have undertaken research in China, and most scientists interviewed for this book discourage such attempts unless you or your adviser have good contacts. Otherwise, the difficulties of starting out in China make this research too risky.

Finally, some students conduct dissertation-level research in China while attending language programs.

STUDY

Most Americans in China with academic interests are students, and most of them are studying the Chinese language. The number of Chinese-language programs organized by U.S. universities has proliferated in recent years. Programs are also offered directly by some Chinese universities and by at least one joint U.S.-China training center. The types of options available are discussed below.

U.S. UNIVERSITY-SPONSORED PROGRAMS   There is a range of summer, semester, or year-long programs organized by U.S. universities and conducted on Chinese university campuses with courses taught by Chinese faculty and supervised by U.S. faculty. Some of these programs are limited to students and faculty at the signatory school, but the programs are often flexible. Study-abroad offices at most universities maintain files and brochures on such programs. Appendix B lists many of them.

The Council on International Educational Exchange and China Educational Tours also sponsor several programs, some of which are for beginning students of Chinese and include field trips and courses in Chinese culture and history conducted in English. These organizations can be contacted at the following addresses:

Council on International Educational Exchange
205 East 42nd Street
New York, NY 10017

China Educational Tours
1110 Washington Street
Boston, MA 02124

APPLYING TO CHINESE UNIVERSITIES   Foreign students may apply directly to selected Chinese schools for study in a range of disciplines, including the Chinese language. Appendix C provides a list of colleges and universities that accept direct applications from foreign students.

The NAFSA Association of International Educators has recently published *Post-secondary Institutions of the People's Republic of China: A Complete Guide to Institutions of Higher Education in China*, which includes profiles of more than 1,200 Chinese postsecondary educational institutions. A full citation is provided in Appendix M. To order, contact:

NAFSA Association of International Educators
1875 Connecticut Avenue, Suite 1000
Washington, DC 20009
Telephone: 202-462-4811

HOPKINS-NANJING CENTER   Chinese and international students live together as roommates at the Johns Hopkins-Nanjing University Center for Chinese and American Studies. Chinese students study about the United States with American professors, and Americans learn about China from Chinese professors. Course work for Americans is in Chinese, and three years of language training is recommended for admission. The program is designed to provide an introduction to modern Chinese history and contemporary affairs. It is directed at people pursuing careers in government, communications, and nonprofit organizations, as well as graduate students pursuing an M.A. in modern Chinese history, politics, or economics. The address is:

Hopkins-Nanjing Program
School of Advanced International Studies
The Johns Hopkins University
1619 Massachusetts Ave., NW
Washington, DC 20036

Chapter 6 is devoted to a discussion of the student experience in China.

TEACHING

American teachers in China are almost as numerous as students. Most teach English, and opportunities have multiplied since 1979 and are available almost everywhere in China. In addition, China recruits U.S. faculty to teach in many areas important to economic development, such as science and technology, finance, banking, business management, law, and computer science. There are several ways to teach in China.

U.S.-SPONSORED PROGRAMS   The best-organized and best-funded program is the United States Information Agency's (USIA) Fulbright program, which recruits American Ph.D.s with at least five years of university-level teaching experience to teach American literature, economics, law, history, American studies, international relations and American politics, journalism, art history, and music at the graduate level at universities and other postsecondary institutions in China. For information on Fulbright lecturing programs, contact:

CIES
3400 International Drive, NW
Suite M-500
Washington, DC 20008
Telephone: 202-686-4023

The Peace Corps has also begun an English-language teaching program. The telephone book should list the number of the local Peace Corps office; the national office may be reached at 202-606-3886.

Beyond these programs, many American universities and exchange organizations have their own, which may be limited to their own students, faculty, alumni, members, or other participants. A list of some is included in Appendix H.

CHINESE-SPONSORED OPPORTUNITIES   Chinese academic institutions also hire teachers directly, most of whom teach English (both literature and English as a Second Language). Many Americans are also hired to teach in other areas important to China's economic development. The Chinese make a distinction between teaching as a "foreign expert" and teaching as a "foreign teacher." It is important to understand these distinctions before applying.

Foreign Experts   Foreign experts are expected to hold at least an M.A. degree, but most have Ph.D.s and hold a faculty position. The number of these positions available is determined by China's State Council, which provides funding for the positions. Payment includes both salary and benefits.

Almost all foreign experts are recruited from their home countries. It is difficult to be designated a foreign expert after arrival. Recruitment is usually done directly by the Chinese institution requesting the foreign expert. Salaries are determined by the applicant's professional credentials, experience, and record, and generally range from Y900 to Y2,500 a month. Well-known scholars, professors, and individuals with special skills may receive more. Housing and one-way international airfare are provided (round-trip airfare can often be negotiated), and stipends for travel within China are available. Salaries are paid in *renminbi*, the local currency, once a month (see p. 142 for a discussion of Chinese currency). If family (spouse and children under 12) accompany you to China, you are permitted to convert 30 percent of your salary into foreign currency. If you do not bring any family members, you may convert 50 percent of your salary.

Chinese institutions with staff familiar with your work and qualifications will be most likely to invite you as a foreign expert. University-to-university linkages provide a good avenue for such opportunities. Alternatively, you can initiate communication directly with a Chinese institution of higher education (see Appendix C) or with the Chinese Education Association for International Exchanges, at 37 Damucang Hutong, in Beijing.

In order to consider your request, an institution will require a copy of your curriculum vitae, including education, professional experience, and publications, as well as letters of recommendation and a health certificate.

Foreign Teachers   The guidelines for recruiting foreign teachers are flexible, but a B.A. is normally required. Most foreign teachers teach English, and most Chinese institutions prefer individuals with some experience teaching English as a Second Language. Given the current demand for English language teachers in China, however, and the wide range of courses language teachers are asked to teach, many institutions are hiring recent college graduates with no previous teaching experience. Foreign teachers are ordinarily recruited directly by Chinese schools or by local provincial or municipal departments or bureaus of education rather than through higher level administrative organizations. The positions are funded by the hiring institution. Often, the institution does not pay for international airfare to China. It is possible to find work as a foreign teacher after arriving in China. Salaries are usually lower than those of foreign experts, ranging from Y600-1,000 a month. The terms and arrangements are diverse but usually include free housing as well. Rules governing payment and benefits for foreign teachers are important, and people contemplating these programs should examine the sample contract for teachers in Appendix J. If you have been invited to teach in China, be sure to request a contract from your host institution that specifies details of your salary, housing, medical care, vacation time, excess baggage allowance, classroom teaching and office hours, and other requirements.

Individuals wanting to serve as foreign teachers in China may apply to one of the American agencies listed in Appendix H, or directly to the relevant college or university.

SPOUSES

Several opportunities are available for employment, particularly in English-language teaching, for accompanying spouses and friends, for whom the same advice applies as cited earlier in this chapter. If application is made through the Foreign Experts Bureau before leaving the United States, inquiries may also be made concerning the availability of work such as training young interpreters, doing editing or proofreading at the Foreign Languages Press, or writing articles for the *Xinhua* (New China) News Agency, *Beijing Review*, *China Reconstructs*, and other English-language publications produced in China.

Many spouses find positions as teachers after arriving in China. Colleges and universities often have positions available, and it is possible to apply directly to them. Other options include teaching language courses to Chinese employees of joint-venture hotels in larger cities, teaching at international schools, or working with foreign firms or international organizations operating in China. If a skill is of use to China's modernization program, such as a knowledge of computers, business, or the stock market, it is likely that, with a little effort, a position may be found. The groundwork should be laid before arrival in China.

2. Preparing for the Trip

The best advice for making a move to China is to be prepared. Preparation depends on type of employment, living arrangements, and length of stay. Clearly, a scientist who will camp for several months on the Tibetan Plateau should make different preparations than the Fulbright professor who will live in Beijing's Friendship Hotel. A young college graduate planning to teach conversational English and prepared to live on a shoestring will make different arrangements than the advanced graduate student carrying out dissertation research. Whether you will live in a dormitory room, a university apartment, or a guest house in the countryside; whether you will be in a big city, a small town, a rural area, or the wilderness; whether you will be alone or with spouse and children, and the type of institutional support available are all major factors determining how you prepare for the trip. The chapters on studying, teaching, and research provide advice germane to those situations. This chapter is devoted to advice that applies generally to everyone planning an extended stay.

The best general advice is to talk to people who have had a recent experience similar to the one you are about to have, particularly those who have been most recently in the place you are about to go. China is in a constant state of flux, and what was true two years ago may no longer be true today. The country, too, is remarkably diverse, and what holds true for Changchun (it is extremely cold in winter but heat is usually—though not always—plentiful) is not true of Chengdu (winters are mild but buildings are unheated and staying warm depends on the layers of clothing worn). The more you know about your destination, the type of employment, and the experiences of those who preceded you, the better prepared you will be.

8

LEAVING THE UNITED STATES

Sponsoring organizations in the United States or China generally provide detailed information on travel arrangements, visas, shipping procedures, methods of payment while abroad, and regulations and procedures governing specific cases. Because there is constant change in regulations, services, and procedures, it is advisable to seek the most current information on these matters from your sponsor. The following is a general guide to what to expect as a long-term resident. Of course, it is not a prescription relevant to every case.

PASSPORTS AND VISAS   U.S. citizens must have a valid passport. Passports may be obtained through a local passport office, which is located in the post office in smaller cities. It may take as much as six weeks to receive a passport after application has been made. If you already have a passport, be sure that it will not expire during your intended stay. A visa is required for entry into China and may be obtained from the visa section of the Embassy of the People's Republic of China in Washington, D.C., or from one of the Chinese consulates in San Francisco, New York, Houston, Chicago, or Los Angeles (addresses and telephone numbers are given below). The consulate, sponsor, or a large travel agency can provide the necessary forms. Copies of two standard forms are reproduced in Appendixes E and F. The application must be filled out in duplicate and mailed with the passport, two passport photos, and the visa fee. The cost of the visa depends on how quickly you want it and whether you request a single- or double-entry visa.

The Chinese government offers several types of visas. Researchers going for less than six months may obtain an ordinary tourist ("L") visa good for three months or short-term ("F") visa good for six months or less. It is now possible to get double-entry tourist visas if you plan to leave and return within the six-month period. Researchers and students going for longer than six months should get an "X" visa. Foreign experts or teachers planning to spend a year or more get a "Z" visa. The consulate will determine which visa is appropriate to the situation, often based on information provided by the Chinese host organization. If the wrong visa has been issued, it can be corrected in China for an additional fee. If your family is accompanying you, they will be issued a visa after the authorization for yours comes through. You will need to send the consulate your family members' passports and a letter of invitation from the host organization. An ordinary single-entry visa, with a two-week waiting period, is $10; one with a three-day waiting period is $20; and a 24-hour request costs $30. The visa section does not ordinarily accept checks; prepare to pay in cash or by money order. For express mail service, include a self-addressed express mail label along with the proper postage.

The PRC government offices in the United States are listed below:

Embassy of the People's Republic of China
2300 Connecticut Avenue, NW
Washington, DC 20008
Main number: 202-328-2500
Visa Section: 202-328-2517
FAX: 202-328-2564

Consulate General of the People's Republic of China
104 S. Michigan Avenue
Suite 900
Chicago, IL 60603
Visa Section: 312-346-0288
FAX: 312-580-7402

Consulate General of the People's Republic of China
3417 Montrose Boulevard
Houston, TX 77006
Visa Section: 713-524-4311
FAX: 713-524-7656

Consulate General of the People's Republic of China
501 Shatto Place #34
Los Angeles, CA   90020
Visa Section: 213-380-2506
FAX: 213-380-1961

Consulate General of the People's Republic of China
520 12th Avenue
New York, NY 10036
Visa Section: 212-868-7752
FAX: 212-502-0245

Consulate General of the People's Republic of China
1450 Laguna Avenue
San Francisco, CA 94115
Visa Section: 415-563-4857
FAX: 415-563-4861

When filling out the visa application, include the exact dates or close estimate of entry into and exit from China. The visa will be stamped in the passport and returned to you within the time frame you requested. Be advised, however, that issuance of anything but a short-term (three- or six-month) tourist visa hinges on the Chinese host unit's approval and its transmission of information to the appropriate consulate, or to the embassy, in the United States. Students' and researchers' visas are approved by the foreign affairs division of the organization governing the institution with which they will be affiliated. Teachers' visas are approved by the State Education Commission, the Foreign Experts Bureau, the ministry responsible for your educational institution, or the foreign affairs office of the provincial government, depending on which higher level unit your institution falls under.

Application for the visa should be accompanied by as much supporting evidence as possible, including *copies* of contracts (keep the originals for your own records), letters of invitation, or other documents that prove you are expected in China. Issuance of the visa requires considerable coordination between you and your host organization, and you will want to monitor the process closely. Sometimes a visa approval is mistakenly sent from China to the wrong consulate or the wrong office or section within a consulate. If delays occur, it is wise to fax the host institution to check on this possibility. Be sure also to check how long the visa will be valid. If it expires during your sojourn in China, it must be renewed with the help of the host unit. Some consulates will offer double-entry visas if you can demonstrate a need to travel outside of China during your stay. Many long-term residents want double-entry visas even if they have no travel plans. If a medical or family emergency requires a temporary leave, re-entry will be simpler with a double-entry visa.

Very often, the visa process is prolonged. Some people report receiving their visa only a few days before scheduled departure. Stay in contact with your Chinese host and a representative at the Chinese consulate so you can work together to smooth the process.

If for some reason the visa authorization does not come through, it is possible to get a tourist visa within 24 hours from the embassy or a consulate in the United States, or from the China Travel Service (CTS) in Hong Kong. This is not the appropriate visa for a student, teacher, or anyone planning to stay longer than six months and should be used only as an emergency measure.

China Travel Service has offices at the following locations in Hong Kong (country code 852):

Alpha House
27 Nathan Road
Kowloon
Telephone: 721-1331

77 Queens Road, Central District
Hong Kong Island
Telephone: 522-0450

U.S. citizens require no visa for a stopover in Hong Kong. China also issues tourist visas at the point of entry into China, but this procedure is not institutionalized and is best avoided by the long-term visitor. Many American residents enter China via Japan or travel there for medical or dental care or for recreation, shopping, or research. U.S. citizens no longer need a visa for short-term visits to Japan. A U.S. passport is good for a 90-day stay there.

INVITING RELATIVES TO CHINA   Relatives can visit for up to three months on a single-entry (or up to six months on a double-entry) tourist visa obtained through one of the consulates listed above or in Hong Kong. For visits of longer than six months, it is best to have the host unit or its parent organization (for example, the State Education Commission, the Chinese Academy of Social Sciences, or the Chinese Academy of Sciences) issue an approval for the visa. Otherwise, your relative would have to return to Hong Kong to get a visa reissued there.

Visiting friends and relatives can stay in tourist hotels, but space should be reserved early during the busy tourist season (from May through October). Students have had varying degrees of success in arranging for guests to stay with them in dormitories. Some warn that there is a policy against accommodating more than two persons in the same room or suite, and only spouses may share the same bed. Parents may keep a small child with them, but not a teenager. However, when the visit is only for a week or two, these rules are often overlooked.

If your visitor wants to travel in China, you will probably be responsible for helping with the arrangements. Host institutions are often willing to help arrange travel for researchers and senior scholars who want to tour the country at the end of their stay, and some will extend the same courtesy to "significant others." If your host institution cannot help with arrangements, the China Travel Service (CTS) will. Every city has a China Travel Service, and many tourist hotels now have small branch offices, though the quality of service varies. Some Chinese speakers with flexible schedules prefer to make travel arrangements on their own, bypassing the CTS. Airline tickets are relatively easy to purchase, either through local ticket offices or through tourist hotels, but round-trip tickets are not generally available. Try to reserve a seat two or three days in advance of your travel since planes often become fully booked. Hotel reservations should also be made well in advance.

HEALTH PREPARATIONS   Despite different standards of sanitation, frequent respiratory flare-ups, and occasional stomach upset, most Americans remain remarkably healthy in China. But the type of provisions you make for health care in China will depend on where you live while there and whether you are bringing children with you. The medical care available in Beijing, Shanghai, and Guangzhou is considerably more advanced and accessible than in smaller towns or remote areas of the country. It is wise to meet with your personal physician in the United States before leaving to map out a health strategy for China. Incidentally, international direct dial telephone communication is now possible in many parts of China (although not in small towns or remote areas) and much anxiety can be relieved simply by knowing that your own doctor is still only a telephone call away. Most doctors will want to prescribe a range of medications for possible ailments in China, and anyone with chronic problems or serious allergies should plan to take along a full supply of medication and perhaps determine what to do should an emergency occur in China. Note that many common medications are not available in the PRC.

Your personal physician should also determine which immunizations to give you before departure—perhaps after consultation with the Centers for Disease Control and Prevention (telephone: 404-639-3311) for their latest recommendations. China does not *require* immunizations unless a traveler enters from an area known to have cholera or yellow fever. However, booster vaccines should be current for diphtheria, tetanus, typhoid, and polio (primary series for polio and typhoid are recommended if you did not take them as a child). The hepatitis-B vaccine may also be recommended if you have not previously received it. The U.S. Embassy suggests having a TB skin test every year. Measles, mumps, and rubella are not controlled in developing countries, and pregnant women should be immunized against rubella.

Viral hepatitis (type A) is widespread in China and many doctors recommend gamma globulin as a prophylaxis for long-term visitors. Gamma globulin is effective only for four to six months and is not ordinarily available in Chinese hospitals. Some long-term residents bring in the serum and arrange to store it. However, the International Medical Center in Beijing now offers the vaccination to U.S. citizens in China for approximately $100 a shot. The dosage is good for six months. The International Medical Center is located at:

Beijing Lufthansa Center
Office/Apartment Bldg., Room S106
No. 50 Liangmaqiao Road
Beijing 100016
Telephone: (86) 1-465-1561
FAX: (86) 1-465-1984

If you will be in China during the warm months, especially outside large urban areas, either you or your doctor should check with the Centers for Disease Control and Prevention to determine whether malaria is endemic where you will be and, if so, what strain is present. Depending on conditions in your destination, your doctor may prescribe a prophylaxis against malaria.

Finally, the U.S. Embassy recommends vaccination against Japanese encephalitis. The disease, which can cause serious brain damage and has a 25-percent fatality rate, is transmitted by mosquitoes and occurs mainly from June through September in rural areas of Asia. The National Center for Infectious Diseases reports that the risk among American travelers is less than one case per year for each million travelers to Asia. The risk for travelers to rural areas, however, is one in 5,000 in a one-month period. In temperate areas of China, there is no risk during the winter. The Japanese encephalitis vaccine is available in the United States under the trade name Je-Vax, distributed through Connaught Laboratories in Swiftwater, Pennsylvania. Your physician can order the vaccine (1-800-VACCINE), which is administered in three doses spread over 30 days.

The International Medical Center in Beijing also provides the three-shot series at a cost of US$60 each. The shots are given in Beijing at one-week intervals.

Your physician should also be consulted about prescribing disposable syringes to take to China, since not all Chinese hospitals use them and since even "disposable" syringes have been reported to be recycled. Some people suggest bringing two types of syringes: one for administering injections and the other for drawing blood. Be sure to bring a copy of the prescription in case you are questioned at customs.

If you are bringing children with you to China, make sure that the child's basic immunizations are up-to-date and bring your family's international health card with a record of basic immunizations. The U.S. Embassy recommends that the encephalitis vaccine not be given to children under 12 months of age unless they will be in a rural area. The hepatitis-B vaccine series is usually begun at the age of one year. The Centers for Disease Control and Prevention now recommends that gamma globulin be given to infants and children as prophylaxis for hepatitis-A.

Useful information about relevant immunizations, diseases, and prevention can be found in the pamphlet *Health Information for International Travel* (publication #017-023-00192-2), available for $6.50 from:

Superintendent of Documents
U.S. Government Printing Office
Washington, DC 20402
Telephone: 202-783-3238

or contact:

The International Travel Clinic

Johns Hopkins University Hampton House
550 N. Broadway, #107
Baltimore, MD 21205
Telephone: 410-955-8931

For anyone planning to stay in China for a year or more, the Chinese government requires a thorough health examination within two months before arrival, including a chest X-ray and an HIV test for AIDS (acquired immune deficiency syndrome), which must be administered less than a month before entry. China will not allow entry to anyone who has tested HIV-positive.

The host organization will provide health forms to be filled out by your doctor or hospital, and a visa will be granted only when the consulate processing your application is satisfied that the forms are in proper order. Your Chinese work unit will review them again on arrival in China. A copy of the form is provided in Appendix G. The procedures are lengthy, cumbersome, and expensive. Individual costs may be as high as $400, and for a family of four the cost will be more than $1,000. All forms must be *original and certified*, and some Chinese work units prefer that the tests be done by a hospital rather than a clinic. To quote one student in China:

> The real nuisance was getting the form certified as genuine. To begin with we had to convince a local notary to go with us to the doctor's office, since the doctor was too busy to go to the notary. The infuriating part was that the Los Angeles Chinese consulate would not accept the single notary seal; they insisted the we also have the California state seal certifying that the Santa Barbara notary was indeed a genuine one. This entailed sending everything to Sacramento by express mail and making countless phone calls to the state office. We had to make three trips to the L A consulate, and finally managed to get the visa the day before departing.

The Chinese Embassy in Washington, D.C. appears to be more flexible in issuing notary seals than are the consulates.

Some people arrive in China after spending much money and time on the health certificate to discover that their institution treats the health forms as an empty formality and that certification could have been done quickly and inexpensively in China. Other Chinese institutions refuse to accept forms that they believe are not properly filled out or certified or that come from clinics rather than hospitals. Some people want to avoid having the health tests repeated in China because X-ray equipment may be older and because physical exams in Chinese hospitals may not be as private as in the United States. To avoid having to repeat the tests in China, it is important that the form be filled out completely and that you bring with you to China the *original* certified health forms and your chest X-ray. If you are planning to be in China less than one year, you do not need to be tested for AIDS. However, if you change your plans and extend your stay beyond a year, you will have to be tested in China.

MEDICAL INSURANCE   You are strongly advised to keep up your existing insurance policies; you should also discuss with your insurance company how much coverage you will have abroad and how to apply for reimbursement of services rendered in China. Most Chinese health administrators will not be familiar with long, complicated insurance forms, and it is unlikely that they would be able to bill your insurance company directly. It is therefore important to clarify the procedures before leaving the United States.

Some long-term residents in China have recommended the Blue Shield International Blue Chip Plan based in Hong Kong, which is generally less expensive than many U.S.-based policies. Write:

Blue Shield International, Ltd.
Causeway Bay Post Office Box 30961
Hong Kong
FAX: (852) 559-8492

Blue Shield International is one of many insurance companies based in Hong Kong offering policies that include the services of SOS Assistance. SOS Assistance allows you to contact a Western doctor in China 24 hours a day and will arrange for full-scale medical evacuations with reimbursement of expenses. SOS Assistance is also available as an independent policy. For information on SOS Assistance, contact:

International SOS Assistance (HK) Ltd.
GPO Box 2981
Hong Kong
Beijing telephone (24-hour alarm center): 1-500-3388 or 500-3419
Philadelphia telephone: 215-245-4707

Another private company offering medical evacuation and insurance in China is:

Asia Emergency Assistance PTE Ltd.
Room 1010, 10th Floor, China World Trade Center
No. 1, Jianguomenwai Dajie
Beijing 100004, PRC
Telephone: 1-505-3521
FAX: 1-505-3526

Note that if you are placing an international call to China, you must first dial the country code 86.

If you will be based near Beijing, you may also want to consider purchasing a membership plan at the International Medical Center (IMC). IMC has a Western medical staff of physicians and nurses and offers a range of services and membership plans. IMC offers a ten percent discount on all fees to members of SOS. See page 13 for IMC's address.

MEDICATIONS AND TOILETRIES   As part of health care management, some people suggest carrying a basic medical encyclopedia. David Werner's *Where There Is No Doctor* is recommended for people living in small towns and villages where medical care is less available. Take with you any prescription drugs you may need, especially if you will be living outside major cities. It is useful to have the Latin names of medications because that is what Chinese medical personnel will recognize. People with a history of asthma, bronchitis, or tonsillitis should be prepared for frequent flare-ups, especially in cities and during the winter. For allergy sufferers, Peking Union Medical College has a good allergy clinic. Allergy medicine can be packed in dry ice, if necessary, and the prescription refilled at Peking Union Medical College. The U.S. Embassy urges residents in Beijing to buy humidifiers for use during the winter months as prevention against colds, and the advice probably applies to all parts of China where winters are dry. Chinese-made humidifiers are now readily available. Almost every newcomer contracts a cold within a few weeks of arrival in China, and some foreigners are plagued with respiratory problems throughout their stay. It is wise, therefore, to take plenty of cold remedies, cough drops, and throat lozenges. You can also ask your local clinic for help; Chinese remedies for colds are mild but quite effective.

A personal first-aid kit might include vitamins, aspirin, lomotil (for diarrhea), antacid, cough drops, deodorant, sunscreen, lip balm, first-aid spray, athlete's foot medicine, shaving cream, dental floss, insect repellent, a lice-removal kit for remote fieldwork, a thermometer, and earplugs. Women who will be living outside Beijing are advised to take a good supply of sanitary napkins and tampons, although many cities now carry O.B. brand tampons. In Beijing, Watson's drug store, now at several locations, Wellcome at the China World Trade Center, and the drug store at the Lido Holiday Inn now have steady supplies of tampons. If you are subject to gynecological infections, bring your remedies along.

Watson's in Beijing sells condoms and over-the-counter birth control pills, but contraceptives are not easily obtained by foreigners in most parts of China and cannot be mailed from outside. Eyeglasses are quite inexpensive in China, but some people have not been satisfied with the quality of the lenses. In any case, it is a good idea to take an extra pair as well as your prescription with you. Contact lens solutions are now available at Watson's and other Western pharmacies in Beijing, but supplies are less reliable in other cities and unavailable in small towns. Contact lens wearers report problems with dust and advise taking a pair of glasses with you as a fallback. A good pair of sunglasses will protect your eyes from dust and debris as well as glare.

Modern dental equipment is still scarce in China, so a thorough dental checkup is advisable before leaving the United States. Beijing, however, does have several good dental clinics, with U.S.-trained dentists, and some people have been quite satisfied with the quality of dentistry there, although you will want to use the department that services foreigners and high-level cadres. Senior researchers and foreign experts will have a better chance of getting an appointment there than will students. The clinics are:

Beijing School of Stomatology
Wei Gong Cun, Haidian District
Telephone: 1-831-0858, x 584; 1-832-9977, x 580
Dr. Lin Qiongguang

Sino-German Polyclinic Dental Facility
located in the basement of the Landmark Tower
Telephone: 1-501-1983; 1-501-6688 x 20903
Dr. Shen

Beijing Jing-Liang Dental Clinic
133 Dianmenwai, Xicheng District
Telephone: 1-403-1330
Ms. Ma (dental assistant)

Chinese brands of soap, shampoos, face creams, and other necessities for personal care are quite good and inexpensive. Familiar Western brands are available in Western drug stores, and Chinese stores are beginning to carry a few Western brands as well.

MONEY, BANKING, AND CREDIT CARDS   Americans who will be paid by U.S. sources while in China can receive money directly in three ways:

1. Money deposited in an American account can be drawn on checks guaranteed by an American Express card at certain branches of the Bank of China.

2. Money can be deposited in a designated account in a U.S. bank that has an international division with correspondent relations with China (many major banks in large cities offer this service); funds can then be wired to a Chinese bank account as needed.

3. Money can be wired directly to a Chinese bank account. Fund

transfers to China for the most part are now routine, but before your departure you should clarify with the U.S. bank how these transactions are managed.

Many people find that by far the easiest method of obtaining cash in China is to write a personal check on a U.S. bank account and then guarantee it with an American Express card. As of this writing, American Express-guaranteed checks can be cashed in the main branch of the Bank of China in the capital city of every province and often at other cities within each province. Counter checks are usually available if you have your account number and the name and address of your bank. A list of locations that have banks where the American Express card can be used is included in Appendix K. A personal check will be honored for up to Y750 with an American Express green card and Y2,000 with a gold card without American Express authorization. (The official exchange rate in February 1994 was Y8.7 to US$1.00.) With American Express approval, you can cash $1,000 every 21 days with a green card and $5,000 every 21 days with a gold card issued in the United States or $2,000 every 21 days with a gold card issued in other countries. American Express approval for these larger amounts can be given immediately only in banks with computers. In banks without computers, a telephone call must be made, which sometimes takes time. If the bank you will be using does not have a computer, you may want to make your request a day in advance or plan to return to the bank several hours after the request has been made. Many people find the American Express arrangements sufficient for ordinary living expenses. When it is necessary to pay large amounts of money for tuition or affiliation fees, however (see Chapter 4), you are likely to find yourself short of cash. Some people recommend taking traveler's checks to cover the large expenditures and using the American Express card to get cash for daily expenses.

If you do not have an American Express card or are not in an area with American Express services, plan to carry a good supply of traveler's checks. All the major brands are honored but American Express traveler's checks can be purchased at designated branches of the Bank of China in many cities. Traveler's checks offer a slightly higher rate of exchange than currency, although a one-percent service fee is charged for cashing them. Traveler's checks can be exchanged at any Bank of China service desk located in airports, major hotels, and stores that serve foreigners, but smaller towns and shops in rural areas are not likely to recognize them, so you should bring enough cash if you are visiting an unfamiliar area. The main office for American Express is in Beijing, but Shanghai, Xi'an, Guilin, Chengdu, and Guangzhou also have offices that can arrange reimbursement for lost checks. Note that while the American Express card can be used to obtain cash at all the locations listed in Appendix K, only the offices in Beijing, Shanghai, Xi'an, Guilin, Chengdu, and Guangzhou can arrange to replace lost traveler's checks.

The American Express credit card can also be used for purchases and hotel payments in most joint-venture hotels and in many Chinese establishments that cater to foreign tourists. New establishments are being added daily. For further information, write for the American Express booklet, *Guide to China*.

Visa and MasterCard can also be used in some locations, both as payment and for cash advances of up to US$500 at designated Bank of China service counters—for a service charge of four percent.

Many people planning to stay in China longer than a few months open a U.S. dollar bank account with the Bank of China. Banking regulations vary from place to place and policies change constantly, so you should learn your bank regulations before opening an account. Payroll and third-party checks cannot be cashed under any circumstances, and personal or bank checks can take at least one month to clear. The Tiananmen experience of June 1989, when most Americans were evacuated and some did not have time to withdraw their money, has made some people cautious about how much money they keep in a Chinese account. You may want to depend on periodic deposits from your U.S. bank account rather than putting all your funds into a Chinese account.

You can also obtain money via international money order. Because there are no standard banking practices in China, policies on cashing international money orders differ from city to city. In some places they can be cashed immediately, whereas in others they may take one to three months to clear.

Appendix L includes prices for selected hotels, food, services, transportation, clothing, and medical care. For further information on currency and banking in China—and for information for people who will receive direct payment by Chinese organizations—see Chapter 7.

CUSTOMS REGULATIONS   Customs regulations as of this writing are in a state of flux. On the final leg of your flight to China, you will be given a customs declaration form on which to list any cameras, tape recorders, valuable jewelry, typewriters, or computers being brought into the country and the amount of currency and traveler's checks on your person. The form will be checked at the customs desk—after the baggage claim area in most airports—and you will be given a copy. In the past, customs officials asked to see the copy when you left the country and could impose stiff fines if you failed to prove that you were taking out all items declared on entry. Fines were also imposed for losing the form. Recently, however, customs officials have not been requesting these forms on departure. Until the changes in customs regulations become clear, you are advised to keep your copy.

One purpose of the customs declaration form is to prevent the sale or gifts of items that are relatively difficult to obtain in China and might have a high resale value or (in the case of reading material) that might be offensive to the Chinese government. If, for instance, you brought in small pocket calculators or digital clocks to give away as gifts, fines of up to 100 percent of their value could be imposed if you leave without them. A few people report having books (such as Orville Schell's *Discos and Democracy*) confiscated on entering China. If, however, reading materials are for your private use, the possibility of confiscation is minimal.

Foreigners entering China may bring up to four bottles of liquor, 600 cigarettes, an unlimited supply of medicine for personal use (in its original labeled container), personal effects, and an unlimited amount of currency and traveler's checks. There are no restrictions on still cameras, 8mm cameras, film, or personal video equipment (for example, cam-corders) but professional film and video equipment may not be brought in or taken out of China without special permission.

Americans going to Shanghai should note that the U.S. Consulate General there has received frequent complaints that Shanghai customs officials routinely assess and collect unusually high customs duties, particularly for supplies forwarded as unaccompanied baggage or sent through the international mail. Shanghai customs has published a pamphlet that lists prohibited and restricted items for all of China and gives some estimates for possible duties. Although this information is not definitive, it does give prospective American residents an idea of potential customs problems. The regulations in the pamphlet apply to all of China, but Shanghai is stricter about enforcing them. The Shanghai consular district includes the provinces of Jiangsu, Anhui, and Zhejiang. You should request a copy of this pamphlet from your Chinese host before leaving the United States.

According to the pamphlet,

- Articles prohibited entry include not only the usual firearms, wireless transmitters, drugs, plants, contaminated foodstuffs, and Chinese currency but also, and much more ambiguously, "publications, photographs, tapes, records and any other material harmful to Chinese politics, economy, culture or morals."
- Certain articles may be brought in only in restricted quantity: wristwatches, pocket watches, and bicycles at one per person; cameras, radios, and sewing machines at one per family.
- Duty is high: 20 percent for grains, flours, medical equipment,

scientific instruments, and electronic calculators; 50 percent for medicines, home and office equipment, tape recorders, tools, televisions, sports equipment, and musical instruments; 100 percent or higher (150 or 200 percent) for all other items.

In addition, some advice for minimizing customs problems includes the following:

• Bring in as accompanied baggage as many personal supplies as possible, since personally accompanied baggage usually receives the most favorable treatment by Chinese customs officials.
• Heavy books and other professional supplies are best shipped separately (the foreign affairs office of the host unit is the best place to send the boxes); the Chinese host institution should be asked to handle customs clearance as part of its support for your activities in China.

Be prepared to encounter what you might judge to be arbitrary and excessive customs duties levied on any packages sent by international mail. Some customs officials can be arbitrary about what cannot be shipped out of China, especially things looking like antiques or handicrafts. One researcher noted that it is easier to mail international packages with the aid of a Chinese friend, and postal clerks are likely to be more cooperative with customers who are courteous and friendly.

Some Americans who will be in China for extended periods have requested information about bringing pets. Personnel at the Chinese Embassy in Washington, D.C., have stated that although bringing animals into China is not prohibited, it is unwise to do so. Chinese customs officers are extremely strict about quarantining animals, and often this results in the animal being quarantined for about as long as the American remains in China.

When you leave the United States, be sure to register with U.S. customs officials any cameras or other equipment subject to duty that you are taking with you to China. Save the receipts to present upon reentry into the United States so that you are not taxed on items made in Asia that you bought prior to departure. A useful booklet, *Customs Hints for Returning U.S. Citizens: Know Before You Go*, is available free of charge from the U.S. Customs Service, P.O. Box 7407, Washington, DC 20044, and from most travel agents. Travelers returning to the United States from China can bring back, duty free, purchases of up to US$400 per person; an additional US$1,000 worth of goods will be taxed at a rate of ten percent. Regular duty charges, which are considerably higher, apply to purchases exceeding the initial US$1,400. Special rates and exemptions are given to Americans who live abroad for more than one year. If you have a letter of invitation or appointment stating that you will reside in China for one year or longer, show it to U.S. customs officials on your return to the United States.

BAGGAGE AND SHIPPING   To avoid excess baggage charges, it is best to travel light. Passengers flying to China from the United States are allowed two pieces of luggage, neither of which may exceed 62 inches (adding all three linear dimensions); both pieces together may not exceed 106 inches. Air China, China's largest international carrier, calculates limits by weight; economy-class passengers are allowed two bags, which may not exceed a total of 44 pounds (20 kilograms). Travel agents advise that carry-on allowances are becoming stricter on all airlines.

Baggage allowances for traveling in Asia, including China, are also calculated by weight; the 44-pound limit applies in most countries. Thus, it is possible that if you travel within China, or if you stop in Hong Kong or Tokyo or Shanghai, for example, before going on to your final destination in China, you may be charged for excess baggage weight even though you stayed within the limit on your U.S. carrier. In group travel, excess baggage charges are based on the total weight for the entire group. You may want to compare the additional cost of extra weight with the cost of sending things airmail. The difference may be marginal and worth it to ensure that you have your materials on arrival.

For long-term stays, items may be shipped ahead by mail (allow two to three months for sea mail) in care of the foreign affairs office of the host institution. However, used clothing, even for personal use, cannot be sent through the mails. Books may be shipped using the special book rates that apply to China; check with your local post office for details. The U.S. Postal Service will supply used post office bags (request "M-bags") that can be filled with boxed printed matter (15 pounds minimum per bag, 66 pounds maximum); the bags go by surface mail (six to eight weeks in transit). Books go for 72 cents a pound; printed matter, $1.32 a pound. Several airlines will accept large parcels as air freight; check with the cargo division of the airlines for details. It is best to schedule air shipments after your own arrival in China so you can pick them up and clear them through customs. Some people report considerable confusion over collecting their packages, largely because it is hard to determine which office is holding them. If possible, get the telephone number and address of the office in China before you leave, and make certain that the office administering shipments is also the same for package pickup. Administrative offices are often in a different location from where your packages will be stored. Take all forms relating to shipment with you when you go to retrieve your packages. Occasionally an entire box is lost or valuable contents stolen. Be certain to register whatever you send.

INCOME TAXES   According to the tax agreement between the United States and PRC, American teachers and scholars in China are exempt from taxation by the Chinese government for three years (either consecutive or interrupted) on payment received for teaching or research activities. However, paid free-lance work in China is subject to Chinese and U.S. taxes. Income for work performed in China by a U.S. citizen or resident alien is subject to U.S. income tax; income in the form of fellowships may also be subject to U.S. tax. If Chinese income tax has been paid, the taxpayer may be eligible for the Foreign Tax Credit, which is computed on form 1116.

There is a foreign earned income exclusion of up to $70,000 for income earned abroad. Generally, the work assignment must be for more than a full year. Information about the exclusion may be found in publication 54.

These tax laws are complicated, and it is best to consult a specialist for details. IRS package 776 contains the necessary forms and information to enable Americans abroad to file their tax returns. To obtain this or other information, contact:

Internal Revenue Service AC (International)
950 L'Enfant Plaza South, S.W.
Washington, DC 20024
Telephone: 202-874-1460
Tokyo office: (81) 3-3224-5466

The U.S. Embassy and consulates in China sometimes invite IRS officers to visit between January and March. The embassy and consulates also distribute federal (but not state) tax forms.

SUGGESTED READING   Many Americans traveling to China for the first time who have not read widely on modern Chinese history and thought should read as much as possible before the journey. Many find it doubly illuminating to read about China while experiencing it firsthand. Appendix M provides a selected reading list of titles in modern Chinese politics, society, literature, and thought.

PREPARING FOR DAILY LIFE

The days when coffee was unavailable even in Beijing are long gone, although coffee connoisseurs may still want to bring along a supply of their favorite brew. The Chinese economy is booming now, and consumer goods that were unimaginable a decade ago are now commonplace in China's major cities. But for Americans, the small towns and villages, while thriving, may still be lacking in goods that many may consider essential. Suggestions for fieldworkers in remote parts of the country are contained in Chapter 4, but the general rule for fieldworkers is still to bring *everything* you will need. And the same advice applies to all others going to small towns and villages. Western clothing for sale in small towns generally does not come in a large variety of styles and sizes. Food, while plentiful, is local. Outside major urban areas it is unlikely to find such items as cheese, coffee, steak, and salad. For many in small villages and towns, the fun is in living as much like the Chinese as possible; some, however, do make periodic forays into nearby cities to replenish their supplies and vacation with Western-style amenities.

China's major cities, particularly those along the coast, offer a wide and fascinating variety of consumer goods. Every Chinese city is dotted with neighborhood shopping areas complete with open-air food markets, hardware stores (stocked with tools, pottery, plastic buckets, and baskets), a *Xinhua* (New China) Bookstore, laundries, restaurants, bakeries, barber and beauty shops, photography shops, bicycle repair shops, tailors, and a general store that carries everything from cooking items, toiletries, and clothing to bicycles and sewing machines. China is now manufacturing many clothes that are sold in the United States, and seconds or irregulars can be found in hotel stores, fancy Chinese-run shops, and numerous outdoor free markets. Some cities, especially Beijing, even have Western supermarkets (at the Lido Hotel and the China World Trade Center) and drug stores—selling goods at greatly inflated prices. Prices of Chinese-made goods are no longer the great bargains of the early 1980s, and imported goods, while available in larger cities, are usually more expensive. Even Chinese cashmere, once a great bargain, is more expensive now, although still considerably cheaper than in the United States. But good prices are still to be found on rugs, embroidered cotton, quilts, leather goods, and down coats, jackets, and vests. Imported wines, candies, shampoos, and makeup are widely available in Friendship Stores and Western hotels.

Outside Beijing (and, increasingly, Shanghai and Guangzhou), it is almost impossible to predict what will be available at any given time. Finding the stores that carry what you need will take time. If you see something you need or like, buy it. It may not be there when you come back.

People who have brought small children to China, even to cities where just about everything is available, suggest bringing a good supply of household cleaning agents, such as liquid detergents for cleaning floors and rugs, and rubber gloves to protect your hands. Older buildings have not been subjected to the strong cleansers that Americans are accustomed to using, and dirt tends to get ground in. American parents often do not feel comfortable letting their children play on the floor until they have satisfied themselves that the surfaces are clean and disinfected.

Within these limits, the less you take, the better. Storage space is limited in hotels and dormitories. Most dormitories and apartments will have only a small free-standing armoire for clothes. A small foot-locker or trunk with a lock is useful for storing and transporting goods; some researchers suggest locking valuables, such as notebook computers, in the trunk while you are out of the room.

CLOTHING   Western and Chinese styles of dress are converging. Dress in China is casual, but not nearly as casual as in the past. Chinese men are wearing coats and ties and women are wearing skirts and dresses. Appropriate dress in China is pretty much the same as that worn under similar circumstances in the United States. Attire will depend on age, status, and the occasion. Men can wear casual slacks and an open neck shirt for teaching, and a coat and tie for meetings, more formal lectures, and banquets. Women can wear slacks, skirts, or dresses to teach, and somewhat dressier attire for special occasions. Nevertheless, the Chinese expect their teachers to be somewhat conservative. Students dress much less formally than visiting Fulbright scholars or researchers, although a certain modest decorum must be observed even on the hottest summer day. Bright colors and tasteful jewelry are quite acceptable now, but extremes of style and ostentation are not considered acceptable for "intellectuals." Bare midriffs, shorts (except for sports), and décolletage are still considered risqué. Bermuda-length shorts, however, are acceptable on men and younger women. No matter what your age or status, you will be doing a lot of walking, so comfortable walking shoes and sturdy boots are essential.

In general, China, except for the far south, has extreme variations in temperature. For example, Beijing is bitterly cold in winter and hot and humid in summer. This is true even in such "southern" cities as Shanghai, Nanjing, and Hangzhou. Residents warn that winters are cold and the heat is turned on late (well into November)—and then only for a few hours a day. Many public buildings, libraries, offices, and laboratories are unheated altogether. Chilblains (*dong chuang*)—where the skin turns a patchy purple, especially on the hands and ears—are a common complaint in southern China in the winter because rooms are often unheated and the air is very damp. Dry exposed skin well after washing and keep fingers and ears covered at night if the room is unheated.

In areas where winters are cold and classrooms are unheated, it is wise to observe the Chinese custom of dressing in layers—many layers. Until Americans become fully accustomed to this necessity, or have suffered one too many respiratory ailments or chilblains, they tend to stop halfway—after three or four rather than the seven, eight—or eleven—layers that their Chinese friends will be wearing. *Duo chuan yifu*—"put on some more clothes"—is an admonition many underdressed Americans will hear frequently from their Chinese friends. Unheated buildings are often as cold as, or colder than, the temperature outside and are damp as well. Chinese wear many layers of socks and sweater-like long underwear together with cotton longjohns, as well as layers of undershirts, cotton shirts, and several sweaters, all covered by thick wool or cotton padded coats or down jackets. The Chinese *mian'ao*, or cotton padded jacket, is less fashionable among Chinese now than in the past, but American students and teachers will appreciate its warmth. Thus layered, even the coldest, dampest room is comfortable, and layers can be peeled as the temperature rises. Cotton or woolen gloves with the tips of the fingers cut out are ideal for writing in unheated libraries or classrooms.

Chinese cities boast good tailors, and many Americans take advantage of the high-quality Chinese silk and wool to supplement their wardrobes. Ask friends, both Chinese and Western, for advice on good tailors, remembering that the cheapest are not usually the best. One strategy is to bring samples of your favorite styles and have them copied—which will mean leaving the original with the tailor until the task is complete. Several fittings will probably be necessary. Zippers and buttons are not of the highest quality in China, so it may be best to bring some of your own.

Chinese cities are usually dusty and polluted, so cleaning clothes is always a problem. Hot water in dormitories is neither abundant nor constant. Because laundry must be done by hand or sent out, clothing should be washable, sturdy, easy to care for, and of preshrunk material. Bring rubber gloves if detergents bother your skin. In a typical Beijing hotel these days, laundry costs Y3 or more per piece and is usually returned in the evening if taken in the early morning. Local neighborhood laundries are cheaper but will take longer. It may be best to wash underwear, socks, and sweaters by hand (bring a mild detergent) and send out larger items such as sheets, towels, shirts, and trousers. A few universities have washing machines installed in the foreign teachers' dormitory. Teachers and researchers sometimes buy small washing machines, and some hire an *ayi* (female helper) to come in once or twice a week to help with cleaning and marketing. Dry cleaning is available but expensive and may be of dubious quality. The best results are usually from the joint-venture hotels, several of which (for instance, the Jianguo and Jinglun in Beijing) have services for the public. One researcher notes that good, inexpensive, private dry cleaning businesses have sprung up in the alleys next to the Jinglun. When sending your clothing out at a Chinese hotel, be sure to specify dry cleaning. More than one Western scholar has found his woolen sports jacket laundered.

Clothing repairs are usually easy to arrange: sewing supplies are common in neighborhood shops; clothing repair shops are inexpensive and efficient; and shoe repairmen offer their services on the streets at reasonable, and often negotiable, prices.

Appendix L lists items that are generally available (with approximate prices) as well as goods that are not easily found. Clothing is stocked seasonally; purchases should be made early in the season as stores run out of the best selections fairly quickly. Again, if you like it, buy it immediately. Size is a factor in determining price: a large sweater costs slightly more than a smaller one because it uses more material. Also, large sizes are often difficult to find, especially in Chinese department stores. Men who wear extra-large clothing (size 44 or larger) or shoes larger than size 10 should either take most of what they will need or plan to use a tailor. However, you should still be prepared for clothes that are cut too short or too slim. As one researcher noted: "Some tailors simply can't grasp that anyone could be so large—especially in the southern cities." Long underwear, pajamas, and silk underwear are generally good buys, but they are simply not available in larger sizes. Because Chinese sizes do not correspond exactly to American sizes, you should always try on clothing before you buy it—a sight, by the way, that often provides a great deal of amusement for Chinese onlookers because stores seldom have private fitting rooms.

The following wardrobe would serve anyone living in a city with wide variations in temperature. Items marked with an asterisk are those best brought from home.

sturdy walking shoes with thick soles for warmth*
leather shoes*
comfortable sandals for summer*
rain boots*
warm socks (of wool and polypropylene)*
umbrella
long- and short-sleeved wash-and-wear shirts
lightweight or cotton trousers*
walking shorts*

turtleneck pullovers
woolen sweaters
long underwear
cotton underwear
bathing suit and cap*
warm bathrobe
warm, sturdy slippers*
flannel and cotton pajamas*
cold-weather parka
rain parka or all-weather coat
knitted cap

You should add to this list *at least* one or two dressy outfits for more formal occasions. Many academics have lamented that they did not bring along enough clothes for such occasions.

The median temperatures below give you some idea of what to expect, but, once again, in unheated buildings temperatures are often lower than outside, and the cold more penetrating. Temperatures may fluctuate considerably during the day. Higher humidity in the south also intensifies the extremes of temperature.

	Winter	Summer	Fall and Spring
Northeast (Harbin)	0°F	70°F	40°F
North China (Beijing)	23°F	78°F	55°F
Central China (Wuhan)	37°F	84°F	62°F
East China (Shanghai)	38°F	82°F	60°F
South China (Guangzhou)	57°F	83°F	73°F

FOOD AND COOKING SUPPLIES   Food in Chinese hotels and dormitories is usually nutritious but can become monotonous after a few weeks, particularly in dormitories. Time constraints usually confine students and teachers living on university campuses to dormitory fare several days a week, but there are many alternatives. Small, independently managed restaurants running the gamut from outdoor carts to modern restaurants with white tablecloths are springing up all over China. Many are surprisingly good and they offer many different styles of cuisine. Students on a limited budget often concentrate on the tiny outdoor stalls and night food markets where *youtiao*, *shaobing*, noodles, and other types of the "common man's" fare sell for mere pennies. Small restaurants offer a wide variety of China's cuisines, with nutritious fresh vegetables and well-prepared fish. Be attentive to sanitary conditions in the small private establishments; some people report stomach upsets after eating at some of the outdoor stands or less-sanitary small restaurants. As a general rule, fresh milk should be avoided, and foods should be well cooked. During the hottest summer months, avoid eating meat from outdoor stands, because it probably has not been refrigerated. Many enthusiasts of the new restaurants carry their own chopsticks or alcohol for cleaning those offered by the establishment—although many places are now using disposable chopsticks.

Free markets are also proliferating in China, and fresh fruits and vegetables are plentiful. Because most Chinese farms still fertilize with nightsoil, the practice is to wash and peel whatever can be peeled (apples, pears, carrots) and to cook the rest. However, some people with hearty constitutions are able to eat well-washed fresh vegetables with no untoward effects. Some markets, like the one on the west side of Beijing's Ritan Park, cater to foreigners and are especially clean.

Foreign teachers often have a small refrigerator and limited cooking facilities in their apartments and some foreign dorms now have a kitchen on each floor, but the time involved in marketing and preparation discourages most people from preparing three meals a day. Some hire an *ayi* to come in and cook occasionally. Students in dormitories sometimes buy inexpensive hot plates, but they are illegal in most institutions because they are unsafe and drain the already overtaxed electrical systems.

Western food is rather expensive; most large cities (Beijing, Shanghai, and Guangzhou especially) offer many choices—from the joint-venture hotels to Kentucky Fried Chicken, Pizza Hut, and McDonalds. Joint-venture hotels sometimes have a delicatessen section, and Friendship Stores now offer a wide variety of often homemade Western foods—from breads, jams, and sweets to cheese and ham for sandwiches. Instant coffee is widely available, but good coffee is not. You may want to take a supply, along with a cup-sized filter and filter paper. Instant soups, hot chocolate, pre-sweetened powdered drinks, and other instant foods can be prepared simply by adding boiled water, usually stored in thermos bottles and kept in your room. Beijing's supermarkets have a wide variety of imported non-perishable foods. Unboiled tap water is not potable in China except in a few joint-venture hotels having their own filtration systems.

For setting up housekeeping in China, most of the equipment can be purchased at local Friendship or hardware stores. As of this writing, only rubber gloves, teflon pans, and sponges seem generally difficult to find in the larger cities.

ELECTRICAL APPLIANCES   Electric current in China is 220 volts, 50 Hz (U.S. current is 110 volts, 60 Hz) so a transformer is needed with enough capacity to handle tape recorders, radios, and any other appliances that must be converted from standard American voltage. Many people recommend buying a transformer in the United States or Hong Kong since they can be difficult to find in China. Franzus and Hoffritz make transformers and a variety of different sized plugs, and Voltage Valet sells transformers for 50, 1000, and 1600 watt units. For further information, write:

Voltage Valet Division
Hybrinetics Inc.
P.O. Box 14399, 225 Sutton Place
Santa Rosa, CA 95407

Appliances with moving parts, such as typewriters and tape recorders, will still run more slowly with a transformer since most only convert volts, not frequency. As an alternative, these items can be converted to 50 Hz in the United States; you also might want to purchase equipment that can be used on either 110 or 220 volts or buy electrical items in Hong Kong, which also operates on 220/50. Extension plugs and extender sockets can be purchased in Chinese general stores and at some Friendship Stores; in some cases, Chinese clerks will even make extension cords and replace plugs. There is a bewildering variety of electrical outlets in China, sometimes even within the same building or room; there is no such thing as a "standard plug." An international travel kit of plugs (Franzus and Hoffritz both manufacture them) is useful, especially since the "universal" plugs sold in the United States usually do not fit Chinese outlets.

You may want to buy some electrical appliances in China. One of the most commonly sought is a small fan; a nine-inch model costs about Y120–150 and larger standing models are priced between Y320 and 500. Chinese-made blow dryers are also widely available. Used appliances can be resold at Friendship Stores and certain other stores (ask your Chinese hosts) at about half the purchase price if they are accompanied by the original sales slip. Some stores will buy back Western-made appliances as well. Much equipment gets passed from foreigner to foreigner as one group leaves and another comes in. Look for possible buys on bulletin boards and talk to friends who are about to leave.

Many people try to circumvent the electric problem by bringing equipment that can be operated on batteries. However, good, long-lasting batteries may be difficult to find in China. AA "penlight" batteries are readily available under brand names such as "White Elephant" and "Golden Bee," but they wear out much faster than foreign ones. Japanese batteries are easy to find in most eastern cities. Some people bring rechargeable nickel/cadmium (NiCad) AA batteries and a 220v 50c or solar-powered charger (available from Radio Shack and Edmund Scientific in the United States). A solar-powered charger can trickle-charge fully drained NiCad batteries over the course of one sunny day. Those who are technically inclined can make solar-powered chargers for larger electrical equipment, including laptop computers, by purchasing the requisite solar cells and connections from Edmund Scientific.

Battery chargers for regular batteries and sometimes NiCads are now available in many Chinese department stores. However, alkaline batteries are best for fieldwork; although they can't be recharged, they last the longest. Recharging batteries during fieldwork is inconvenient, especially if you are constantly on the move. Take a couple of hundred batteries for extensive tape recording. If you run out of American or Japanese-made batteries, try to get brands manufactured in the larger Chinese cities.

Bring an adequate supply of batteries for cameras, calculators, wristwatches, and micro-cassette tape recorders since these specialized varieties are difficult to find in China.

OFFICE EQUIPMENT   The necessary supplies and equipment will depend on the work there. Many teachers find that a typewriter is sufficient for their needs. A standard manual typewriter will give the most reliable service because there is no need to worry about electrical transformers and there is no problem finding repair shops, which also sell ribbons. Some teachers bring typewriters with wide carriages for typing stencils. It is also easy to purchase a good manual typewriter in China for approximately Y300. Many units with foreign teachers will have such equipment.

Some teachers bring electric or battery-operated typewriters. The most efficient electric typewriters are those that can be operated on both 220 and 110 volts. People who bring 110-volt typewriters and use a transformer report difficulties because the transformer converts the voltage but not the frequency. The result is a slow machine and light print, and it is impossible to make carbons. One disadvantage of battery-operated typewriters is that some require special paper that cannot be bought in China.

Many researchers bring computers to China and have few problems using them once they are properly set up. Deciding which equipment to bring and how to protect data against brown-outs can be daunting, however. For a full discussion of various options and pitfalls, refer to the article by Norman Bock in the Fall/Winter 1991 issue of *China Exchange News*. Discussions with others who have had experience with computers in China may also prove useful. Computers are now widely used and many earlier problems are easier to manage with improved and updated equipment.

Electricity can be sporadic in China. Unless the computer has back-up batteries to guarantee power when electricity goes down or, with a desktop computer, there is an alternative power source, there is always the risk of losing all the data. When using a computer, it is wise to save the document after every page. A voltage regulator is useful in protecting against voltage shifts. Dust and humidity are problems with computers; running a fan directly into the disk drive slots may keep the screen from jumping in hot weather.

Battery-operated laptops and notebooks are now the most popular choice of researchers in China, and they can be brought in as baggage with no problems from customs officials. This is also a disadvantage, however: small computers are easy to steal, and you should take precautions against theft. Many companies, including Apple, Compaq, and Toshiba make models that operate on either 110 or 220 volts, which solves the problem of a transformer. Often a power supply is purchased separately from the computer. It is a good idea to buy one that senses automatically which voltage is used.

In addition to the transformer, you will need a surge protector (*wen ya dian yuan*) to guard against voltage spikes. Surge protectors must be designed for 220 volts, and good ones can be purchased in China, although you are cautioned to buy a high-quality machine and check while in the store to be sure that it works. The transformer is then plugged into the surge protector. One researcher noted that he had found a device at a computer store in China that combines the functions of voltage conversion and regulation with surge protection (*zidong xiaoliu wen ya dian yuan*). They are rather expensive, however. Regardless of which system you use, note that transformers become quite hot when left plugged in and may burn out if overheated. If you are planning to use your computer or other equipment requiring a transformer for long periods, training a fan on it will keep it cool. Otherwise, the transformer should be unplugged when not in use.

Bringing in a desktop computer is more cumbersome than bringing in a laptop and is more difficult to get through customs. Some people recommend buying one in China, where the prices, particularly in Beijing, are now only somewhat more expensive than in the United States. Advantages of desktop computers include the larger, easier-to-read screen and the fact that many Chinese work units use them. You could also buy a screen in China and plug it into the video port on your laptop. If your desktop unit includes a port for a 5 1/2" disk, which is most commonly used in China, you will avoid the problem of transferring data on different-sized disks back and forth between your own machine and those of your work unit.

In large Chinese cities, brown-outs are not as common as they once were. However, if you do use a desktop computer it is advisable to have a back-up power supply to protect your data against brown-outs. An uninterruptible power supply (UPS) can be bought in China for several hundred dollars. Although most do not have the capacity to supply electricity for more than a few minutes, they will give you enough time to save your data and turn off the machine before the data are destroyed.

Setting up a printer in China can be problematic, because successful operation requires conversion of both volts and cycles. A few brands, such as Canon Bubble Jet, have portable models that run on both 110 volts 60 Hz and 220 volts 50 Hz. Many people suggest buying a printer in Hong Kong, where you will pay about ten percent extra for the 220/50 capacity.

As mentioned above, long-lasting batteries are difficult to find in many parts of China. Researchers using nickel cadmium batteries, which can be recharged, report that they need to be drained frequently when using a transformer. Some people prefer to use short-lived batteries and keep an ample supply on hand. They warn, however, that batteries can lose power suddenly, so it is necessary to save every page.

Since computers have come into wider use in China, it is now possible both to purchase and repair them in some cities. Large foreign computer companies have offices in major cities, and the Haidian district of Beijing has several computer shops selling disks, programs, and a variety of computer accessories. There is now a Computerland in Beijing, on Xizhimenwai Dajie, 1 Wenxingjie (phone 832-1279; fax 835-

0777). They do not ordinarily sell parts and accessories, but they occasionally supply parts and do repair work for name-brand computer equipment such as Compaq and Hewlett-Packard.

Opinions on Chinese software vary. Many people have been quite pleased with computer software purchased in China. Others warn that viruses are rampant and recommend bringing anti-viral software with you, although some of the viruses are unknown in the United States and your anti-viral software could prove ineffective against them. One researcher recommends asking your Chinese hosts to lend you their anti-viral software, noting that it is effective, easy to use, and updated periodically.

Finally, customs regulations with respect to computers are changing. Portable computers brought in as luggage are now routinely waved through without being registered. If, however, you bring in a desktop computer that is registered with customs officials, you are technically supposed to bring it with you whenever you leave China, even for a short visit, unless you get authorization from your work unit to leave it behind. People who have had to get such authorization report that obtaining it can be extremely time-consuming, and the documents are not always accepted by customs officials.

As of this writing, bringing a personal fax machine into China continues to be problematic. It is difficult to bring one in as personal baggage, and customs officials often confiscate them temporarily. You will want to ask your work unit in advance whether they can help with arrangements. Even so, some people report that authorization from a work unit does not guarantee that customs will let it through. Some people advise against surrendering the machine to customs officials. If you must, however, get a receipt, stamped with an official red seal, and get the badge number of the customs official.

Some researchers use computers with a built-in fax, and fax machines are now available for sale in large Chinese cities at little more than what they cost in the United States. The use of fax machines in China is somewhat more complicated than in the United States. Most telephone lines available to foreigners must go through a central switchboard, which necessitates manual transmission and receipt of messages. Moreover, some domestic Chinese telephone lines are full of static, which affects the quality of transmission. Faxes on domestic direct dial (DDD) and international direct dial (IDD) lines are much better. For further information about faxes, see the article by Norman Bock, mentioned above, and Chapter 7.

Some office supplies may be unavailable in China. Lined notebooks, good-quality typing and printer paper, and felt-tip pens are particularly hard to find outside of Beijing or Shanghai. If you have a computer, bring adhesive labels for computer disks—some Chinese brands do not adhere well. It is recommended that you also bring correction fluid, carbon paper, manila file folders, tape, paper clips, a good pencil sharpener, book mailers, colored pencils, glue sticks, magic markers, and, if you will be teaching, colored chalk and blackboard erasers. Manila envelopes, file cards, and boxes are usually available at stationery stores. Desk lamps in dormitory rooms are often fluorescent; some travelers prefer to bring their own high-intensity lamps.

RADIOS AND TAPE RECORDERS   A small AM/FM worldband transistor radio is useful for language practice and for news from outside China. Beijing Radio offers a special Chinese-English program (for schedules, see *China Daily*); Voice of America (VOA) schedules, which change four times a year, can be obtained from the U.S. Embassy. The British Broadcasting Corporation (BBC) airs programs at several frequencies between 5:00 and 9:00 a.m. *China Daily*, the English-language newspaper available in most major Chinese cities, offers useful information about television and radio broadcasts in Chinese.

If you buy a shortwave radio, be sure that the shortwave bands go at least to 23 KHz to tune in VOA and U.S. Armed Forces programs. Small transistor radios can be purchased in China and are adequate for local stations, but they are not powerful enough to bring in broadcasts from outside the country. Most foreign- made radios and tape recorders can now be repaired in Beijing and Shanghai. Imported and Chinese-made cassette recorders also can be purchased now in China, but they are expensive. Blank cassette tapes are easy to buy, but they are not of the best quality; taking a supply with you is worth the trouble if you plan to use them for music. Locally purchased cassettes should be adequate for making language tapes. In most cities you can purchase recorded music, mainly classical Chinese and Western selections, but Western and Chinese pop music is available, too. Most foreigners take their favorite music with them, wish they had brought more, and find that these tapes make fine gifts for Chinese friends and teachers when they leave.

CAMERAS AND FILM   Photography has become popular in China in recent years, particularly among the more affluent young, and many have become avid photographers. Both the purchase and development of film is easier now than several years ago. Kodak and Fuji film are easy to buy in large cities, but it is advisable to bring film if you will be in out-of-the-way places or to ensure that the film you are using is fresh. Print film is generally easier to buy than slide film. Foreign black and white film and high ASA (over 400) film are still hard to find. Disk and Polaroid film are generally available only in the more expensive joint-venture hotels and in Guangzhou's Friendship Store. Print film prices in China are about the same as they are in the United States. Chinese-made black-and-white film is easily purchased and processed, and many hotels and local shops offer color-film-processing services. The Jianguo in Beijing has one-day service, and so does a shop in the China World Trade Center. The Friendship Hotel develops print film reasonably (Y35 for 36 color prints). The quality of film processing in China is uneven; scratching of negatives is common and the fluid used to coat prints may not be up to standard, causing color to fade faster. However, many long-term residents feel that it is safer to process exposed film than to carry it through airport inspections or to store it in extreme temperatures. Slide film is quite expensive in China. If you have it processed in China, be sure to tell the service personnel that you want the slides mounted. Some places process prepaid Kodachrome film, but it can also be sent to Hong Kong or Australia. Some post offices provide film mailers, and there have been few reported problems sending film out of China.

A word of caution about Polaroid cameras: they are still a novelty in China, and if you use them in public or crowded places, expect to receive a lot of attention and, possibly, requests from people wanting instant photos. In less touristed areas, people who have seen Polaroids work may expect you to produce instant photos for them even if you are using a standard camera. One researcher using his 35 mm camera in a remote region of China was followed for several blocks by the subjects of his photograph who demanded that he produce instant photos for them as a previous photographer had with a Polaroid.

Videocassettes are a special case. Technically, they cannot be taken in or out of the country without inspection and special permission; however, some researchers report that customs officials have not even bothered to examine videocassettes that they are carrying. Still, it is probably best to err on the side of caution. If you travel to Hong Kong during your stay in China to purchase photographic equipment, be sure to check with your host unit about customs regulations.

In the past, travelers were cautioned about taking pictures of airports, bridges, harbors, military facilities, soldiers, policemen, and wall posters. Sensitivities have eased considerably in recent years, but military facilities are generally off limits to foreigners and thus should not be photographed. Always ask permission before taking a picture of an individual. Taking pictures without asking permission is considered discourteous and has led to some incidents in which film has been confiscated. The elderly are particularly sensitive about being photographed, and some rural folk, who may never have seen a camera, may be frightened. Chinese parents, though, often enjoy having their children photographed, and many people find it fun to have their picture taken with a foreigner.

BICYCLES   Bicycles are the preferred mode of transportation for many American residents in China, and both new and used ones are easy and inexpensive to purchase. A new bike costs Y340-800; used ones are about Y200. Ask around or check your local bulletin board if you want to buy a used one. Used bicycle shops are fairly common in larger cities. The quality of brands varies, and some carry a certain measure of status. Ask your Chinese and foreign friends for advice before you buy. All bicycles must be registered. Ask your host unit for guidance.

Bicycle repair shops—usually independent entrepreneurs who set up their tools along the street—are everywhere. Repairs are inexpensive: a complete overhaul may cost as little as Y10. Check any new or used bike carefully, however, before leaving the shop, and make certain the salespeople tighten all the parts. Buy a bicycle light and reflecting tape for the front and back fenders for safety. Many riders carry repair kits with lock washers of various sizes and other tools for repairs on the road. Theft is not uncommon in China, and Chinese-style bicycle locks are usually part of the purchase. Chains and locks are also sold in most bicycle stores. Some people recommend bringing a Kryptonite lock from the United States. Park in a bicycle lot to minimize the possibility of theft or confiscation by campus police, who sometimes pick up bikes not properly parked. If your bicycle is missing, check first with the police.

If your stay in China will be relatively short, you might want to rent a bicycle. In large cities, the rental shop is often found just opposite the Friendship Store; personnel at tourist hotels or local China International Travel Service offices can provide information on rentals in other areas.

I.D. PHOTOS   When you register with the local public security bureau, you must provide passport-sized photos for library cards, swimming passes, and diplomas. You should take along ten or more extra copies of photos or have them done in China (the turnaround time is about two days).

READING MATERIAL   Beijing has an eclectic selection of reading matter in the stores catering to foreigners, but rarely the latest bestsellers or much serious nonfiction. A selection of Western newspapers and magazines is offered in Friendship Stores and joint-venture hotels—*The Asian Wall Street Journal, International Herald Tribune, Time, Newsweek, Reader's Digest,* and *Far Eastern Economic Review.* Chinese-run English language bookstores in big cities often have a good selection of English-language novels as well as translations of Chinese novels, poetry, and art books. Some familiarity with Chinese classical and popular writing is both informative and educational; it also provides a rich source of conversation with Chinese colleagues and friends.

One important publication for the foreign community is *China Daily*, which is published in English, distributed free in some hotels, and sold for Y0.30 in certain stores. *China Daily* notes restaurant specials and art exhibits; provides local entertainment schedules; reviews current theater, opera, and films; lists Radio Beijing and TV programs; publishes daily exchange rates; has a crossword puzzle and bridge column; and provides minimal coverage of Chinese and world news. The editorial section, in particular, is invaluable to the non-Chinese speaker because major pieces from the Chinese press are often translated there.

GAMES   Board games can be fun for relaxation with friends, both Chinese and foreign; and word games like Scrabble and Password provide novel ways of teaching English. Puzzles, too, can be useful for long winter Sundays and they make thoughtful gifts for Chinese friends with families when you leave. If you are taking children with you, it is a good idea to pack their favorite toys and a few special decorations and treats for American holidays.

GIFTS   Purchasing gifts to take is a problem for the prospective China traveler. Gifts to Chinese colleagues and friends and to those who help out along the way—drivers, for example—must be chosen and given with care. Too lavish a gift will create embarrassment, and yet the days of giving ballpoint pens and picture postcards are long over. For any gift you are given, a reciprocal gift is expected. Most Chinese prefer gifts that are clearly both Western and "modern," but many of your Chinese acquaintances will have been abroad and have accumulated some of the trinkets that were once deemed satisfactory gifts. As one student warns, beware of underestimating the sophistication of your Chinese friends. Chinese drivers often smoke and generally appreciate American-made cigarettes, such as Marlboro, which can be bought in China. For advisers and academic colleagues, well-chosen books and scholarly materials are always appropriate, especially a copy of your own book or monograph. Scholars also appreciate Chinese calligraphy manuals, which are expensive in Chinese terms. Tapes of Western classical music are easier to buy in China now than they once were, but they are still a good gift. Art books and colorful calendars with scenes of U.S. life also are appropriate presents, as are English dictionaries and study guides and tapes for learning English.

Something with your school emblem is a good gift for academic hosts. One researcher took a beautifully printed greeting from the president of his university to his Chinese hosts, who enjoyed the calligraphy. If you are invited to a home for dinner, you might take along some imported candy or wine, or cookies in a decorative tin, all of which can be found in Friendship Stores and hotels. On these occasions, presenting gifts to the women and children of the family is appropriate.

Many Chinese are avid stamp collectors and appreciate the variety of stamps produced in the United States. Bring a selection along and save those that come on your letters. One teacher who brought a Vogue pattern book for her own use discovered that her female students loved it and began sharing it among themselves. Posters of historic or scenic sites in the United States or poster reproductions of Western art are also good gifts. Intricate jigsaw puzzles are popular gifts for children. You should not be surprised, however, if the recipient does not open your gift immediately; it is customary to wait until later.

Taking friends, colleagues, or advisers out to dinner is still an excellent way to say thank you or repay hospitality. For more formal obligations involving officials at your institution, a Chinese banquet may be in order. See Chapter 3 for details of this ritual. Special friends and colleagues may appreciate being taken more informally to a local restaurant or even to a Western-style coffee shop in one of the joint-venture hotels. And if children are invited, an excursion to Kentucky Fried Chicken, McDonald's, or Pizza Hut can be a great adventure. Remember, too, that while China's economy is booming and many are getting rich, the intellectuals with whom you are ordinarily in contact will be on very tight budgets. Most cannot afford restaurants except on the most important occasions. Expect to treat, even in the most casual and informal circumstances, unless it is very clear that you have been specially invited as the guest.

As restrictions on contact with Chinese friends continue to ease, relations have become more casual. Today you can simply ask a Chinese friend for advice about gifts and courtesies. Your Chinese acquaintances, in turn, may well let you know what they want or need. But if some of the mystery has gone out of gift giving in China, courtesy demands that you nonetheless remain sensitive to the obligations and implications of a gift in that culture.

PREPARING FOR PROFESSIONAL LIFE

The chapters on research, teaching, and studying in China provide information that will help you decide what to bring to China for the work you will be doing there. This section offers some general suggestions.

Business cards printed, if possible, in both Chinese and English are essential in China. You will be handing them out and receiving them from almost everyone you meet. If you can have some made to bring with you to China, you will be able hand them out immediately. If not, business cards can be made inexpensively in China or Hong Kong.

A standard survey of Chinese history, guidebooks that describe your particular Chinese city, and up-to-date tourist handbooks are useful references to have in China. *The Cambridge Encyclopedia of China*, edited by Brian Hook and Denis Twitchett, is useful as is *The China Guidebook* by Kaplan, Sobin, and de Keijzer. Lonely Planet's *China: A Travel Survival Kit* is a favorite among travelers. Nagel's *Encyclopedic Guide to China*, a more detailed and scholarly work, offers historical information and is well worth the price ($65) in the opinion of some academic tourists. *In Search of Old Beijing*, by L.C. Arlington and William Lewisohn, and Juliet Bredon's *Peking*, published earlier this century, are fascinating guides to exploring the new city and noting the extensive architectural changes. Similar guides are available for other Chinese cities. Many of these guidebooks are now for sale in hotels and Friendship Stores in Beijing; see Appendix M for complete publishing details. A subscription to *China Daily* or *Beijing Review* for a few months before departure is good preparation for current events in China (both political and cultural). To order *China Daily*, contact:

> *China Daily*
> U.S. Distributor
> 15 Mercer Street
> New York, NY 10013
> Telephone: 212-219-0130

Multistandard videocassette recorders (VCRs) are widely available but frequently are standard play (fast speed) only. Persons taking NTSC extended or long-play tapes to China may have difficulty. VHS is the most common format, although many institutions also have 3/4-inch Umatic or Beta formats. Equipment must be 220 volts, 50 Hz; as noted, 120-volt transformers are available in China but are expensive. The more serious consideration is frequency, since electricity in China is 50 Hz as opposed to 60 Hz. Those planning to take videocassettes to China are advised to inform their institutions early on and to inquire what sort of equipment is available. Moreover, Chinese customs officials may want to examine videotapes being taken into the country and may confiscate tapes deemed to be pornographic or politically sensitive.

RESEARCHERS   Researchers should take an updated resume, offprints of relevant publications and books, and copies of major papers (with Chinese abstracts, if possible) to distribute to colleagues in China. Most scholars with experience in China advise taking all printed materials that are essential for your research and writing, including reference works. Libraries and bookstores in China are treasure troves, but new publications are often sold out soon after they reach the stores and the availability of, and access to, library books is unpredictable. Even major secondary works in your field may not be available. And dictionaries published in China are sometimes hard to obtain, so take the ones you need.

Experienced bibliophiles have discovered that books can now be ordered direct from publishers based in China or obtained from distribution centers. Out-of-print books and back issues of journals sometimes can be found in used bookstores, especially those in out-of-the-way spots. Bookstores in Liulichang, the newly renovated antique district in Beijing, often are a good source of books on early China. Cities such as Xi'an and Lanzhou, for example, have stores devoted to ancient history, stocking items that are hard to find in the larger cities. Ask your Chinese colleagues for advice, and offer to share your finds with them. Many scholars report that they have borrowed books from Chinese academics who have better private collections in their field than some libraries. In any case, if you see a book that you need, it is wise to buy it immediately.

Periodicals in Chinese may be ordered at the post office. A useful guide, arranged by subject, to newspapers and periodicals published in China is available from:

China International Book Trading Corporation (Guoji Shudian)
P.O. Box 2820
Beijing, China

(Sections on access to materials and the post office can be found in Chapters 4 and 7, respectively.)

If equipment is essential to your research, write ahead for information on available equipment and ask for precise specifications. Some researchers have been supplied with manual or electric typewriters, whereas others have no access to school equipment. Only a few of the people surveyed for this book were able to use computers supplied by their host institutions. If you will need a tape recorder, it is best to bring your own. Hong Kong is a good place to purchase excellent tape recorders at reasonable prices. Calculators are easy to buy in China. If you will be in a small town or village and gathering and copying materials is essential for your work, you may want to take a portable copier with a heavy-duty transformer. Canon's Personal Copier series comes highly recommended. Duplicating facilities are far more available in Chinese cities today than a few years ago, although most shops are located outside university gates and sometimes a good distance away.

Duplicating costs start at Y0.30 per page, and if you are teaching, your department may have only a minuscule budget for copying materials. (See also the previous section on office supplies and machines.)

Scientists whose research relies on specialized equipment should be particularly attentive to the question of what equipment to bring. Although some of China's laboratories are very well equipped, the quality varies widely. Check whether the laboratory in which you will work can meet your specific needs. A fuller discussion of this issue appears in Chapter 4.

If you will be working with interpreters, a dictionary that specializes in the technical terminology of your discipline can be of great use. If you will need audiovisual equipment, write ahead to your hosts to let them know exactly what you need. Some organizations have overhead projectors, but you should bring your own transparencies and marking pens. Most also have slide projectors, although screens apparently are scarcer and quite often the projectors are not in working order. With equipment, then, as with all other aspects of life in China, you can only try to plan ahead—and then be patient when your plans fail and grateful when they work. In such matters, a sense of humor is invaluable.

TEACHERS   In addition to the guidebooks on China mentioned earlier, an excellent book, specifically for teaching in China, is written by two Americans, Tani Barlow and Donald Lowe, who taught literature and history in Shanghai from 1981 to 1982. Their thoughtful and detailed account, *Teaching China's Lost Generation: Foreign Experts in the People's Republic of China*, is well worth reading.

Most returned teachers recommended that you write ahead to your host unit for details on what books and equipment will be available, because the availability of books and equipment varies considerably from school to school. "Key" universities with substantial government funding ordinarily have better teaching aids than smaller, locally run schools. The teachers surveyed for this handbook taught a variety of subjects in China, and they all strongly urged prospective teachers to take with them as many books and materials as possible. There is in general a serious shortage of English-language books in China, and books in fields that have only recently been introduced, such as law and management, are in particularly short supply, though many Western works are now being translated into Chinese. Many university libraries have difficulty keeping their English-language collections up to date, and student access to these holdings is often limited. Although some department libraries have excellent collections, the books are often reserved for faculty rather than student use. It is probably best to take important books in your field with you and plan to donate them to your

Chinese host institution when you leave. If you will be teaching English, you should also obtain information about the Test of English as a Foreign Language (TOEFL) and take TOEFL books and tapes with you. Certain U.S. or community funding agencies offer grants for books. If you apply early enough, you may be able to have materials sent ahead for use in your courses. The Fulbright lectureship includes a book allowance with which to purchase materials; check with the U.S. Embassy and with consular USIS staff.

One way to circumvent the shortage of books is to photocopy or ditto articles. But don't count on it. Duplicating facilities are limited at most institutions; some have only mimeograph machines and photocopiers are still scarce within institutions. In large cities, photocopying services are easy to find. Even if your institution has a copier, your funds for copying may be limited and you may have to pay for copying yourself. Moreover, with such heavy demands on copiers and limited repair service, teachers report that their university duplicating machine is often out of order. If you plan to use unbound materials, you should either take multiple copies with you or plan to have them copied at a hotel or neighborhood copy shop at a cost of Y0.30 or more per page.

Some teachers have typed course assignments on ditto masters and made direct transfer stencils of materials which were then duplicated in China. Duplicated articles about current events from *The New York Times*, *Newsweek*, *Foreign Affairs*, and other periodicals are avidly read by students and are a good form of language instruction because of their sophisticated vocabulary. You may also want to clip articles of current interest from magazines and newspapers to use as the basis for class discussions. Chinese students are accustomed to the lack of textbooks. They take meticulous notes, and if lectures are concise and well constructed, they can manage quite well without textbooks, although they often use their own reference books in Chinese to supplement English lecture notes.

Information about higher education in the United States is always welcome in China, and your hosts and students will appreciate any catalogs, course syllabi, or descriptive material that you can share with them. Many will be looking for ways to study in the United States and you can expect your students to call on you for advice and help. The U.S. government has placed collections of educational reference materials at 18 sites in China; the locations of these collections and the list of their materials are in Appendix P. U.S. colleges and universities have been requested to send their catalogs to these sites.

Finally, regarding books to take to China, teachers who have come back from China recommend the following: as many basic reference books as possible, several good dictionaries and encyclopedias, your favorite books at various levels on the subject matter you will be teaching, anthologies of American and British literature, Bartlett's Quotations, references on American culture, a copy of the U.S. Constitution, novels, a good atlas, standard grammar books, maps of the United States and the world in English, and a world almanac. As one teacher put it, "I can't think of anything not to take, except maybe pornographic literature. That is frowned upon, but the Chinese are remarkably open about what you bring for your own reading or for sharing with Chinese friends."

If you plan to use audiovisual aids, find out from the host institution if they have what you need. Some institutions do have overhead projectors, but teachers have found that at times their classes were too large to use transparencies as a teaching aid. Slide projectors are fairly common and teachers do recommend taking slides to use in classes. Also, reel-to-reel tape recorders are frequently available. Cassette recorders are becoming more and more common, but high-quality tapes are still difficult to find. Some teachers found that they could arrange for films and videotapes to be shown, but if the department for which they work does not have the necessary equipment, it may be charged for the use of such equipment. Also, both the equipment and the rooms for viewing must be reserved in advance, and in some cases, tapes must be submitted to institution authorities to be reviewed one week in advance of the showing.

If your institution does not have the necessary equipment, consider taking your own, such as a slide projector with transformers, if you think it worth the effort. Be sure to read the preceding sections on equipment and review the customs regulations on tapes and films. If you plan to donate equipment to your Chinese institution when you leave, be certain when you arrive to have your unit register it with Chinese customs officials as a duty-free educational item.

There is a great deal of curiosity in China about life in the United States, and American teachers are often asked to give talks about American culture. You should be prepared to talk knowledgeably about a variety of topics—from current slang and films to intricate workings of the U.S. Congress. Take along any references that might be useful to you in answering wide-ranging questions. An almanac, according to one teacher, was "worth its weight in gold—we used ours every day"; a good paperback English dictionary and thesaurus are handy and make appropriate gifts for Chinese friends when you leave. The press and cultural section of the U.S. Embassy has a library that can be tapped, but its holdings are limited. You may want to bring slides and photographs showing various aspects of your life in the United States. For example, shots of your city, school, family, and holiday celebrations, as well as pictures taken in your neighborhood, such as supermarkets, city and street scenes, farms, parks, schools, subways, and airports can be of great interest to Chinese students who have had little opportunity to glimpse everyday life abroad. Returned teachers also stress balancing "the good and the bad" when discussing life in the United States.

3. Settling In

Just as opportunities for getting to China are diverse, so are the experiences of people who travel there. Few say that living in China is easy, and most people report wide swings between exhilaration and frustration. Most leave feeling their lives have been enriched by what they have learned, both about China and themselves, and many continue to return year after year. To reduce the richness and variety of life in China to a single picture would be unfair. But returning "veterans" have a fund of anecdotes and insights, and certain patterns do emerge. Their experiences can help prepare you.

ARRIVING IN CHINA

An experienced travel agent in the United States can acquaint you with the many ways of entering China, and the China guidebooks listed in Chapter 2 describe the various options. You may also want to consult the China National Tourist Office in New York (212-867-0271). There are now direct flights from many parts of the world, especially Tokyo and Hong Kong, to numerous cities in China, including Shanghai, Beijing, Guangzhou, Xiamen, Guilin, and Chengdu. Some travelers prefer to stop in Hong Kong or Tokyo for a day or two of rest before proceeding to their destination in China, and some even arrive by ship or the trans-Siberian railway. In Hong Kong, the China Travel Service can supply information, tickets, and even last-minute visas. Addresses and telephone numbers for China Travel Service's two Hong Kong locations are provided on p. 11. The China International Travel Service (CITS), which serves non-Chinese visitors exclusively, has an office in

South Sea Centre
Sixth Floor, Tower Two
Tsimshatsui East
Kowloon
Telephone: (852) 721-5317

Representatives of host institutions often meet senior faculty, teachers, and researchers at the airport. If you are worried about getting to your new residence on your own, ask to be met. But the sheer volume of academic travelers to China has placed such a strain on host organizations that they may not have the personnel. Students are not ordinarily met, although some programs sponsored by U.S. universities will arrange to meet you.

If you want to be met, be sure to tell them so, and communicate your travel plans to your hosts clearly and early on. You can telephone or fax from Hong Kong if final plans are made there or you can fax from the United States. If possible, try to avoid a weekend arrival. Most units are open on Saturday morning, but Saturday afternoons and Sundays are typically days of rest and offices will be closed. If your flight is delayed en route, try to fax the unit so staff do not make unnecessary trips to the airport. Airports are usually located a considerable distance from the city, and making the trek is time-consuming. Try also to notify all the organizations involved in hosting you. For example, if you are to be associated with a unit in the interior that has a parent organization in Beijing or Shanghai, do not assume that the two organizations will communicate with each other. Specify which unit should meet you, however. Otherwise both may make the trip. One scholar suggests taking a taxi to a predetermined hotel where your hosts can meet you. This saves everyone time and effort.

You will have to proceed through customs on your own. Hosts are not allowed to enter the baggage claim or customs area.

The baggage claim and customs process is often hectic. Sometimes several flights arrive at once, and baggage carousels in many places are inadequate for the volume of traffic, even with the recent expansion of many international terminals.

If no one is to meet you at the airport, your first adventure will begin. Bring the telephone number of your unit so you can call if you arrive during working hours. Many airports have China Travel Service booths with English-speaking personnel who can help you call or even assist in getting you to your destination. If you cannot reach your work unit, you will need to change money at one of the foreign exchange booths in the airport and hire a taxi.

Taxis have recently proliferated, as the Chinese say, "like bamboo shoots after a spring rain" and most airports will have a line of waiting cabs. Regulations require the taxis to line up at a designated stand and for customers to form a line. But more aggressive drivers often assemble where passengers are exiting from customs, promising cheap fares and good cars. You would be wise to refuse their offers. Sometimes their cars are not properly registered and fares can be exorbitant. One researchers says, "never, unless you are very desperate, go in a vehicle with anyone who approaches you in a train station or airport. Either the vehicle will turn out to be a kidney-jarring wreck, or you will be badly overcharged, or both."

Insist that you want to *paidui*—line up—outside. Taxis charge different rates depending on the quality of the car, and the rate is posted along the rear windows. Mercedes, Volvos, and other upscale cars are more expensive than older models that have been around for a while. If the driver is not using a meter, be sure to negotiate a price in advance.

If you will be staying in the city where you have just arrived, you can communicate better if you have the name and address of your destination written in Chinese. The driver will be able to find it. If not, ask for assistance from someone who speaks English. Few taxi drivers have more than a rudimentary command of English. Look around to see if there is a minibus from a joint-venture Western hotel. If you go to one of those hotels, English-speaking staff will help arrange for you to get where you want to go. If there are no minibuses and all communications fail, the taxi driver will probably take you to one of the joint-venture hotels with an English-speaking staff who can give instructions to the driver or help with other arrangements. If you must make your own arrangements for travel to a final destination, someone at the hotel can direct you to the nearest office of the China Travel Service—which might be in the hotel.

One American researcher who spoke no Chinese arrived in a remote city with no taxis and no one to meet him. He took a bus, got off when he saw a hotel, and walked into the lobby to find his Chinese hosts waiting for him there!

THE TENOR OF LIFE IN CHINA

THE WORK UNIT   Every foreigner who lives and works in China is assigned to a work unit, which in Chinese is called a *danwei*. For the foreign visitor, as well as most Chinese, the *danwei* is the organization through which most official activities are filtered.   Whether it be a factory, research institute, or university, the work unit is a microcosm of Chinese society, with its own political hierarchy, networks of personal and professional relationships, services, and, in most cases, living quarters.

It is primarily through the work unit that the Chinese government exerts its influence on the life of the individual, because, in addition to work, the *danwei* also provides many of the necessities of daily life, including housing and dining halls, and permission to marry, to bear a single child, and to travel. The work unit also entitles its members to state-supported medical care and issues the identification card that marks the bearer as a working member of Chinese society. The unit acts as a go-between contact between its own members and members of other organizations. Lateral relations among *danwei*, even those engaged in similar activities, are cumbersome. Each unit is a more-or-less autonomous compartment.

Temporary movement in and out of the *danwei* is common for Chinese intellectuals and administrators. Until recently, an individual assigned to a work unit remained there for his entire working life. Now, many people are leaving *danwei* to join newly formed research institutes, joint-venture companies, or to strike out on their own, although permanent exit from a work unit often requires considerable negotiation.

The nature of the work unit is changing, however, and travelers will witness the remarkable transition currently under way. One of those changes is the growing commercialization of academic institutions. While universities and research institutes still rely on government funds, they are being called on to become more self-sufficient economically by starting money-making ventures. Most university students are still supported by the state, but the trend is shifting. More students are paying their own way, and state funds are largely concentrated on those in critical disciplines or on promising students with severe financial constraints.

Departments within universities—both academic and administrative—are being asked to raise funds as a way of both increasing faculty income and providing money for university-wide operation and expansion. Faculty members are encouraged to generate new sources of income. Many money-making activities within universities and research institutes are academically related. Some departments are holding international conferences and charging registration fees to foreign participants in addition to living expenses. Others are conducting training courses for people outside the university. Southern universities are organizing educational tours to Hong Kong. Computer science departments are assisting in the computerization of businesses and writing programs for them. Some departments are offering preparatory courses for students planning to take graduate-level exams. History departments are training archivists and working to put classical texts on computers. Funds generated are shared among faculty, departments, and university-level administrative units.

Relations within the *danwei* are invariably complex, particularly within universities and research institutes. Older staff members may carry scars from the various political campaigns that swept China from 1957 until the death of Mao in 1976 and often pitted colleague against colleague and friend against friend. During the most tragic of those movements, the Cultural Revolution (1966-1976), Chinese universities and research institutes were torn apart, and senior, Western-educated intellectuals in particular were subject to prolonged abuse. Despite the passage of time and the infusion of new staff and students, persecutors and persecuted, enemies and friends, continue to live and work side by side.

The effect of the Tiananmen Square incident of 1989 was less divisive. Many faculty and administrators supported the students who demonstrated, and others were sympathetic. Although most universities have returned to normal, activities at Peking University, as of this writing, continue to be closely scrutinized.

The complexities and strains within a work unit will be invisible at first. Over time, as you make Chinese friends, you will learn that the surface cordiality among coworkers may mask larger tensions—not only the remnants of previous political campaigns but also the result of new competition for scarce resources. There may be two candidates for promotion and only one space available, for instance. Or several faculty might have invitations to study abroad when the department can spare only one. Pressure to make money for the university is creating new strains. Some faculty who might want to befriend you may have been criticized in the past for becoming too close to foreigners.

The presence of a foreigner, even if temporary, can create further imbalances, both in interpersonal relations and over such scarce resources as office space and assistants who may be reassigned to you. More important, the Chinese members of the *danwei* who associate most closely with a foreigner become both more visible and more vulnerable to criticism by their superiors and colleagues. You will want to be discreet with Chinese hosts and friends. Never flaunt close friendships and do not discuss your relationship with Chinese friends to others. It is also wise to avoid writing letters that detail relationships or conversations with Chinese friends. To do so would betray their confidence and risk intervention by their superiors.

You, too, will become a member of this highly structured society, and you can accomplish little without learning to work within its boundaries. Membership in a *danwei* will make life simpler and more secure. Many of the basic arrangements for daily life will be made for you. But foreigners may also feel confined and deprived of a measure of freedom when they realize how dependent they must be. Most need to break out now and then—whether for a bike ride or walk through the back alleys of the city, a visit to friends who have nothing to do with their work unit, a hike through the woods, a picnic at the Ming tombs or some other scenic spot, a shopping spree, a splurge at a joint-venture hotel, or late night dancing at the local disco.

THE FOREIGN AFFAIRS OFFICE   Figuring out how a unit is organized, who has formal authority and who has actual power, and how to couch your requests will take time. The first introduction most new arrivals have to their work units is through the *waishi banshichu*—literally "the office for outside business," but usually referred to simply as the foreign affairs office or *waiban*. The foreign affairs office exists in virtually all organizations and administrative units that have contact with foreigners. For students, the *waiban* office is usually called the *liuxuesheng bangongshi*, the "office for overseeing foreign students," or *liuban* for short.

The foreign affairs office looms large in the lives of foreigners. It provides the mechanism whereby you can work within the unit without becoming fully integrated into it. The responsibility of the *waiban* is to make living arrangements and to serve as a liaison with other units and with different departments within the unit itself. Formal introductions to people you wish to meet in other units will often be made not directly by you but by the *waiban*. If anything goes awry during your visit, if you are sick, hurt, or robbed, the *waiban* will be called on to help.

Foreign affairs officials sometimes have training in a foreign language (usually English), but few have spent any significant time abroad and most are not scholars. Their task is complicated by the fact that they are dealing with people from all over the world and from many different cultures. What they know about U.S. culture is likely to be influenced by what they read in the Chinese press and by their experience with other Americans who came before you. If your institution has hosted many Americans in the past, the *waiban* is likely to understand that Americans are diverse, with different tastes and personalities and different capacities to adapt. If you are one of the first Americans at your institution, the *waiban* official's initial perception of you is likely to be colored by his experience with the last American he hosted. If the last American did not like Chinese food and complained about the plumbing, the foreign affairs office may fear that your attitude will be much the same. As such, you are, unwittingly, a representative of all Americans. It will take time for both of you to understand who the other really is.

Your status, linguistic capabilities, prior contacts with the *danwei* and outside networks, as well as the unit's own history and style of dealing with foreigners, all influence your relations with the foreign affairs office. A major factor affecting how you are treated is the number of other foreigners under the care of the office. Busy foreign affairs personnel may have been told little about you or why you are coming to China, and thus may not be certain at first of your status. The result of so many people coming in through the "open door," one scholar points out, is that "China seems to find it difficult at this stage to discriminate among her visitors with respect to their usefulness, seniority, etc. As a consequence, allocations of all kinds seem to be made literally on a first-come, first-served basis."

The *waiban* will be interested in determining your status, because the extent of services provided is also a function of where the foreigner falls in the hierarchy. A distinguished scholar will be accorded more help than a student. An American student in a university crowded with students from all over the world can expect less help and even, at times, a lack of cooperation from overburdened officials.

What students lack in comfort and attention, however, they are compensated for by a relative degree of freedom to make their own arrangements. Students can make their own travel plans, for example, and thus they can determine the style and schedule of their trips far more easily than the honored foreign guest who tours with an entourage or is met along the way with interpreters, guides, formal banquets, and photo sessions. Ironically, without the mediating influence of the *waiban*, students also have the opportunity to understand how the bureaucracy works for the Chinese, because they often come face to face with it. Such experiences, although often frustrating, also provide insights into Chinese society that are not always so easily glimpsed by those sheltered by status.

Advice on how to deal with the foreign affairs office is difficult because the office varies so much from unit to unit. Recent descriptions from academics in China portray foreign affairs personnel ranging from saints to devils. Some China veterans try to ignore the foreign affairs officials as much as possible and to work through academic colleagues who are likely to be more understanding of and sympathetic to their academic goals. Others argue that functionaries must be courted. One graduate student laments that he heeded warnings to avoid the foreign affairs office: "It has been my experience this year that if you get to know them well and have requests which are within their power to grant, they will be granted. This is not unlike bureaucrats and administrators in the West."

He goes on to point out, however, that help from Chinese bureaucrats often hinges on personal relations. Of one particularly powerful official, he says, "If he does not like you, he will use every means to prevent you from achieving your goals."

The traits that may help you win your *waiban*'s cooperation include good cheer in the face of adversity, respect and understanding for the limitations of particular offices, and the ability to offer criticism constructively—which means, among other things, that when frustrated you should not slander the socialist system or Chinese culture but rather focus on the particular problems at hand.

With the increased autonomy of Chinese universities, many are in the process of reorganization and, in some places, new names are being given to the offices for managing foreigners. A few foreign researchers have reported delays in getting set up because they could not determine who was responsible for them. If you are having trouble deciding where to turn, ask another foreigner in your unit with a status similar to your own.

The *waiban*'s tasks are not confined to foreign guests. The office also handles the unit's external relationships, including arranging for its Chinese members to go abroad, receiving delegations, and negotiating exchange programs. With the recent call for *danwei* to begin earning money themselves rather than relying exclusively on funding from the state, universities and research institutes are also looking for ways to make money. In some parts of China, *waiban* are being assigned new roles. Because of their ties with foreigners and with other work units, *waiban* are particularly well placed to organize money-making activities, and scholars in China report instances of *waiban* officials disappearing for long periods to organize such endeavors. Scholars and students have come to recognize that their presence is often seen, quite frankly, as a means of making money. But the situation is different in every *danwei*, and among foreign affairs personnel as well. Many have proved exceedingly helpful to American teachers, researchers, and students.

Interactions are almost always restrained when Chinese and Americans first meet, even when friendships later develop. Meet your own *waiban* with an open mind and no preconceived notions. Allow time to see how your relationship is likely to evolve. Then you can decide whether your *waiban* can become an ally or whether to turn to others for help.

THE QUALITY OF LIFE   Every work unit is a minisociety with its own personality—its traditions, folklore, factions, history, and style of working with foreigners. The flavor of daily life differs among *danwei*. The city in which you live, the size and personality of the foreign community there, the nature of the *waiban*, and your institution's relations with other organizations will all affect your life. A small, less prestigious teacher's college may be either more defensive and rigid with its foreign guests or more welcoming and open than a large key university. A research institute that has never hosted foreign guests may be eager to establish new ties or, alternatively, suspicious and hesitant at first. Generalizations about daily life can only be made with caution.

Nonetheless, themes do emerge from reports and conversations with foreigners who have lived in China for any length of time. One frequent observation is the lack of privacy in China. As one American comments, "Some things are difficult to get used to—the absolute lack of privacy is one. There are people hovering about me from 6:30 a.m. until I retire. They are all well-intentioned, trying to make me comfortable and trying to help. But it's hard to adjust to and in many ways sets up a barrier between me and the society I am studying. I am gradually finding ways to get around this, but the key here is patience."

There is, says another, a "different concept of privacy in China—people walking into one's room freely, inspecting personal items, reading mail, asking questions. An adjustment is needed." The boundaries in China between acceptable questions and embarrassing intrusions are different from those in the West, and you will face all sorts of questions that Americans generally consider taboo: about how old you are and how much money you make, about how much your clothes cost and where you have been that day or plan to go tomorrow.

On the other hand, Chinese colleagues and friends—especially the older generation—will rarely take the initiative to delve into questions about your personal life beyond a polite concern for health and family matters, nor will they volunteer details about theirs. Some foreigners have learned only by accident, for example, that a longstanding Chinese friend is divorced, married, or about to get married. As one senior scholar observed, "It often took a genuine effort to establish a dialogue that moved beyond the superficial aspects of daily life, especially with my older Chinese colleagues."

One researcher who travels frequently to China carries pictures of his family, his house, and the town where he lives and shows them to new acquaintances as a way of making friends. Lively exchanges usually ensue. Topics of common intellectual interest can also be the source of lengthy and fascinating conversation, and can open windows on Chinese society that mere observation cannot.

Younger people are sometimes far more open. American students can expect a great deal of curiosity about U.S. life (from rock stars to sex and romance), and they may, in turn, learn about Chinese family life, courting behavior, and marriage expectations. Often the most intense encounters occur when you are traveling, for many people talk more frankly with people they will never see again.

The nature of the *danwei* system allows little separation between one's personal and professional life, especially for those who live on the campuses of their work units. Your apartment may double as your office, and you may find that visiting hours are open-ended. Not even the hotel dweller in a far corner of the city is immune to frequent visits from anxious colleagues, especially in the first few weeks when hosts may be concerned about how quickly you are adapting to a new environment. Indeed, hosts are right to worry: many foreigners develop colds or feel otherwise out of sorts initially, and many report frustration over how long the process of settling in and buckling down to work can take.

Although first meetings with Chinese colleagues may be very formal, once a relationship is established, friends and colleagues feel free to stop by, without phoning ahead (because most scholars do not have telephones), simply to visit. Or they may make vague plans to meet, leaving you bound to your room for hours waiting for a friend or student who promised to stop by "sometime in the afternoon." Sometimes Chinese colleagues and friends will appear without notice at times when they are least expected—early on a Sunday morning, for instance. The only time you can be relatively sure of time to yourself is during the *xiuxi* or rest period, from noon until 1:30 or 2 p.m.—and even that is changing.

In China, your housing belongs to the *danwei*. One teacher in southern China whose apartment had a small spare bedroom was informed that the university would be renting the room to short-term foreign visitors as a way to make some extra money. Only persistent negotiations on her part finally convinced her hosts that both her privacy, and conceivably her safety, would be compromised should the spare bedroom be converted to a hotel room.

Despite the concerns of some foreigners, rooms are rarely searched and people are rarely followed. As one researcher declares, "Nobody is following you—you're not worth the effort." The exceptions are generally cases when the political activities of the foreign guest become cause for Chinese government concern. When cleaning people at one dormitory reported that a student had scrawled "Down with Deng Xiaoping" on the wall of his room, university security officials were called in to inspect not only his room but the rooms of others as well. Researchers with close ties to dissidents have been followed. And one researcher who stepped beyond the bounds of what Chinese officials considered acceptable behavior for someone in her status reports "both my activities and those of my visitors and guests are monitored, recorded, and sometimes submitted to the police for review. . . . Warnings and cartoon stories about foreign spies cover the walls and display stands at police stations, and other lingering fears about even casual contact with foreigners clearly still abound." If you are ever involved in political activities and rouse Chinese government suspicions, even nonpolitical Chinese friends could be called to task. Unless they clearly indicate otherwise, they will be less subject to scrutiny if you stop seeing them, at least temporarily.

What Chinese officials regard as appropriate behavior on your part depends on your status in China. Suspicion of a foreigner's activities is most easily aroused when the outsider steps out of the bounds of the category in which he or she originally has been placed.

Foreigners who behave in a manner inappropriate to their status (particularly journalists reporting on tourist visas or journalism teachers who publish in U.S. newspapers) risk reprimand (or, in rare cases, expulsion). A Ph.D. candidate subject to the two-week-per-semester limit on fieldwork who makes private arrangements to carry out fieldwork for longer periods risks being declared an "unwelcome scholar" for not going through official channels. Those who travel to China to carry out serious work of any kind must have the sanction of officialdom at some level.

At a recent briefing for Fulbright lecturers about to depart for China, "patience, politeness, and perseverance" were taken as the watchwords for getting by in China. Indeed, the word "patience" comes up repeatedly when Americans offer advice. "Patience is the most valuable trait to take to China," says one. Says another: "Be sensitive to Chinese personality traits; they are much more patient than we, and a quick temper will get you nowhere. Never take yourself, or the Chinese, too seriously; they are extremely modest, a trait we Americans should learn to practice more assiduously."

A combination of patience, politeness, and perseverance can help Chinese colleagues and friends understand and respect your need to balance privacy with friendship and collegial interaction. The Chinese recognize vast differences between their own culture and that of the United States, but they often do not know exactly what those differences are. You can explain. You do not have to answer questions that you regard as personal. Most Chinese will appreciate a friendly explanation that in the United States such questions are ordinarily raised only among family and close friends. Most want to understand Western values. Some Americans assert their right to privacy by establishing hard and fast visiting hours and posting them on their doors, with a polite explanation that they need time to work or be with their families. In one university, the results were so successful that Chinese professors began posting similar signs.

Foreigners often face conflicts between the personal difficulty of living with far less space and luxury than they are accustomed to in the United States and the knowledge that their living conditions are usually vastly better than those of their Chinese friends and colleagues. Despite rapid construction in many parts of China, most organizations remain constrained by a severe shortage of space. Few of your Chinese colleagues enjoy the luxury of a private office—or any office at all—and their living quarters are often cramped. On the one hand, foreigners are embarrassed at being given housing and office privileges so clearly superior to their Chinese counterparts. Researchers feel vaguely guilty to realize, for instance, that their office had once accommodated six or eight of their colleagues, who had to move out to free up space. Some scholars working in the countryside discover that special quarters—with showers, kitchens, and personnel to staff the establishment—have been constructed just for their use. Such luxurious accommodations place them far above the living standard of their Chinese neighbors.

On the other hand, researchers and teachers have been equally dismayed at the condition of their apartments, dormitories, laboratories, and classrooms, which are not generally heated or well-maintained and are sometimes downright unsafe. One scientist, for example, discovered asbestos materials filtering through the heating system, and others have complained about inadequate fire escapes in dormitories and hotels. Only after visiting a Chinese home, or understanding the daily working conditions of colleagues, or seeing a Chinese student dormitory, do many foreigners finally understand what a privileged position they enjoy.

The shortage of space, and the fact that many members of the *danwei* live on campus, are the main reasons that professional business is often conducted in the room or apartment of the foreign guest. The foreign visitor's room may be the only available space to hold language tutorials, conduct financial negotiations, arrange for travel, and so on.

PERSONAL RELATIONSHIPS   **Friendship**   The Chinese concept of friendship is powerful, and nothing has been more moving about the "opening up" of China than the renewal of friendships between Chinese and Americans that had been severed for 30 years. But Chinese friendships are often slower to develop than those made in the United States. Making Chinese friends can be a long and painstaking process, and friendships usually result only from conscious acts of will on both sides. But once a friendship forms, you can expect it to last for life.

The opening up of China to Western science, technology, and business has at times been coupled with equally strong admonitions against Chinese citizens becoming "tainted" by Western values. The official press periodically inveighs against "peaceful evolution" and Chinese friends will tell you about the policy of being open on the outside while maintaining tight political control within. Many Chinese delegated to work with foreigners are warned by their superiors that *neiwai youbie*—there is a difference between what you can share with insiders versus outsiders.

Opportunities for friendship and informal contact are far greater now than in the early stages of academic exchanges. However, many Chinese are still wary of contact with foreigners, and residues of earlier restrictions, including the registration of visitors at many student dormitories, remain, although the number of people cleared to have contact with foreigners has grown. In general, friendships are easier with people who have official reason to be in contact with you—colleagues and students, in particular.

But one dissertation-level student doing research at a Chinese academy reports that a professor who was offering informal guidance was warned by his superiors to minimize contact. Meeting with her, he was told, was part of "foreign affairs" and therefore had to be officially reported. Faculty elsewhere not specifically designated to engage in "foreign affairs" may be under similar constraints, which is one of the reasons so many American graduate students and researchers are disappointed that they interact so rarely with potential colleagues in their units.

Less formally, it is possible to find good excuses to make Chinese friends. If getting to know the Chinese people is one of your goals, be sure to ask your Chinese and American friends in the United States to give you the names, addresses and telephone numbers of friends they think you would like to meet. Be prepared to treat them to meals, and do not be insulted if you cannot be invited to their homes. Contacts are still sensitive, and home visits by foreigners, however discreet, are usually public events. Many researchers, on the other hand, are often invited to friends' homes.

The waxing and waning of Chinese politics will affect how often and whether you will be able to meet your Chinese friends. Many temporarily severed their contacts with foreigners after the Tiananmen Square incident of 1989, only to resume them when the situation eased. Longtime residents in China learn to read the subtle changes that indicate a political tightening—as when guests are required to register again, or university gates swing closed, or your old friend at the library suddenly becomes distant and requests for materials are refused. Protecting your Chinese friends means *never* pushing to see them when they tell you it would be "inconvenient." They stand to lose far more than you by risking contact during times of political tension.

Guanxi   One of the first words foreigners in China learn is *guanxi*, a traditional concept meaning relationship or connections. To get anything done in China, you must have *guanxi*. In a society of scarcity and strict institutional control, getting what you want—a good doctor, a scarce consumer item, the right job, acceptable housing, a chance to travel abroad—depends on having good *guanxi*. Thus, Chinese cultivate *guanxi*. The use of *guanxi* (who owes you a favor, or who thinks you might be of use in the future) is just as important as the formal lines of authority. For example, if you have offered help to your Chinese friends, they will almost surely feel obligated to draw on their own *guanxi* to repay the debt; others might help you with the anticipation that you may repay them in the future—in the form of help to study abroad, more immediate access to scarce resources, practice with English, or some other form of entry into the Western world.

In *Teaching China's Lost Generation: Foreign Experts in the People's Republic of China*, Tani Barlow and Donald Lowe describe the rich network of human relationships they both inherited—as a result of Donald Lowe's family connections in Shanghai—and developed, as foreign experts at Shanghai Teacher's University from 1981 to 1982.

> The term *guanxi* describes social connections based on concrete, reciprocal exchange of favors and goods among family members and others. In a sense, *guanxi* is the way people organize relationships outside the *jia* (family), transforming strangers into kin by extending them favors and incurring obligations. All pseudo-family ties are cemented by this process. And ideally all relations between people should have a familist[ic] overtone. A Chinese doctor usually does not try to intimidate patients through a show of professionalism. Patients play on the familist[ic] ties between parent and child, making the doctor a parent through *guanxi*, usually giving the latter food or gifts. In return, the doctor is expected to treat the patient's entire being, including feelings and fears which Western doctors tend to consider "psychological" and hence not a part of their responsibility. This kind of relationship cannot develop unless both sides accept the obligation to give and receive concrete favors as tokens of the *guanxi*.

Barlow and Lowe then describe how *guanxi* works in practice:

> If you have no previous *guanxi* (perhaps you have neglected to give the clerk at your local grocery a piece of candy or new year calendar), your chances of getting what you want are pretty slim. When mothballs come on the market once a year, there is a frenzy of *guanxi* reaffirmations. People give cigarettes, generally in exchange for good cuts of meat. . . . The more powerful the recipient, the more expensive the gift.[1]

With both the growing commercialization in China and the desire of so many young people to study in the United States, Americans are seen as a particularly good source of *guanxi*. We are often perceived as having the "connections" in the United States that can make study there possible. Some Chinese, knowing how *guanxi* works in their own country, hope that American acquaintances have *guanxi* with a consular official who can be persuaded to give them a visa. Because Americans are perceived as generally rich and good at doing business (and because certain advantages accrue to joint-venture enterprises with foreigners),

---

[1]Tani E. Barlow and Donald M. Lowe. *Teaching China's Lost Generation: Foreign Experts in the People's Republic of China*, pp. 104-105. San Francisco: China Books and Periodicals, Inc. Reprinted with permission.

they are also seen as potentially helpful in fostering money-making enterprises.

Americans confronting the distinction between friendship and *guanxi* for the first time are often distressed when a relationship they believed was friendship turns out to be one of *guanxi*. While Chinese friendships naturally involve a measure of *guanxi*, there is a real distinction between the two. Your closest and best Chinese friends will be loathe to call on your *guanxi*. Among very good friends, the ties of *guanxi* are so natural that they are hardly noticed. Many Americans who have formed close friendships with bright and promising students or colleagues likely to thrive in a U.S. academic environment are enthusiastic about helping their friends with the procedures. But nearly every American who has spent time in China has faced situations where "friendship" was being sought almost exclusively for the purpose of *guanxi*, and many feel used when they discover this. With limited time and resources, many Americans have to decide whom to help—usually close friends and particularly bright and worthy students or colleagues—and whom they will have to refuse. Difficult though it might be, you may be put in a position of having to explain that your limited time and resources make it impossible for you to help. Your *guanxi* is limited.

Reciprocity   Between pure friendship and opportunistic *guanxi* is a notion of reciprocity more like the concept of social obligation in the United States. Anyone who steps beyond the confines of his or her formal authority to ease your way in China assumes that you will find a way to repay them. But social obligations are not necessarily as simple as your inviting friends to dinner in return for a similar invitation from the Chinese hosts, and you may wonder how to respond to such hospitality. As one senior scholar points out:

> When a friend insists on inviting you to a restaurant for dinner—inevitable, because so many people do not have big enough apartments to hold a dinner—along with a few other people, the evening may well cost him his month's salary (as well as a couple of hours spent holding the table until his guests arrive). A return banquet doesn't begin to make this up to him, so what do you do?

Hosting a return banquet, or a meal in a joint-venture hotel, only partially repays your obligation. Your friend might also ask for your help in getting him or his relatives to the United States.

Ritual   Senior professors and researchers, teachers, and students will be expected to participate in ritual activities that still govern professional and social encounters in China. Ritual is a polite way of getting to know you while still maintaining a distance, and it helps to clarify the participants' ranks in the social hierarchy. How and by whom you are greeted at the airport, the order in which officials enter a room, and the seating patterns at a welcoming banquet all place hosts and guests in their proper place in the hierarchy. Foreigners are expected to at least attempt to play by the rules, and you can learn a great deal in the process as well. It is important to know what to expect and the meaning of ritualistic signals.

Almost every major occasion in China (be it a welcome, departure, banquet, or formal meeting) opens with an exchange of name cards followed by tea and a superficial exchange of pleasantries. Arrivals and departures are treated with great care. The host unit will, if at all possible, send a representative of suitable stature to the airport or train station to greet or see off an official guest. Many Chinese train stations have special lounges set aside for the rituals associated with meeting and departing—and to shield privileged travelers from the noise and bustle outside as they sip their tea.

Banquets are another form of Chinese ritual, and both distinguished foreign guests and young students can expect to be treated to a welcoming banquet. Student banquets are usually held in the university dining hall where dishes are more plentiful and better than ordinary fare. Distinguished guests will be hosted in the special rooms or screened portions of rooms in well-known Chinese restaurants or some older Chinese hotels.

The welcoming banquet often provides newcomers their first opportunity to witness the structure of authority in the *danwei*. The host is always the highest-ranking person present and is almost always seated facing the door; the most honored guest sits to the right and the second-ranking host sits directly opposite or at a corresponding position if more than one table is used. Interpreters are situated for practical rather than ritually correct reasons. Banquets usually begin with a cold plate and end with a soup and a simple dessert, usually fresh fruit. They are punctuated with toasts, which for students may be sweet Chinese soda (*qishui*) and in rural areas is likely to include a devastatingly powerful local liquor akin to China's fiery *maotai*.

However, beer and Western-style red and white wines are increasingly being served in the larger cities by establishments accustomed to foreign tastes. Except in the countryside (see the section on fieldwork), those who do not drink alcoholic beverages can toast with soda, and women will be expected to consume far less than men. Many Chinese women, even in large cities, do not drink, and Chinese will not press American women to drink, either.

Those who do not (or cannot) eat some of the exotic delicacies served at banquets can move them politely around their plate. Chinese who

have hosted Americans in the past will understand you do not appreciate such dishes as much as they do. It is correct to use a toothpick
(covering your mouth with a hand) after dinner, but not to fiddle with
your chopsticks (which are supposed to rest, together, at the edge of
your plate). Your hosts will use their serving chopsticks to place food
on your plate, which you should refuse, cheerfully insisting that you
can help yourself, after the first couple of times.

You can expect a great deal of bantering and good will at a welcoming banquet. Your host will signal when the meal is over by standing
up and wishing you good-bye. There is little lingering after the meal,
and inexperienced Americans often find the evening ending abruptly
and early.

If you have any dietary restrictions, especially if you do not eat pork
or seafood or are a vegetarian, it is best to inform your hosts in advance.
Banquet dishes are heavy on meat and fish, and you may wait in vain
for the vegetables. Anyone with allergies to nuts should know that
peanut and sesame oils are commonly used in cooking. Your hosts
could lose face if you do not eat, and most hosts are happy to accommodate your requests.

Researchers whose work takes them to several sites will invariably
be treated to a welcoming banquet at each one, even if the visit is only
for a day. Many researchers agree with the assessment of one who
found "this way of doing research stultifying and lifeless, not to mention emotionally and physically draining. . . . And yet, this is the form
which governs the Chinese model of the research trip. . . . The banquet,
despite its highly ritualized form, does lead to a more relaxed atmosphere in which a more genuine connection can be made. Dour officials, reciting facts from memory, unwind to become genial hosts who
are quite happy to make unofficial asides on what they just spent most
of the morning dishing out to the visitor."

A return banquet at the end of your stay is the best way to express
appreciation. To ensure that you depart with warm feelings and a good
impression, ask a Chinese friend or assistant to help plan the event.
Your favorite restaurant may not be the favorite of your Chinese hosts
or the most ritually correct place to hold your farewell dinner.

The cost of your banquet will vary according to where you are (countryside, town, or big city), your status, and the status of those you are
hosting. Students hosting their teacher at a local restaurant will pay far
less than a senior professor hosting high-status guests. It is possible to
find good restaurants charging Y50 per person, but the price will be
considerably higher for a high-status banquet. One senior researcher
recently paid $1,000 to host the high-ranking officials he had inter-
viewed. Student researchers at smaller institutions may look into banquet facilities at the institute—they may be much cheaper than outside

but still quite acceptable. Get advice from your adviser or someone in the foreign affairs office.

Be sure, when making arrangements, to find out what kind of drinks are included, and remember that most alcoholic beverages are not included in the price of the banquet. Wine, beer, and soft drinks are usually served, and you will want to consider whether to serve *maotai*. Remember to arrange for transportation for your guests and to pay for the drivers' meals, which will add to the cost. Open the dinner with a short toast of gratitude and expectations of continuing friendship, be sure to serve your guests with your serving chopsticks, encourage them to eat more, and relax as everyone settles in to their ritual roles and the enjoyment of the food.

While it is always a plus when a foreigner understands the rituals well, attitude is more important than superficial correctness. The banquet table is not the place to discuss unpleasant business or to remind your hosts of the glitches in their arrangements. In fact, the banquet can be used to smooth ruffled feelings and get your plans back on track. One researcher who had experienced more stalling than cooperation from his unit, which had never hosted a U.S. scholar, received his welcoming banquet several months after his arrival in Beijing. He made a point of being polite and positive on this public occasion. "My unit was very concerned that I would let my frustration show at my long-delayed welcoming banquet, and they were pleased to no end when I behaved like someone who understands China and can be a good guest."

Steven Butler describes using a banquet to bolster the standing of the local officials responsible for the day-to-day implementation of his work with a visiting official from their parent organization in Beijing. After demonstrating through relaxed, genial behavior how well everyone got along and toasting the importance of individual cooperation, he reports:

> The cadre from the Academy left for Peking [Beijing] feeling that he had been well entertained, that my project was proceeding well, that local cadres had been doing an excellent job helping me out, and, most important, that his own work arranging my field research had been successful. The local cadres, in turn, were pleased because I had made them look very good in the eyes of someone whom they regarded as influential. It is by taking advantage of opportunities like this that the researcher can find ways to reduce the heavy burden which he places on almost everyone with whom he comes into contact.[2]

---

[2]Anne F. Thurston and Burton Pasternak, eds. *The Social Sciences and Fieldwork in China: Views From the Field*, p. 121. Boulder, CO: Westview Press, Inc., for the American Association for the Advancement of Science. 1983. Reprinted with permission.

Stick to safe subjects during the meal—the locality and its customs, Chinese food, your travels or plans for travel in China, and the food—and be profuse in your thanks for the help your hosts have given.

Ritual life in China is by no means confined to banquets. It is just as important to try to observe some of the proprieties on less grand occasions. When a Chinese guest comes to your dorm or hotel room, for instance, be sure to pour tea or coffee, or a soft drink on a hot day, no matter how short the visit or how loud the protests. If you offer your friends a choice of beverages, they may refuse them all. Insist that they have something. Having tins of cookies, fruit, or candies on hand for unexpected visits is always a good idea. When making appointments with Chinese friends or officials and teachers, avoid the rest period. It has been said that 10 a.m. and 3 p.m. are ideal times to schedule meetings. Remember that punctuality is essential.

Take a small gift if you are invited to a Chinese home. The guidelines presented earlier (see the section on gifts in Chapter 2) can give you some ideas. Giving gifts to individuals in front of others outside the family setting is considered impolite; either save it for a more private time, or give a gift that can be put easily into a pocket or bag. Do not press an individual to accept a gift when he or she seems genuinely embarrassed or frightened, but keep in mind that it is good form in China to refuse any offer, no matter how attractive, three times. Always give your Chinese friends a fourth chance to accept or decline whatever it is that you are attempting to give them. If you have a driver while you are in China, periodic gifts of cigarettes or music tapes will be appreciated.

One of the great advantages of the current openness in China is that you can ask Chinese friends for advice and help in negotiating the labyrinth of behavioral expectations. And most Americans agree that although the Chinese appreciate sincere attempts to respect Chinese culture by emulating some of the modes of behavior that ease potentially awkward situations, there is no need to lose your own identity in the process. As Scott Seligman observes:

> It's important to emphasize that no Chinese seriously expects a foreigner to behave appropriately in all of these situations. Allowances will be made for you whether you want them or not, and you will never be held to very stringent standards. But a small gesture which indicates an awareness of Chinese expectations will go a long way toward complimenting your host. Even in China, it is viewed as the most sincere form of flattery.[3]

---

[3]Scott Seligman, "A Shirtsleeves Guide To Corporate Etiquette." *The China Business Review*, January-February 1983, p. 13. Reprinted with permission of the China Business Forum.

LEGALITY AND ETHICS   Foreign residents are expected not only to respect China's customs but also to conduct themselves in accordance with its regulations and laws. Since regulations are not publicized, are often local, and change frequently, even the most conscientious foreigner has difficulty knowing what they are. Appendix D contains the rules and regulations governing foreign students in China. Several situations sometimes faced by foreign scholars are not covered in these documents:

1. Visas. Make certain your visa is up to date. If, for instance, you enter on a three- or six-month tourist visa, the Public Security Bureau may extend it for a month. Beyond that, you must leave China (most people go to Hong Kong) to have it renewed. Remember, also, that your behavior in China is expected to be in keeping with your visa status and that stepping too far beyond the boundaries will be frowned upon.

2. Travel permits. Some parts of China are still officially closed to foreigners, and special permission must be obtained to visit them. Make certain before you set out on a trip that the areas you plan to visit are open. If not, ask for help from your *danwei* to arrange the necessary permissions.

3. Off-limits areas. Some areas are also off-limits to foreigners, especially military installations. Warning signs are usually posted, in both Chinese and English, at the crossroads where entry is prohibited, but some foreigners miss the signs and have been caught inside prohibited areas. If you have made an honest mistake, the authorities will usually recognize this and let you off the hook. You are likely to suffer only inconvenience and embarrassment. But individuals who have deliberately ignored the signs have been expelled or made to write confessions.

4. Changing money. One of the first English phrases Americans along the tourist routes hear is, "Hello, change money?" The black market value of dollars is ordinarily considerably higher than the official rate of exchange, and black market money-changing is pervasive. Some restaurants and stores in south China charge different prices depending on the currency with which one pays. The practice of changing money on the black market is still illegal, and when officials recently caught one longtime foreign resident changing money, they stamped the crime on her identification card, which must be shown for many routine transactions.

5. Registering with the Public Security Bureau. Foreigners are required to register with the Public Security Bureau wherever they are. Ordinarily, your work unit does this for you, and by registering in any hotel you are also registering with Public Security. If you stay over-

night at the home of a relative or friend, however, you are expected to take the initiative to register. If you do not, the local residence committee will quickly learn of your presence and you will be asked to register. Permission can be denied if the Public Security Bureau thinks your accommodations are not appropriate for foreigners.

6. Taking cultural relics out of the country. Sale of antiques is strictly controlled in China, and written permission must be obtained to take cultural relics out. In the past, few antiques were available for sale, but the recent commercialization of China is changing that. If your travels present an opportunity to buy, keep the receipt and make certain the sale also includes permission to take your acquisitions out.

7. *Neibu* (internal) materials. Much information in China, including high-quality maps, is considered *neibu*, or classified. Many scholars nonetheless are given such materials, and a few scholars have had difficulty when their possession of such materials became known. On rare occasions, suspected *neibu* material is temporarily confiscated for official review (and on even rarer occasions the scholar has been detained as well). If you have not received permission to take such material out of the country and your luggage is inspected when you leave, the material can be confiscated. Even non-*neibu* materials may be questioned if your luggage is inspected. If you are carrying non-*neibu* materials, one scholar recommends getting a letter with an official seal attesting that all copies are legitimate.

The problem of *neibu* materials raises larger ethical issues for U.S. researchers. Individual Chinese sometimes put themselves at risk by sharing information with and voicing personal opinions to U.S. academics. When this information is important to your research project, not to note it runs the risk of vitiating scholarship. Publishing it may violate ethical norms of protecting one's informants. How to balance the two concerns remains a problem for some researchers that is not easily solved.

Teachers also sometimes confront the dilemma of balancing Chinese sensitivities to the content of their courses with their own standards of academic freedom and the unhindered exchange of ideas. Many labor over decisions of when to present material that challenges or offends their hosts and when to compromise or pull back. Most American teachers report considerably more academic freedom than they had expected, but occasional incidents occur—as when a teacher showing videotapes of the Clinton-Bush presidential debates was asked to edit out the section dealing with U.S.-China relations.

8. Taxes. American teachers remain exempt from Chinese taxes for three years and become subject to taxation thereafter. If you are planning a long-term stay in China, acquaint yourself with the law and the tax agreement between China and the United States.

9. Religious activities. While many religious organizations sponsor programs in China, religious proselytizing is prohibited.
10. Romance between Chinese and foreigners. Romance at the undergraduate level in China, even between Chinese, is ordinarily frowned on, and teachers and student class monitors often intervene when they observe the blossoming of romance. Mores, however, are changing rapidly, particularly in the cities, and reports of student behavior from American teachers interviewed for this book differed widely. Romance is inevitably complicated when an American is involved; Americans who have married Chinese in China have invariably reported bureaucratic interference and delays. Casual dating, particularly by young Chinese women, is still not widely accepted, though the situation is changing in the more Westernized cities. Many young Chinese women are likely to assume that a marriage is in the making after a few public dates with an American. Americans need to be sensitive to the cultural differences when dating Chinese.

Conversely, the periodic campaigns against "spiritual pollution" and pornography from the West have portrayed Westerners as prone to loose morals. Some Chinese men view American women as more *suibian*—casual—in their sexual relations, and misunderstandings have resulted. Similarly, some American men have suspected Chinese women of pursuing them romantically as a means of getting to the United States and obtaining a green card.

Finally, several couples in mixed marriages—American husband and Chinese wife—report considerable discrimination against the Chinese wife. One couple suggests keeping openly affectionate public behavior to a minimum.

The brighter side, however, is that romances between Chinese and Americans do blossom, that Chinese and Americans do, despite the bureaucratic obstacles, get married. Nevertheless, Americans on the verge of romance need to be particularly sensitive to the cultural and bureaucratic differences.

Only on extremely rare occasions have Americans been jailed in China. The more likely route when an American's behavior becomes unacceptable to Chinese authorities is temporary detention followed by immediate expulsion. If you should ever be detained for any reason, try to contact the U.S. Embassy or the closest U.S. consulate immediately—or have a friend do so. The Consular Convention between the United States and China provides that Chinese authorities must notify the U.S. Embassy within 48 hours of an apprehension of an American.

For an excellent article on the different concepts of guilt, procedure, and trial in China and the United States as they were revealed in the prosecution of an American who was imprisoned for causing a hotel fire in which ten people died, see Stanley B. Lubman and Gregory Wajnowsci, "Criminal Justice and the Foreigner," in *The China Business Review*, November-December 1985.

Americans should also be warned that theft in China is much more common now than several years ago, and numerous people, particularly students who ride buses frequently, report having their pockets picked. Women also report mild forms of sexual molestation on crowded buses. Thefts of computers from dormitory rooms are also on the rise. Make certain, particularly in crowds, to keep your money and passport close to your person (definitely not in a backpack). Many people with small laptop computers advise locking them in a suitcase when leaving the room for any length of time and suggest that the fewer people who know you have such equipment, the safer it is.

THE FOREIGN COMMUNITY   The foreign community in China has grown dramatically in recent years, especially in Beijing and major coastal cities. Academics will find not only diplomats and journalists in many large cities but foreign businesspeople, too. Some Americans, particularly students intent on immersing themselves in Chinese society, eschew contact with other foreigners. Others, particularly those with little Chinese, turn to foreigners for friendship, support, and exchange of information about a wide variety of topics. Contact with the business community can provide an insight into China's far-reaching economic changes that the academic community has little opportunity to experience firsthand. Although "Western-style" activities are becoming more common in China, many universities are located far from the center of town, and "getting into the city" is a major excursion usually reserved for weekends. And such diversions are usually expensive, requiring a cash outlay that many students and teachers cannot afford. It is still possible to feel isolated and cut off from the outside world.

Many U.S. students, teachers, and researchers live in foreign enclaves—foreign student dormitories, special residences for foreign faculty, hotels, or the huge Friendship Hotel in Beijing, built in the 1950s for Soviet foreign experts. The foreign community in these places provides friendship and support when contact with Chinese is limited. Many welcome the opportunity to live with people from all over the world and like the more Western ambiance of the enclaves. Some find the challenge of living among so many nationalities equally as great as the challenge of adjusting to Chinese culture. In fact, some of the most disruptive clashes occur not between foreigners and Chinese but among foreigners who live in close quarters without clearly defined rules to guide their interpersonal relations.

Thus, living in a foreign enclave provides a different set of challenges. On the one hand, because information in China is scarce, foreigners learn to seek it out, and new information passes rapidly throughout the foreign community—just as it does among the Chinese, through what they call "back alley news." Such information is an important way of keeping abreast of change and one of the facets of life in China that make it so interesting. But not all such information is accurate. China is a place of rumors, too, and passing "information" so quickly by word of mouth often amounts only to gossip.

Many people in China report wide swings in mood, from exhilaration to depression—the high, for instance, when an interview you hoped to have finally comes through and the low when a request for material is denied. The long, cold winter months tend to be the most difficult, particularly when holidays like Thanksgiving and Christmas are celebrated alone without the usual family festivities. These moods can be contagious within foreign enclaves, and the worst periods in China are when the "blues" seem to hit everyone at the same time. There is no easy way to escape the down times. Nearly everyone experiences them. But when the mood pervades the foreign community, short-term escape may be in order. The fact is that there is much to do in China, and much of it is free or very inexpensive—long visits to local markets or historic sites or parks, curling up with a good novel, a determined effort to meet with Chinese friends, walks through a city's little alleyways, a long distance telephone call home, a Chinese massage or facial or a new regimen of ginseng, or an afternoon in the lobby of one of the Western hotels. For the young and young at heart, there are discos and karaoke bars. What is most important to remember is that the ups and downs are part of the experience, and many people return home to recognize that in the process they have learned a great deal not only about China but about themselves. And many people have struggled through a difficult situation only to reach a breakthrough that becomes one of the most rewarding experiences—whether professional or personal—of their lives.

HOUSING

Housing in China will depend on your status and the type of program you are in.

Students are almost always assigned to a campus dormitory reserved for foreigners. Most colleges and universities do not allow Chinese and foreign students to room together (the Johns Hopkins-Nanjing Center is an exception, which is one of its attractions to U.S. students). The definite trend in the larger schools is to segregate foreign students in separate dormitories.

How much students pay out of pocket is determined by the kind of program in which they enroll. Most U.S.-sponsored language programs charge a flat tuition, room, and board fee that covers all the essentials including meals; other programs include only partial payment to the Chinese organization for these services. Graduate students and undergraduates who make their own arrangements with a Chinese institution of higher learning will pay all expenses directly to that institution. In addition, there are a variety of agreements between Chinese and U.S. institutions for student exchanges that include remission of tuition or room-and-board costs. See Appendix D, "Regulations Concerning the Admission of Foreign Students in Chinese Schools, 1986."

Chinese schools have separate dining halls for foreign students. However, foreign students may, if they wish, have meals in the canteens for Chinese students. They should observe the regulations of the dining halls and canteens and maintain order in them. Chinese schools provide dormitories for their foreign students. In general, two students share one room. No special accommodations are available for married couples or for a student's family members. In some schools, if space permits, students can occupy a room alone—if they pay for the unused bed. Room rates vary from school to school but they generally range from $5 to $10 a day for a single room with public bath. Some schools require lump-sum payments at the beginning of the semester, but timing is often negotiable.

Teachers, whether Fulbright lecturers, "foreign experts," or "foreign teachers," will have housing provided, usually free of charge, by their work unit. In some cases, housing is on campus—either in rooms or apartments on campus or, in Beijing, in the Friendship Hotel. As noted earlier, the regulations governing foreign experts state that the housing provided by the hiring party will also include furniture, bedding, a bathroom, a television set, a refrigerator, and facilities for heating and air conditioning, although the quality and condition of these amenities vary considerably.

Researchers, whether dissertation-level students or more advanced scholars, are considered guests and must pay for their housing from their own funds. If your research affiliation is with a university, it is often possible, with a little negotiating, to find housing on campus. Each campus often has several possibilities—foreign student housing for the single graduate student, foreign teachers' or foreign experts' housing for the more senior researcher or any researcher traveling with family, and, in some places now, guest houses or even hotels. Some have lived in apartment buildings housing Chinese faculty.

The prices of these options vary widely, not only among the accommodations but also within any accommodation according to your status, how you have been introduced to the place, and how well you or your Chinese friend or host may be negotiating on your behalf. Some good negotiators have been able to reduce the cost of their housing by

15 to 20 percent by pointing to longstanding "friendships" or arguing that the length of their stay—anything more than two weeks—justified a reduced rate. Some people have relied on their academic adviser to negotiate reductions of up to 50 percent. Researchers on a shoestring have persuaded university officials to house them in cheaper student dormitories. The budgets of younger scholars in particular dictate looking into several possibilities and negotiating for reasonable accommodations at reasonable prices. Be prepared to stay a week or two in more expensive accommodations until long-range housing can be arranged.

The researcher affiliated with an institute that does not have housing for foreigners faces a more complicated set of choices. As one recent researcher writes, "Finding a reasonably comfortable, clean, quiet, secure place to live, with adequate and functional plumbing, located a manageable distance from one's workplace is a chronic problem in China—for everyone."

Many Chinese research institutes have arrangements with one or two local hotels to house their foreign guests, where they get a special rate. But if you find the hotel too far from your work, too noisy or expensive, you may want to find a place on your own. This can take time. Someone in your research institute, or other Chinese friends, might be able to suggest a place. So might other foreigners who have lived in the city longer than you. Inquire widely and be prepared to spend some time investigating. Inexpensive housing for foreigners is in short supply almost everywhere in China.

Finally, one scholar points out that housing and other costs can become very expensive when your research institution has made *formal* arrangements for you to visit a similar institute in another city. She writes that if a formal request goes from one unit to another, her institute required that she "be placed in an international hotel, be assigned (for a fat fee) an academy car and driver, etc., and pay the host unit one-half again the total cost of all things arranged by them." This is obviously extraordinarily expensive and other institutes operate under different rules, but if informal arrangements would get you the same access to the scholars you hope to meet or the research materials you want to peruse, economics may suggest going the informal route.

Researchers who travel or work in the countryside have been housed in a variety of accommodations—from dormitories to moderately priced hotels. In recent years, many work units have begun charging flat daily sums for research in rural areas which include housing, food, transportation and overhead. Some field scientists report paying between $200 and $300 a day, but others are able to work much less expensively. Choice of accommodations is limited in the countryside and the researcher is more dependent on his hosts. Persistent reminders to your hosts that your budget is limited will help keep down costs.

Below are descriptions, by category, of the physical set-up of student dormitories, campus apartments, and a range of hotels.

STUDENT DORMITORIES   If your physical accommodations are important to you, you would be wise to inquire about what type of dormitory space is available for the study programs you are considering. Some Americans prefer to duplicate as closely as possible a Chinese student lifestyle. (Chinese students, however, live six to eight to a room, while foreign students generally live two to a room.) Others are more comfortable in more modern facilities. New dormitories for foreign students have been constructed on many university campuses that host large numbers of foreign students, and some represent quite a departure from the earlier buildings. A few even have air conditioning, private bathrooms, and 24-hour heating.

On campuses where new construction has not taken place, dormitories are remarkably uniform in their outward appearance and furnishings. Almost all are gray, cement edifices with communal shower rooms, communal bathrooms with Asian-style squat toilets, laundry rooms equipped with washing machines, washboards and clotheslines, a television lounge, and a reading or reception room. In many dormitories, boiled water for drinking may be fetched from a boiler room. Hot water for laundry or showers is usually available only a few hours each day, often right after the dinner hour. Not all older dormitories are heated, and those that are usually have heat for a few hours in the morning and again in the evening. When the heat is on, the rooms are quite comfortable, but hallways and communal rooms can be cold and dark in the winter. Many people suggest putting up polyethylene sheeting as storm windows. Electricity can be erratic, especially in the evenings. Room sizes vary. Some (for example, in the Shaoyuan Lou Guesthouse at Peking University) are small (3 meters × 4.5 meters); others are quite large, even by Western standards.

Regardless of size, however, rooms are typically furnished with a bed and desk for each occupant and at least one bookcase and wardrobe. Rooms are spartan: whitewashed cement walls, gray cement floors, and a stark fluorescent light overhead. Newcomers are routinely issued a thermos for storing potable water, mosquito netting, a padded cotton quilt, woolen blanket, two sheets, and a washbasin. With imagination and effort, rooms can be decorated and arranged to suit individual tastes, and you might want to bring a bright cotton bedspread or a few posters and trinkets from home to brighten up your surroundings. Plants are very inexpensive, and free markets are filled with inexpensive kitsch, some of which is worth bringing home for the beginnings of a longer-term China collection.

The dormitory community on most campuses includes foreigners of many nationalities, teachers (Chinese and sometimes foreign), and Chinese caretakers (*shifu*), all living together. The *shifu* answer telephones, clean the hallways and common rooms, distribute newspapers and mail, and generally watch over dormitory residents and their guests. In many dormitories, Chinese visitors are required to register. Mail comes in twice each day and is generally placed on a hall table or in mailboxes designated by nationality. Most dormitories have only one or two telephones for incoming and outgoing calls, and residents are notified of calls by loudspeaker or a knock on their door. Some of the dorms that have been built recently have better telephone facilities. The Shaoyuan Guesthouse at Beida, for example, has a telephone on each floor, and the apartment suites have their own telephones.

A student housed at a dormitory for both Chinese and foreigners describes her living conditions:

> Foreign students. . .are housed in a 12 story building which also houses Chinese students, some faculty, departmental offices and the dining halls. Female foreigners are on the 8th floor, male on the 9th, and for all the rumors I heard about puritanical strictness, there was mingling between floors. On the 9th floor there is a rather barren lounge area with a TV. Each room has a radiator and mine was pleasantly warm all winter long. Each floor has one phone, and the connection is always dreadful; 2-3 shower stalls which provide hot water for showers from about 9:30 in the morning to 9:30 at night. If one wants hot water for any other purpose, it must be obtained from the shower. One small kitchen—4 gas burners and a sink in a very small, very dirty unventilated room. Even if one doesn't cook, one generally boils one's own drinking water. A washroom with ample sink space for various sorts of washing, and space to hang clothes to dry. A *cesuo* [bathroom] with 2 squatting and one sitting toilet. Smells bad, but usually functions.

Foreign students can eat at the foreign student dining hall for a few yuan a day, or they can eat at the Chinese students' canteen for even less. Some institutions allow students (Chinese and foreign) to eat in the teachers' dining hall, which may be a bit more expensive than the student dining halls but may have better food. The latter are crowded and lively; some have no tables or chairs, and students are responsible for bringing their own bowls and utensils. Most students complain that the food is monotonous and sometimes greasy and cold. Chinese and foreign students alike devise ways to cook in their rooms using hot plates (which are usually forbidden) with ingredients from local stores and markets, where there is plenty to choose from and prices are cheap. With the burgeoning of small, privately owned restaurants, most neighborhoods have at least a few good, inexpensive places for eating out.

The main complaint of students in dormitories is noise. Late-night parties are common in many foreign student residences, and no formal rules govern foreign student dorm life. Nor is there a student organization to make such rules. Many dormitories are now renting rooms to short-term nonstudent guests, and serious students complain about their late-night, noisy returns. Programs run by U.S. universities and supervised by U.S. faculty provide a means for more structure, with group meetings to formulate mutually acceptable rules. Former students suggest that the Golden Rule is still the best way to live harmoniously with many different students from many different countries.

Some married students have reported great difficulty arranging to live together, and many schools will not bend the rules to let them do so. One couple reports having to move to a higher priced hostel on campus in order to live together. Students bringing their spouses should check with their host institution in advance about the regulations and what alternative arrangements can be made.

CAMPUS APARTMENTS   Campus housing, and people's reactions to it, is diverse. For a description of the variations, several representative occupants speak for themselves:

> Housing excellent, though we were compelled to fight for such necessities as laundry facilities, heat in November, and a decent phone. . .Furniture excellent. We had two bedrooms and a big living room, a modern kitchen (with oven) and a full bathroom. One problem—no double bed.

> Our first reaction to the flat was "You mean we're going to live here?" It was hot and dirty and nothing was clean or ready. . .but our nesting instincts started to come out and we worked at making things better. The best way to describe the housing is that it is small but adequate and you learn to adjust. Even though the carpeting is considered a luxury. . .it has been the most frustrating part of trying to keep the apartment clean. Everything sticks to it and the dirt is almost impossible to remove—especially with a Chinese broom! [Some people recommend bringing rug cleaner from the United States.]

> The unit consists of one large room (20 ft × 15 ft), a small room (13×10), a medium sized bathroom, and a small entrance hallway. The unit is carpeted, air-conditioned and well-heated in winter. It is not new but reasonably clean; bathroom is grubby. When we first moved in there were some roaches, but now just about gone.

> Housing adequate by Chinese standards, but not by ours. "Bathroom" is a shower stall with a toilet in it. Cooking is difficult but not impossible— kitchen has a 2-burner "stove" at knee height, a piano-bench-sized table about mid-thigh height, and a hip-high sink—the *only* sink we have. Flat has an entrance hall, off of which open the living-room, kitchen, "bathroom," bedroom and office/workroom. Flat is "cozy" for two—*crowded* for more than that. Building is roach-infested, although we have managed to keep our flat pretty clear of them—combination of Combat and

Chinese "magic white powder." Some flats have roaches in the refrigerators! They live under the door gaskets. Heating is on only from Nov. 15 to March 15 and there may be some chilly weeks before heat goes on and after it goes off.

Overall, the most common housing problems include poor and leaky plumbing, insufficient heat, a lack of hot water, inadequate storage space, poor lighting, erratic electricity, and difficulty cleaning. Roaches are common, but most people manage to control them after a while. Insect spray is available in the Western supermarkets in large cities, but some people recommend bringing a supply of roach killer or "cockroach hotels" from the United States. Mice are not unknown, but they ordinarily seem to occupy the lower floors.

Cooking was another commonly mentioned problem. Most people, even those with kitchens, adopt a multipronged strategy, doing some cooking in their apartment and eating other meals in the campus dining hall (where the most common complaint is that the food becomes monotonous) or nearby privately owned restaurants. Some hire an *ayi* (recent reports indicate that a privately hired *ayi* from the countryside is generally Y2 to 3 an hour) to come in and cook occasionally, and sometimes a group of three to five people hire an *ayi* to cook for them as a group. Some people have formed "eating clubs" and pay their dining hall chef extra (Y10 per person) to cook a special meal once a week. "Eating clubs" also make weekly excursions to local restaurants, which are always more fun with more people because you can order more dishes to share. Some people find that the food in small restaurants is too oily or salty. Experimentation may be necessary before you find a few favorites.

HOTELS Hotel accommodations in China range from the very expensive joint-venture hotels (some of which have five-star ratings), offering Western amenities and service at Western prices, to very modest establishments that house Chinese travelers as well as foreign guests. In most cases, if Chinese hosts make arrangements, they will place you in medium-priced lodging, usually at one of the older Chinese hotels. As mentioned earlier, the problem, particularly for graduate students and young faculty on limited budgets, is to find an acceptable hotel at a reasonable price. Many Chinese hotels have recently been renovated, and prices are going up fast. One scholar in Beijing describes the fruits of his search for a reasonable hotel:

> At Y80 a night, the Jiangsu offered considerable savings over the cheapest tourist places. The hotel was built only a couple of years ago and already shows signs of considerable wear, but the owners had aimed high and the accommodations are fairly comfortable. The rooms are small, but the beds and hot water are excellent. The rooms contain the standard ameni-

ties: bathroom (not very clean), telephone, television. The staff was very courteous and helpful, a pleasant surprise, and the hotel tries to provide nice touches here and there (complimentary copies of *Beijing Ribao* are delivered daily). The restaurant also was surprisingly good and inexpensive (Y10-15 for dinner). In addition, there are several excellent *getihu* [privately owned] restaurants in the street directly opposite the hotel. . . and a variety of decent, but slightly more expensive, restaurants can be found farther south.

Typical suites in Chinese hotels include one or two rooms, a private bath, very small closet or wardrobe, bureau, desk, telephone, and color television. The amount and type of furniture in each room is fixed by regulations, which allow for little maneuvering within the system. Most long-term residents find ways to decorate their room with plants, prints, and extra furniture purchased outside. Aficionados learn to frequent the local antique stores where good quality wooden furniture can be purchased relatively inexpensively, although prices, as for everything, are going up.

Kitchen facilities are rarely provided in hotels, but refrigerators are becoming more common, and all hotels have a dining room. Some offer both Chinese and Western food. Hotel fare at the more modest establishments is usually relatively inexpensive (about Y10 to Y15 per person for a simple lunch and Y30 for a dinner with several dishes), and eventually, like dormitory food, it becomes monotonous. (The fancy joint-venture hotels usually have several restaurants offering different national specialties at Western prices.) A few people have mentioned that some hotels require their guests to pay for three meals a day in their own restaurants—a matter most people would want to negotiate in the interest of taking advantage of the better neighborhood restaurants or those in other hotels. And everyone occasionally wants to buy food from the market and find creative ways to eat "at home."

Some hotel residents have lunch at their work unit for a few *mao* per meal, eating only breakfast and dinner at the more expensive hotel restaurant. Some units strongly advise their foreign guests against eating in the canteen—sometimes to maintain the separation between foreigners and *danwei* personnel, but sometimes because the quality of canteen food is not good. One researcher who insisted on principle that he be allowed to take lunch at the workplace was told repeatedly by colleagues that the food was not up to minimal standards of cleanliness. When he finally won the right to eat at work, he became violently ill. In larger cities, some people find ways to bring their lunch to their work unit by taking advantage of the bread, peanut butter, cheese, and other "delicacies" available in Friendship Stores or joint-venture hotels; others return to their hotel for lunch and rest or to prepare for the afternoon's activities.

Hotel life in China can also become monotonous, and the sense of isolation on the part of long-term hotel guests is probably stronger than for those who live in foreign communities. The same advice about overcoming the sense of isolation and the inevitable "downs" in China offered previously on pages 68–69 thus applies even more strongly to the long-term hotel resident.

The problem of privacy may also be greater in inexpensive hotels. Most floors have a service desk on each floor staffed by *fuwuyuan* (service personnel). Keys are usually kept there, and service personnel are generally very attentive to the comings and goings of hotel guests and their visitors. If you do much work in your room, you may also have to negotiate when the *fuwuyuan* come to clean, since some hotels send five or six people to visit the room every day, each with a different task— from cleaning the bathroom to watering the plants. One person reported a week of negotiations before the routine was worked out. On the positive side, getting to know hotel personnel and understanding how the hotel functions as a workplace offers another interesting perspective on Chinese life.

ARRANGEMENTS FOR ACCOMPANYING SPOUSES AND CHILDREN

Chinese regulations prohibit undergraduate students from bringing spouses and children to China (although some manage to do so anyway). Dissertation-level students, researchers, and teachers may be accompanied by their families if prior permission has been received from the host institution. Not all institutions may agree, however; some have problems providing accommodations for families because of acute housing shortages, and some places charge extra for family housing and food.

Not all cities have adequate pediatric care (see pages 12–16). Some host institutions are concerned about finding proper schooling for children. For these reasons, host institutions may be reluctant to accommodate families. Nonetheless, most people who come with families work out satisfactory arrangements, and many find that having children breaks the ice when meeting Chinese. One couple with a blond-haired toddler report groups gathering around them every time they went out, and requests to have pictures taken with the child were frequent (which, fun at first, became tiresome after a while).

Couples with children ordinarily are given apartments with an extra bedroom, although in at least one instance the apartment assigned to a single parent and child had only one bedroom, a living room, and a bathroom.

Researchers with families and tight budgets living in dormitories face the greatest challenge. One researcher accompanied by her husband and two children describes their living situation:

> Our living conditions. . .were quite spartan. The four of us lived in a single room in the old foreign students dorm, with a gas ring and bathroom down the hall. As we were on the third floor, we frequently had water stoppages due to the low water pressure in Nanjing. There was a communal washing machine available, but it was frequently on the fritz. . . . We had to haul hot water up three flights to wash diapers and children. After the first few months. . .we were able to get a second room as a study. The biggest problem for us was our 6-month-old son who was just learning to crawl. The rotting wooden floors were uncleanable and it seemed impossible to find for him a place that was reasonably clean. We finally enclosed him within a structure we made of numerous hempen mattresses and their bench-like supports.

Several parents interviewed in China expressed concerns about the difficulty of keeping floors clean while children are still crawling. People living outside Beijing recommended bringing a gallon of chlorine bleach from the United States as a cleaner and disinfectant. Parents with small children also pointed out that plastic bicycle seats for children are not available, and many preferred those to the less sturdy bamboo constructions commonly used in China. They suggested bringing a bicycle seat and a child's helmet from the States if children will ride with you. Cotton swabs and disposable wipes are also difficult to obtain outside the most Westernized cities.

Schooling options for families with children are varied and include a limited number of international schools in several large cities, Chinese schools, and home schooling. Many people with preschool children hire an *ayi*, at least part time. With continuing economic decentralization in China, capable *ayi*s are relatively easy to find, although people urge you to rely on the recommendation of a good friend. An American doctor in Beijing suggests obtaining a health certificate guaranteeing that the *ayi* does not have tuberculosis, which is fairly common in China. In addition to helping care for your child (and for additional money), people have relied on an *ayi* to wash diapers, do housekeeping, cook, and market.

Many people with nursery- or kindergarten-aged children put them in Chinese schools, with great success. The family described above put their four-year-old daughter in a full-time nursery school:

> It was difficult for her at first, as she was one of two foreign children, but she quickly adjusted and learned quite fluent Nanjing dialect by the end of the year. Her teachers were extremely solicitous and caring of her. We paid Chinese rates for this child care and it was an almost unbelievable bargain.

Indeed, the reported experiences of virtually everyone whose children attended Chinese nursery school and kindergarten were positive. However, one couple who brought their children with them to live several years ago suggests that parents give strict instructions to their children's preschool not to give them any medications or vaccinations without prior parental approval. There had been a serious health incident at the school when the wrong medication was mistakenly given to a large number of children. While the parents believed this was an isolated incident, they suggested that other American parents give similar instructions to the school against administering medicine or shots.

At the elementary school level, a few big cities, such as Beijing, Shanghai, Shenyang, Tianjin, and Guangzhou, have international schools. Beijing now has a Montessori school. Tuition at most of the international schools is expensive, but reports on school quality are overwhelmingly positive. Children seem to have few problems with academic readjustment when they return to U.S. schools. The International School of Beijing is a coeducational day school for English-speaking expatriate children in kindergarten through twelfth grades. It operates in a four-story building in the Lido (Holiday Inn) Hotel complex located in the northeastern suburbs of Beijing. (The school is accredited in the United States only through the eighth grade, and is currently seeking full accreditation for the high school.) Tuition is $8,100 a year per child. Fulbright faculty are given stipends to send their children to international schools. One parent whose son attends the International School of Beijing at the Lido Center writes "It is an excellent school, even better than American schools." Writes another:

> Our daughter attends the Beijing International School [and] is in the 9th grade. We have been quite satisfied with the school and [our daughter] has enjoyed it very much. She has made very good friends on an international scale—Denmark, Norway, India, Iraq, etc. The curriculum is similar to U.S. high schools and the faculty seem to be mostly very good. There are some limitations in the upper school as to classes available. The languages offered are Chinese and French. The classes are small. . .and there are 18 students in her class. I have heard very good comments about the lower and middle schools, also.

Space is limited. If you are interested in the school, you should submit an application as early as possible before your proposed arrival in China. For further information, write:

Mr. David Eaton
Principal
The International School of Beijing
Jiang Tai Road
Dongzhimen Wai
Beijing 100004
People's Republic of China

The Montessori School is located at the Lufthansa Center in downtown Beijing. Courses are in English, but there are many Chinese teachers, and children also learn Chinese. There are 160 children from 70 to 80 countries, including China.

The U.S. Consulate General in Shenyang has established the American Academy, which is located in the consulate compound. The curriculum consists of an accredited correspondence course administered by an American teacher. The school operates only if there are sufficient students and an available teacher.

The U.S. Consulate General in Shanghai also runs a U.S. school in one of the consulate's buildings for prekindergarten through ninth grade. In 1993, the tuition was US$9,750 per year, with an additional $750 transportation fee. The school is located at 155 Jianguo Road, Shanghai. The telephone number is 21-252-1687.

The American School of Guangzhou is located on the fourth floor of the Office Tower in the Garden Hotel. The school accommodates children of kindergarten age to the eighth grade. Tuition for the school year is US$8,200.

In Tianjin, MTI has established an international school. Further information on these schools can be obtained from the appropriate American consulate.

One difficulty with the international schools is that they are often a considerable distance from one's residence. Traffic in China's cities is becoming increasingly congested, so children sometimes spend more than two hours each day commuting back and forth, and often special rides have to be arranged at additional expense.

Parents who have placed their children in Chinese elementary schools have also been pleased. Writes one Fulbright lecturer in answer to a question about schooling:

> Excellent! Our seven-year old daughter was welcomed into the first grade of the local elementary school, where she was fully integrated into the school program. She was treated wonderfully by students and teachers alike and within four months was fully conversant and feeling "at home" in school.

Others write:

> Both of our two children attend local schools. One goes to an elementary school, the other attends a local middle school. Initially, they had a difficult time in adjusting. Now they are getting along quite nicely and their Chinese has improved significantly (starting almost from ground zero).

> If you come with young kids, by *all means* send them to a Chinese school. The Chinese kids are real friendly, and in a month, after a few days of crying, your child will be conversant. In a year they'll be bilingual!

Your Chinese host institution can assist you in finding appropriate Chinese schools.

Beyond elementary school, if children cannot attend the International School in Beijing, parents rely on several options. In Beijing, one father sent his son to the Beijing Language Institute.

> My second son, 16, has been going to Beijing Language Institute. There are about 1,500 foreign students studying Chinese at the Institute from some 50 countries. It is about a 20-minute bike ride from where we live. He has done well thus far and covered two years of college level Chinese in about 4 months. The tuition is about $1,500 a year.

Some families opt for a combination of Chinese middle school and college-preparatory correspondence courses or home study, and some rely exclusively on either correspondence courses or home study. The books *Home Style Teaching: A Handbook for Parents and Teachers*, by Raymond and Dorothy Moore, and *Homeschooling for Excellence*, by David and Micki Colfax, are recommended by people involved in homeschooling in China. Other children have taken correspondence courses through the University of Nebraska School of Continuing Education, the American School in Chicago, and the University of Wisconsin extension. Many parents hire Chinese (and even French) tutors for the children, and some parents have tutored their children themselves in coordination with their children's teachers in the United States.

THE ACADEMIC CALENDAR

The academic year in China is broken in two by the Spring Festival or Lunar New Year (*chunjie*), a celebration that symbolically marks the end of winter. The month-long holiday after *chunjie*, which usually falls during the last week of January or the first of February, marks the end of the academic term that begins in late August or early September. The second term begins around the end of February—depending on the date of *chunjie*—and runs through late June.

The pace in most work units slows considerably during these holidays because staff often travel to visit relatives or sightsee. Many foreigners enjoy celebrating these holidays with Chinese friends and colleagues, where gatherings involve the making of traditional Chinese New Year's dumplings. If your research plans require meetings with specific scholars or continuation of work during one of these holidays, be sure to make arrangements as far in advance as possible, recognizing that your plans could force your coworkers to give up their vacation time.

Foreigners are given time off to observe Chinese holidays, and many institutions schedule trips or other activities during semester breaks.

This is a time many Americans take off, often traveling south to warmer climates. Shorter holidays, such as National Day (October 1) and May Day (May 1), may offer opportunities for two or three days of travel. Foreigners are not entitled to time off for their own national or religious holidays, but many units arrange for celebrations of Christmas, Hanukkah, and other holidays. Americans have reported great success throwing Halloween, Christmas, and Easter-egg parties—and even celebrations of Thanksgiving without turkey—and inviting Chinese students, colleagues, and friends. These are good occasions for friendships to develop.

4. Research

This chapter focuses on opportunities for research in China, both for advanced graduate students and more senior scholars. It is based on numerous reports from scholars who have conducted research in China, interviews with many of them, visits with a few in China, and published accounts—especially from *China Exchange News*. Reports from scholars in the field provide detailed accounts of individual experiences—problems faced and obstacles surmounted, the joy of new academic discoveries and the need to adapt to changing opportunities, and daily life in China. It is impossible here to do justice to those accounts. Rather, this chapter will try to outline the range of research being conducted in China today, offer advice about how to go about conducting research, and describe how some have managed the complexities of the research process. A distinction is made between archival research (where the scholar's time is devoted largely to gathering documentary materials in libraries or archives), laboratory research, and field research. The concept of field research is broad—from the social scientist who lives in the city and conducts interviews with respondents outside his own work unit, to the rural fieldworker who spends weeks or months in a county seat or village, to scientists conducting research on animal behavior or geology in remote parts of the country. Several general rules apply.

THE RESEARCH CLIMATE

The trend toward economic self-sufficiency in universities and research institutes affects the foreign scholar in several ways. In many respects, the climate for foreign researchers is improving. Greater academic autonomy means more flexibility, and universities or research institutes that want to help foreign researchers have greater maneuverability now.

"China is a pretty flexible place," points out one researcher. More Chinese scholars are doing research on topics of interest to Americans, and Americans are being invited to more conferences, where Chinese and foreign scholars can interact and find out what colleagues in their field are doing. Collaborative research projects are increasing, and social scientists are beginning research on topics that would have been difficult in previous years. Nonetheless, research in the social sciences and humanities remains much more sensitive than that in the physical sciences.

Work units that remain skeptical of foreign researchers are still tough to crack. A few major collaborative projects have begun in archaeology. In general, however, archaeological collections, to quote one researcher, "are under the control of the excavator and his *danwei*," and access for foreigners remains difficult—in his case, impossible. The new demands on Chinese faculty to raise money often means that they are busier now and have less time to spend with foreign colleagues. As one researcher pointed out in early 1992, "It is obvious that even compared to my 1991 visit, scholars are much busier, spending less time discussing topics and more time providing consulting and other services to earn additional income." In some universities, personnel in the foreign affairs offices (*waiban*) who were attentive to the needs of long-term, serious, financially constrained researchers have turned their attention to short-term moneymaking "China experience" packages for U.S. undergraduates. Some foreign students and researchers are discovering that personnel in the *waiban* assigned to assist them are away working with newly formed enterprises.

Finally, as in many other countries, research fees are becoming a standard requirement for doing research in China. The trend is a departure from the early years of exchanges and has taken many foreign scholars by surprise, particularly those with previous research experience in China. Some are concerned that the profit motive is excessive. As one researcher argued, "Money is the only thing that matters to most people now and they do not seem to care a bit about whether foreign researchers come to China in the future so long as they can squeeze maximum profits from them now. Closely related to this development is the fact that *guanxi* has become absolutely critical for getting anything done."

This trend is likely to continue, despite protestations of American and other foreign researchers. Knowing when to negotiate and when to accept the reality of higher costs will be essential to any researcher's psychological equilibrium.

Successful research in China usually operates at three levels—a formal institutional affiliation, the more informal collegial and personal ties of *guanxi*, and the concept of mutual benefit. Banquets still include toasts to friendship between the Chinese and the American people. The most successful projects are those where a measure of friendship does develop and where researchers return—as friends and colleagues—again and again.

The concept of "mutual benefit" suggests that the benefit to U.S. scholars of gathering research data should be balanced by benefits to the Chinese scholars. These benefits could take the form of opportunities to study in the United States, practical contributions to the process of development, gifts of equipment, or research fees.

LAYING THE GROUNDWORK FOR RESEARCH

Before attempting to undertake a project, and to ensure a successful research experience, it is important to meet with Chinese colleagues at international conferences, within your own university, or through short-term academic visits.

Research is likely to proceed more smoothly if a preparatory visit to China is made to lay the groundwork. For instance, short-term study (for a student) or lectures at Chinese academic institutions (for a teacher) could be combined with meetings to make research arrange-ments. As one scientist observes, "In the final analysis, there is no sub-stitute for advance personal contact between participating scientists to optimize conditions for joint investigations. The expense involved is well justified."

IMPLEMENTING YOUR PLAN

THE IMPORTANCE OF YOUR HOST UNIT   Almost everyone needs a host unit in China, and finding an appropriate host is vital to the success of any research project. Planning for a research project re-quires selecting and securing the cooperation of a host unit, and ar-rangements to do research can be made only when formal affiliation has been assured. Because the question of appropriate affiliation re-mains vexing for many researchers, this section discusses the search for an appropriate host.

Conversations with colleagues who have done research in China can be especially useful. Researchers have had diverse experiences, and their insights and advice will be invaluable. Most are happy to share with others what they wish they had known before going. For ex-ample, both Chinese and American colleagues can provide advice on the most appropriate host units for your work. Opportunities and pit-falls are so diverse that you will want to weigh a variety of possibilities.

Check into various possible affiliations before deciding which are best. There is no need to jump at the first opportunity, because local research academies have now been given considerable autonomy. In the early years of exchanges, only national academies, universities, and ministries had the right to issue official invitations, so affiliation at the national level was almost a prerequisite to research. Today, however, authority has been decentralized, and it may be more useful to affiliate with an institution in the locale where your research will be conducted, thereby removing several layers of time-consuming bureaucratic communications and working directly with the unit that will make your research arrangements.

When considering potential affiliations, obtain answers to two questions. Most important is: can the proposed host unit make all the arrangements necessary for your project? Some foreign scholars have identified Chinese colleagues with whom they wanted to collaborate only to find upon arrival that the foreign affairs office at the university or institute was unable or unwilling to make arrangements necessary to carry out the research.

Second: is the cooperation of a single unit sufficient for your needs? If it appears that the cooperation of more than one unit will be necessary for your research, you need to consider the relationships between or among those units. The Chinese bureaucratic structure is quite different from that within the United States. Understanding that structure can help you work within it. Chinese institutions are highly compartmentalized. Each *danwei* is part of a larger system, or *xitong*, and cooperation across *xitong* can be awkward. Knowing to which *xitong* your proposed *danwei* belongs is important.

The university system under the direction of the State Education Commission (SEDC) is one *xitong* with which many American scholars affiliate. The SEDC determines important educational policy and administers all national-level universities, exercising control over their budgets, curricula, and the allocation and promotion of faculty. It also issues regulations governing research by foreign scholars hosted by universities under their jurisdiction. Several recent social science field researchers—both advanced graduate students and university professors—have noted an SEDC regulation stipulating that scholars affiliated with universities under its jurisdiction are permitted only two weeks of fieldwork each semester. The rule has rarely been applied, and many people have found informal ways of circumventing it. But at least one researcher recently decided to switch her affiliation to a local social science academy that permitted her to spend several months in the field.

Similarly, the SEDC currently has a rule that Chinese social scientists under its jurisdiction must first get national-level permission to conduct collaborative research with foreigners. And a 1989 decision to impound survey data gathered under a collaborative project sponsored by Peking University was made not by university officals but by officials at the SEDC, who then ordered the university not to release the data (the data have since been released).

Some universities and scholars are willing to bend SEDC rules, and the SEDC is likely to become more flexible in the future, but scholars hoping to conduct field research through a host unit under SEDC jurisdiction will want to assure themselves early that their proposed research and collaboration are possible. If a local social science academy is an equally attractive affiliation, arrangements there may be easier.

Universities under the jurisdiction of local governments are not directly administered by the SEDC, although most comply with the spirit of SEDC directives. But local-level universities are often more flexible than centrally administered ones, and their position in the educational hierarchy allows them a degree of local autonomy.

Research on localities is often easier at a locally administered university. Even in a province distant from Beijing, a centrally administered university is less likely to have ties with the locality. For instance, a graduate student studying local administration in one southern city found that his affiliation with a university administered by the SEDC in Beijing was not particularly useful in gaining him entrée to local officials. By establishing a less formal affiliation with a locally administered university, he was able to get introductions to many officials in the local government. Conversely, a researcher hosted by a municipal foreign affairs office found that city officials could not make contact for her with the centrally administered university there.

Even at the national level, there are differences among *xitong*. The Chinese Academy of Social Sciences (CASS) is administered by the State Council and is not part of the SEDC *xitong*. Cooperation between CASS and universities under the SEDC can be difficult. Moreover, in contrast with the SEDC, the national-level CASS has no vertical line of command to provincial and local level academies. Although relations between CASS and local-level academies may be close and cooperative, local academies have the autonomy, for instance, to decide for themselves whether to accept foreign researchers. And local-level academies are able to sponsor foreign researchers who might be refused by the national-level academy.

The Chinese Academy of Sciences (CAS) is also administered by the State Council. It is a different *xitong* from both the SEDC and CASS and is subject to different regulations. What may be possible for a foreign researcher within one CAS institute may not be possible under SEDC or CASS. Thus, although CASS instituted a moratorium on rural fieldwork by foreigners in the early 1980s, U.S. scientists under the auspices of CAS continued to conduct research in rural areas. And, unlike CASS, CAS does have administrative authority over its branches.

Similarly, each ministry under the State Council constitutes a separate *xitong*, and some ministries also operate their own universities and research institutes. Some Americans, particularly scientists, choose to carry out research under ministry auspices.

In addition to institutions falling under clearly defined *xitong* are numerous local government and party organizations that sponsor research of importance to them, some of which have established their own, relatively independent, research institutions outside national jurisdiction. These institutions tend to be relatively flexible and adaptable, and a few foreign researchers who have established *guanxi* with them have also been able to conduct research under their auspices. This type of affiliation, however, is apparently open only to more established scholars. Advanced graduate students seem to be required to affiliate with either universities or research academies. Moreover, working with these organizations requires such good *guanxi* that only people with long-term, close relations with Chinese colleagues are likely to be able to make the arrangements.

Horizontal communication among *xitong* is difficult, although cooperation across *xitong* is somewhat easier in the sciences than in the social sciences and humanities. Since the mid-1980s, in an effort to bring scientific research in China up to international standards, China has instituted several dozen "open labs." These promote horizontal mobility between research institutes under the CAS, scientists at universities under the SEDC, and ministries, and at least one foreign scientist sits on the governing board of each of the open labs. A fuller discussion of laboratory research appears later in this chapter.

The social sciences and humanities have yet to reach this level of cooperation. A researcher affiliated with CASS's Institute of History, for instance, has access to the library at his institute but may face difficulties obtaining permission to use the library at Peking University, which is under the administration of the SEDC. One graduate student doing research on the revival of temples in southern China discovered that different temples were administered by different *xitong*—the Office of Religion, the Tourist Bureau, the People's Political Consultative Conference, and the Cultural Bureau. Relations between these organizations were often strained, and communications between them were difficult. Access to one of the organizations made it difficult to work with the others. Similarly, a researcher in archaeology discovered that relations between the research institute with which he was formally affiliated had terrible *guanxi* with a museum whose cooperation he needed.

The complexity and compartmentalization of China's institutional structure serves to highlight the importance of talking with as many colleagues as possible—both American and Chinese—before deciding which affiliation best serves your research needs. Only with time and experience do the complexities of institutional relationships become clear.

The compartmentalization of institutional relations in China is one reason why *guanxi* is so important. While formal horizontal communications among *xitong* are often difficult, informal ones are not—if you, or more likely your Chinese associates, have a friend or relative in the *xitong* with which you want to communicate. One scholar recently had great success conducting field research with a younger Chinese faculty member who had been sent to the countryside during the Cultural Revolution. They returned together to the village where the Chinese professor had lived for several years and where her ties of *guanxi* were still strong.

Cultivating *guanxi* is much like networking in the United States. Informal ties can often open doors that formal affiliations cannot.

THE RESEARCH PROPOSAL   After finding an appropriate host, you will usually be expected to submit a detailed research proposal outlining the purpose of your research, specifying how the research will be conducted, and stating what you expect to accomplish, who will be involved, and what types of collaboration, cooperation, and training can be expected. Virtually every field researcher working through formal channels has stressed the importance of the proposal, because after the Chinese agree to it, the proposal will become, in effect, a contract from which deviation will require further negotiation. If you are a scientist and your research requires camping, make certain that everyone on your team (including the driver) is prepared to camp, too. Americans whose research proposals have not specified the importance of camping report having to leave their research site and drive two hours to sleep in less than commodious hostels. Similarly, research requiring work outside normal hours (generally 8:00 a.m. to 5:00 p.m. with a two-hour rest period around noon) should also be spelled out. Researchers for whom early morning photography is important have been stymied because their proposal did not specify the necessity of early morning visits to their field site. Fieldworkers observing animal behavior have been frustrated because prior agreement had not been reached for the team to go to the field at sunrise or during the noon rest break, when the animals were active. Without specifying your research needs in precise detail, key members of your Chinese team could balk, legitimately claiming that they had not understood the terms of the agreement—or even that your demands are a violation of the contract.

In working out the details of the project's work schedule, remember that the ordinary Chinese work day is eight hours long and five-and-a-half days a week. The Chinese weekend usually begins at noon on Saturday. Respecting your colleagues' work schedule is important and will allow them time for family responsibilities and rest.

The question of intellectual property rights should also be spelled out clearly in the proposal. Jointly authored papers are commonplace in academic exchanges with China. U.S. researchers, however, still report instances when articles based on their collaboration were published under exclusively Chinese authorship without mention of U.S. collaboration or funding. Conversely, Chinese have published articles claiming joint U.S. authorship when the U.S. author had not been actively involved or consulted.

Similarly, the need to bring specimens, questionnaires, or other raw data out of China should also be spelled out in the proposal. Some researchers expecting to take raw data with them have been stymied by restrictions on data export. Agreement in the proposal should start with delineation of responsibility for investigating export restrictions and for getting necessary documentation. The proposal should include agreements on data collection. For example, it should clearly state what data the Chinese are supposed to produce, sampling techniques, and data processing methodologies. Be wary of the spoken or written phrase, "according to Chinese conditions." It can cover different interpretations about objectives or methodologies. It is important to understand potential differences early on and make sure comfortable resolution can be found for them. Finally, the proposal should address how data will be collected across institutes and *xitong*.

Researchers also advise that you bring to China your proposal and all correspondence related to your project. If modifications must be made, you will need to refer to your written understandings.

Finally, the agreement on cooperative research between the National Science Foundation (NSF) in the United States and the Chinese Academy of Sciences, the Chinese Academy of Social Sciences, the State Education Commission, and the Chinese National Science Foundation stipulates that the receiving side pays all in-country fees of the scholars in their program (that is, the Chinese pay per diem expenses of U.S. scientists in China and the United States pays the costs of Chinese in the United States). However, researchers should be flexible in interpreting this agreement. The agreement works well when scientists are working in laboratories without extraordinary additional costs. Field research, however, is more expensive in terms of the number of personnel involved, equipment, and cost of cars and trucks transporting researchers and equipment to the site. Chinese research institutions ordinarily cannot afford to pay the additional costs of field research. These costs thus should be worked into the budget of the funding proposal to the NSF or any other institution operating under a similar agreement.

FEES   Researchers should expect to pay research-related fees in China. It is important, when negotiating a proposal, to ask for clarification of what those costs will be. Specific types of fees will be discussed in the sections on archival research, laboratory research, and fieldwork. The most common are affiliation fees for more advanced scholars and either affiliation fees or tuition for dissertation-level graduate students. Most people also pay a variety of service fees, and additional costs are incurred when host units arrange outside visits that last overnight or longer. Many scholars, having been housed in more expensive guest houses when equally comfortable, cheaper accommodations are available nearby, suggest trying to negotiate to stay in dormitory rooms or cheaper accommodations. In fieldwork, additional fees may be charged for the salary and costs of staff who accompany you to the field.

Fees now vary widely from institution to institution and, within institutions, even from person to person, often depending on the researcher's status (for example, advanced graduate student or senior scholar), ability to pay, and *guanxi* with the host organization. Some researchers with longstanding relations with their work unit pay no affiliation fee; some have paid $300 a month, others $100. One senior scholar paid a $1,000 affiliation fee for a research stay of three weeks, which included conducting interviews, sending and receiving faxes, and photocopying some materials. This amount should be considered too high in almost every case. In general, short-term researchers pay more than long-term ones, and senior-level researchers pay more than junior-level ones.

Graduate students engaged in research are generally required to pay either affiliation fees to a research institute or tuition to a university, even if they do not attend classes. The cost to students varies, but it seems generally to run between $1,000 and $3,000 a year. In negotiating this fee, it is important to clarify what types of assistance you will be offered in return; for example, guidelines from an adviser, use of the library, assistance in making outside contacts and arranging for interviews, or help in negotiating fees for interviews. Costs for preparing questionnaires, photocopying, computer time, and transportation are usually extra.

FINALIZING A PLAN   After reaching agreement on the proposal and fees, you will usually be issued a formal invitation, signed by an official of the institution with which you will be affiliated (usually a dean of a university or a vice president of a research institute).

Scholars who have worked in Chinese institutions have discovered that no arrangement is predictable, permanent, or self-executing. The experience of the CSCC is telling. Research proposals of students and scholars selected by the Committee on Advanced Study in China are approved by the appropriate Chinese organization prior to the grantee's departure for China, and placements are negotiated with host institutions. Yet most researchers discover that the implementation of these carefully laid plans requires continuous negotiation with their host units. Some scholars adjust their project to fit available materials and resources. Proposals must be flexible enough to accommodate different opportunities.

The last edition of *China Bound* noted, "The most serene reports come from individuals who manage to combine a Taoist philosophy that everything will eventually work itself out with low-key but persistent negotiations with Chinese hosts."

Reports from more recent years suggest that that approach is still best. One researcher writes:

> Working successfully in China seems to require the development of a kind of Zen-like mental balance that allows you to take in new and often challenging information without having it obscure your original vision. . . . If I ever encounter a similar situation, I hope I will be able to arrive quickly to a state of resignation and not waste so much mental energy being mad.

ARCHIVAL RESEARCH

Historians and other scholars in the humanities have benefited greatly from the opportunity to do research in China's vast archival and library collections. As Beatrice Bartlett, a leading expert on China's Ming-Qing archives, writes:

> China's dazzling wealth of archives and plethora of archival organizations, preserving 30 million fascicles (*juan*) of materials at both the national and local levels, have attracted many foreign researchers. In addition to the three enormous chronologically-demarcated institutions for central-government holdings—the Number One in Beijing for Ming and Qing documents, the Number Two in Nanjing covering the Republic, and the central archives in Beijing for the post-1949 era—there are more than 2,000 local depositories. In theory, every county (*xian*) or district in China has its own archive; this should also be true for most townships (*xiang*) as well. Faced with this information, foreign scholars may be led to devise extensive research plans worthy of this latest manifestation of the fabled riches of the East. Nevertheless, researchers are well advised to proceed with caution. Direct inspection of a local archive is likely to yield considerable deviation from expectations.[4]

---

[4]Beatrice Bartlett, "The Number Three Archives of China: The Liaoning Provincial Archives." *China Exchange News*, Fall-Winter 1991, pp. 2-6.

China has more than 200,000 libraries, including the national library in Beijing; 1,732 public libraries; 700 college and university libraries; 100,000 middle school and elementary school libraries; 1,000 scientific and specialized libraries; and 110,000 trade union libraries. Detailed descriptions in Chinese and English of Chinese and foreign holdings along with addresses of important libraries can be found in the *Directory of Chinese Libraries*.

Foreign scholars have used only a fraction of China's holdings, but each year a few researchers begin work in previously unexplored collections. Scholars who have done research in Chinese archives urge others planning to use archives to read the articles by Bartlett in the *National Palace Museum Bulletin*, as well as her book, *Monarchs and Ministers: The Grand Council in Mid-Ch'ing China, 1723-1820*, and the Fall/Winter issue of *China Exchange News*, which is devoted to reports on archival research. Bartlett's admonition to users of the Qing archives holds true for library collections around China. The archives, she writes, "were saved for the Chinese, to be developed by the administrative vision and genius of Chinese curators. Foreigners are welcome, but as readers, not owners of the documents."[5]

Scholars planning archival research will also find useful *Archives in the People's Republic of China: A Brief Introduction for American Scholars and Archivists*, by William Moss, director of the Smithsonian Institution Archives. The publication includes description of several central, municipal, and provincial archives and includes translation of archives laws including the July 1992 law on archival work by foreigners (provided in Appendix N). The report is available free of charge from

Alan Bain
Smithsonian Archives
Arts and Industries Bldg.
Room 2135, Mail Stop MRC 414
Washington, DC 20560

The following section is devoted not to a description of the collections in archives and libraries but rather to the practical experiences of those who have used them.

RESEARCH AFFILIATION   Access to archival or library holdings requires a research affiliation, so it is advisable to seek affiliation with the organization most likely to be helpful in arranging for the access needed. For most library or archive users, that affiliation will be either a university or a research institute.

---

[5]*Times Literary Supplement*, July 4, 1986, p. 734.

In considering affiliation with a university, it is important to know that humanistic research in Chinese universities is often focused on events and personalities of local importance. For example, scholars at Shandong University have conducted research on the Boxers while those at Wuhan often study the 1911 revolution. Scholars at Nankai write about the economic history of the Tianjin region. And in Nanjing University, the focus is on the Jiangnan region. Faculty at these universities often can introduce the foreign scholar to colleagues in museums, libraries, publishing houses, and other universities who are working on similar topics.

Some university departments may be oriented toward a particular historical era rather than toward local interests. Peking University has aided scholars working in Shang and Qin-Han history because its departments are strong in those areas; it is also strong on May Fourth literature.

For access to holdings outside the library at the institute or university with which you are affiliated, a letter of introduction from a scholar at your host organization, together with a description of your research project and the types of materials you need to use, are usually required. Sometimes several weeks pass before the request is granted. In other cases, permission is immediate. Some libraries, such as those at CASS's Institute of History and at Peking University, are open only to people who are directly affiliated with the institution. Scholars affiliated with research institutes often have difficulty obtaining permission to use university libraries and vice versa. On the other hand, an introduction from someone who already has access is often sufficient for permission to work there temporarily. Some archives with years of experience with foreigners, such as the Ming-Qing holdings, have institutionalized procedures, making these archives relatively predictable and easy to use. Access to other holdings must often be explored on a case-by-case basis. Occasionally, students have obtained access to municipal libraries with only student identification, but some libraries are still closed to foreigners. Additional pressure from an adviser or colleague is often necessary before requests to work in other libraries are accommodated. In library research, as in other aspects of Chinese life, good relations with colleagues are important to achieving your goals.

USE OF COLLECTIONS   Researchers report that card catalogs for some collections are difficult to use. Chinese categories for arranging knowledge are different from those in the West, and many card catalogs are incomplete, making it difficult to be certain about holdings or their contents. Fortunately, there is a growing literature on the kinds of materials available and reference guides for further information, all of which can be very useful when preparing to work in China. It is wise to read all the secondary literature and consult catalogs (that is, of Chinese holdings now increasingly available outside China) before your arrival so you can be prepared to ask for particular holdings. Most collections have one or two staff members who are knowledgeable about their holdings, and their cooperation has been invaluable to foreign researchers.

Access to particular materials can be limited even after receiving permission to use an archive or library. Rare books are carefully protected and generally may be read only in certain areas of a library and often under supervision. While one scholar using twentieth century sources at the National Library of China describes it as "unbelievably modern and user-friendly," scholars working with its rare books collection complain of a rule, issued in 1991, that a letter of introduction allows a scholar to look at only four (one scholar says five) rare books. Some scholars have circumvented the regulation by obtaining several letters of introduction, and one such scholar was able to see well over 80 books by bringing in new letters. Others who have used similar tactics have been told that the rule is four books per research project. "This drastic restriction on the single most important collection for the study of premodern Chinese history is a serious blow to scholarship," writes one disappointed researcher.

Occasionally, researchers find that materials are out of circulation for microfilming or that some portion of a collection is not open to foreign researchers. One researcher found he was not allowed to copy everything he wanted because the person in charge did not want him to obtain "systematic" records. But many people, after spending some time working with collections, find one or two people who are sympathetic to their research needs and knowlegeable about the collection who become very helpful in gathering and copying materials. "What is needed," writes one researcher "is much persistence, a judicious amount of insistence tempered with courtesy, and good luck."

FEES   Costs for using China's libraries and archives may include fees for access to collections, user's fees to examine materials, preservation fees, and reproduction costs. Usually your host organization will not charge additional fees for use of its own library, although some do. But places where you have no formal affiliation may charge an entrance fee even before you use the holdings. Students can usually negotiate smaller fees than senior scholars. One graduate student, for instance, was able to negotiate a fee of Y100 to use a rare books reading room for a year, while a senior scholar who came at the same time paid $US200 to use the same holdings for two-and-a-half months. Other scholars have reported paying nothing or as little as Y2 a day for library use.

On June 16, 1992, reports one researcher, the Chinese government announced a decision to define archival work as a "third industry." Archives, like universities and research institutes, were made responsible for raising money for their operating costs. The result has been higher fees both for using collections and for reproducing materials, although as of this writing, the guidelines have not been uniformly enforced. One researcher was able to copy a portion of the new guidelines for increased charges on library use. The portion he was given detailed the costs to Chinese users. Foreign users, the researcher was told, are to be charged five times the Chinese price, although sometimes this cost can be lowered considerably by judicious negotiation. The prices listed below are for the Chinese:

Storage fees
1. User's fee (the cost of examining a document or microfilm reel) for "ordinary" historical documents: Y2/*juan*
2. User's fee for "special" historical documents: Y10/*juan*

Preservation fees
3. User's fee for Qing dynasty documents: Y2/*juan*
4. User's fee for revolutionary history documents: Y1/*juan*
5. Republican material: Y0.8/*juan*
6. Material on the founding of the PRC: Y0.5/*juan*
7. All microfilm material, all periods: Y5/reel/day

Reproduction
8. Large, 11×16 sheet: Y0.8; 11×8.5 sheet: Y0.5
9. Microfilming, color: Y10/frame; black and white: Y2/frame. (Microfilming costs vary according to the size of the original document.)

People have found it possible to negotiate these prices. Some have continued to pay Chinese prices or a combination of Chinese prices for use and preservation and foreign prices for reproduction. For most scholars working in archives, duplicating costs are the most burdensome, and some have found it cheaper to hire an assistant to hand copy documents than to have them mechanically reproduced.

LIBRARY RULES   Rules regarding access and duplication of materials vary among libraries. Most stacks are not open and fetching materials generally takes more time than in libraries in the United States. Often, collections and reading rooms are separated, sometimes in different parts of a city. In some cases, books or periodicals must be ordered as much as a week in advance.

Photocopying facilities, while more common now than in the past, are usually limited. Photocopying and microfilming are ordinarily done by the staff and also require a wait—sometimes days or weeks. In some cases, however, researchers have been permitted to photocopy materials themselves. Some places limit duplication of materials to 500 sheets. Some archives and rare book collections require that notes be taken only on specially supplied paper, in pencil and in Chinese. At the Ming-Qing archives, all notes must be inspected and stamped when they are taken out. At the Peking University Library, only 30 sheets at one time can be photocopied, and the turnaround time is at least two days. String-bound books and most pre-1800 materials may not be photocopied, although in some libraries they may be microfilmed. Usually, microfilm readers must be reserved in advance. Research assistants to help with transcribing materials by hand may not be admitted to some facilities. Some libraries do not allow their old books to circulate during the hottest months of the summer. Learning the rules early and planning your time accordingly can increase efficiency.

LIBRARY HOURS   Library hours also vary. The National Library of China is open six days a week (closed on Saturday) and does not close for the noon lunch and rest hour. Many others, however, are open only five days a week and take two-hour breaks at lunchtime. Some allow foreign researchers to continue working in small sitting rooms during that period, but others require that the facility be shut down. Some researchers say that facilities open later than the posted hours and that staff members leave earlier than closing time. Most libraries are not open at night.

In conclusion, Beatrice Bartlett's general advice to scholars in China's libraries and archives is as sound today as it was in 1985:

> The situation is constantly changing, however, and frequently one is gratified when a curator's generosity is employed to prevail over a narrow interpretation of the rules. In view of the fact that the materials in all Chinese archives are magnificent, offering much to the scholar willing to search, patient submission to the rules while at the same time quietly attempting to negotiate improved terms is a worthwhile posture, likely eventually to produce desired results.[6]

FIELDWORK

Fieldwork by U.S. scientists and social scientists has been a vital part of academic exchange with China and can be especially rewarding, but the bureaucratic procedures required to conduct fieldwork continue to puzzle potential researchers. For the purposes of this book, fieldwork

---

[6]Beatrice Bartlett, "Archive Materials in China on United States History." Pp. 504-506 in Lewis Hanke, ed., *Guide to the Study of United States History Outside the U.S., 1945-1980, vol. 1.* White Plains, NY: Kraus International Publications, 1985.

is defined as almost any research that requires extensive contact outside the host unit, from interviewing workers or enterprise managers in the city, or carrying out systematic survey research, to conducting anthropological research in a rural village or doing on-site studies of animal behavior. Making arrangements to conduct fieldwork is more complicated than affiliating with a research institute, university, or scientific laboratory and requires time to plan. As Otto Schnepp observes:

> Conducting fieldwork in China. . .is in many respects unlike carrying out field investigations in the US and other foreign countries. The reasons for this difference are many but for the most part may be attributed to the structure of the Chinese bureaucracy, the undeveloped nature of some rural areas where fieldwork takes place, China's own priorities in scientific development (which may not always match our own), and, to some extent, basic cultural differences between Chinese and foreigners involved in joint projects.[7]

This section provides an overview of opportunities for fieldwork in China, details the steps that must be taken in order to carry it out, and provides information and advice on how to ensure that fieldwork goes smoothly.

Scientists often find it easier to identify opportunities for field research in China than do social scientists. Many institutes within CAS operate field stations in various parts of the country, and many stations welcome cooperative projects with foreign scholars. Projects in earthquake geophysics, paleontology, mining, forestry, botany, epidemiology, and oceanography were among the early successes.

Social science fieldwork, especially survey research and anthropological studies of rural villages, is always more sensitive, and identifying appropriate opportunities is often difficult. Until very recently, CASS had been the principal sponsor of social science fieldwork. The National Science Foundation and the CSCC's National Program for Advanced Study and Research in China both fund American field research in China. The Luce and Ford Foundations also sponsor collaborative research projects, while a number of U.S. institutions and scholars have been able to make their own, less formal arrangements.

Several anthropologists were among the first group of scholars sent to China under the CSCC's Program for Advanced Study and Research in the late 1970s. However, it was not easy to get official authorization to do fieldwork then, especially in rural areas. In 1981, after the conduct of an American anthropologist had provoked controversy within both the U.S. and the Chinese academic communities, the Chinese government instituted an informal moratorium on social science fieldwork in rural areas. Nevertheless, scientific fieldwork continued and several

---

[7]Otto Schnepp, "Fieldwork in China." *China Exchange News*, March 1984, pp. 1-3.

social scientists were able to make their own arrangements through informal channels. In 1985, the Chinese Academy of Social Sciences and the Zouping County government in Shandong Province agreed to permit a team of CSCC-sponsored researchers, including anthropologists, political scientists, economists, historians, sociologists, and ecologists, to conduct long-term fieldwork in Zouping. At about the same time, institutional restrictions appeared to ease, anthropologists were again given permission to conduct village studies, and anthropological fieldwork was revived.

Proposals to do social science research continue to raise sensitive questions and official concerns remain, but the increased autonomy of universities, provincial social science academies, and local research institutes in recent years has made fieldwork easier to arrange than in the past. Today, social scientists are conducting field research on a wide array of topics, including China's "floating population," the development of the stock market, enterprise management, linguistics, and local administration.

The ingredients for successful research in China described in the previous section—formal institutional affiliation, *guanxi*, and mutual benefit—apply equally to fieldwork. Stanford University's joint research with Chinese earth scientists demonstrates the interrelationship of all three elements and thus stands as a model for successful scientific fieldwork. Cooperation in the geological sciences between Stanford and China dates from the turn of this century. When an international meeting in 1979 provided the opportunity for Stanford and Chinese geologists to meet after a hiatus of 30 years, the old ties of *guanxi* were immediately revived. The multifaceted, long-term research project that has resulted combines both theoretical and applied science. The implications of the research for the development of China's petroleum industry make the project of interest to the Chinese Ministry of Geology and Mineral Resources, the China National Petroleum Corporation, and U.S. oil companies interested in petroleum exploration in China. The NSF has provided funding for the project, and U.S. oil companies make yearly contributions. Several Chinese graduate students have received Ph.D. degrees at Stanford as a result of the joint collaboration. More than one hundred scholarly papers have been published. The practical benefits are unquestionably mutual.

The 10-year study of a rural village by Edward Friedman, Paul Pickowicz, Mark Selden, and Kay Johnson demonstrates how successful good *guanxi* can be. The authors were seen by authorities in Beijing as friends of China and in 1978 were allowed to begin research in a north China village, where they returned 18 times over the next decade. As the Chinese government's policy of opening to the West continued and the U.S. researchers won the respect and confidence of village lead-ers, their access to the details of village life expanded. In contrast to scholars working with formal affiliations, they have never paid research fees. Their book, *Chinese Village, Socialist State*, is a detailed analysis of rural life in China.

Few American projects will approach this complexity or these ideals. Such projects require considerable experience and sophistication. But several important considerations will greatly increase your chances of success. Following is a brief discussion of what they are.

COSTS   Field research, because so many people are involved, is generally more expensive than archival research. Costs naturally vary depending on the subject to be researched, scope of the project, and number of people involved. Costs for field research are not institutionalized, nor are the names given to different fees consistent.

In addition to affiliation fees mentioned earlier, field researchers may be asked to pay additional administrative costs (*guanlifei*) as compensation for arrangements made on behalf of the project, work compensation fees (*laowufei*) to the work unit where interviews take place, fees for reproduction of questionnaires, equipment, transportation fees, gifts and banquets for people who have helped you, fees and living expenses for the people who accompany you to the field, as well as your own living expenses. For collaborative projects, some of these fees may be waived, especially costs related to Chinese personnel involved. The China Health and Nutrition Survey, a cooperative survey research project between sociologists and health economists from the University of North Carolina and nutritionists and biostatisticians from the Chinese Academy of Preventive Medicine in Beijing, is one example. Although major funding comes from several U.S. organizations (the Ford Foundation, the National Institutes of Health, and the National Science Foundation), the Chinese side contributes both its expertise and hundreds of hours of work. Data collection takes place in China, but much of the analysis is done in the United States, and many of the younger Chinese collaborators come here to work for extended periods, often obtaining graduate degrees in the process. The NSF provides funding for senior Chinese collaborators to stay in the United States for up to six months.

Chinese approval of fieldwork depends on a demonstration that the project will be beneficial to all concerned. For the American, the opportunity to conduct research constitutes a benefit. The benefit to the Chinese host varies. For Chinese scholars, the benefit may be the opportunity to work with (and sometimes publish together with) an American with similar research interests or to come to the United States. With the recent decision to encourage every Chinese work unit, including research institutes and universities, to generate their own income, Chinese hosting organizations may also see foreign research projects as a way to make money. Many local officials regard it as an honor for their unit to be the subject of study, but they will also expect financial benefit from the research. So long as the current trend continues, foreign researchers can expect the cost of their research to rise.

You will want an accurate estimate of your research costs before you go to the field. This is difficult. Many Chinese collaborators will be reluctant to discuss finances with you. Some institutions prefer to delay discussions until you are actually in the field; some researchers agree, hoping first to develop ties of friendship that may serve to lower their costs. Other researchers caution that you should negotiate as many of your costs as possible before arriving in China. Whether before or after your arrival, honest, up-front discussions of budget limitations and funding sources may help to establish guidelines within which to work. Many local officials appear to believe that Americans are wealthy enough to afford whatever is asked—a belief that is confirmed by the few scholars who do pay whatever is asked.

You may be charged a lump sum without any itemization of costs. China hands suggest negotiating over costs and encourage their colleagues to ask for a breakdown of costs by category. Similarly, some researchers have found it effective to spread payments out over time rather than dispersing funds in a single lump sum, reserving a hefty portion of the total payment for the end.

Service fees (*fuwufei*) are another category you will want to scrutinize. Some researchers, for example, have been charged a daily fee to cover such services as making travel arrangements and being picked up at the airport. In a few cases, people report having been charged for services that were never rendered, and some prefer to save money by making arrangements themselves.

Expect to pay more than the cost of salary for your research assistants and interpreters. Some portion of what you are charged for them will be going toward institutional overhead.

Finally, with corruption now widespread in China, there is no easy way to distingish between unreasonable research fees and outright corruption. Fieldworkers urge you to consult American colleagues who have already been to the field when attempting to decide what are reasonable costs for your research. Prices vary by region and by the status and wherewithal of the researcher.

Negotiations can be time-consuming, and the ill will that can result from bickering over money can hinder your research efforts, which is another reason for trying to negotiate your expenses before you leave for China. Researchers who can spend only short periods of time in the field may find it simpler to pay the requested sums with few questions asked. Indeed, short-term researchers whose projects can be completed in one or two visits can expect to pay more than researchers conducting long-term projects where the ties of *guanxi* and friendship have had time to develop. The best way to come up with a realistic budget is to begin with a good sense of legitimate costs and ask for a precise breakdown of costs by category, presenting your own financial situation honestly, negotiating—and compromising—on the basis of all these factors.

PLACEMENT IN THE FIELD Scientific fieldworkers are often based in established field stations. However, social scientists often prefer to work in locales (such as villages) that are outside the *xitong* with which they are affiliated. Technically, most host organizations do not have the authority to place a social scientist in the field. Field placement still depends on *guanxi* and necessitates that representatives from the sponsoring organization persuade local-level officials and organizations to accept your project. If your Chinese collaborator has close ties to the area, as in the case mentioned earlier where the Chinese partner was returning to the village where she had lived during the Cultural Revolution, that process may be quick and smooth. Often, however, a process of courtship is required—including hosting banquets and offering gifts—to convince local officials that hosting a foreign researcher is to their advantage.

For anthropological research, this process may have to be repeated in several places before local officials are willing to sign on. Unless you have already developed personal friendships with local officials, they will expect compensation for making your research possible, for seeing that you are properly housed and fed, and for ensuring that local people will be cooperative.

THE RESEARCH TEAM If you rely on a host organization to get to the field, a complicated cast of characters is likely to be involved—administrators from the host organization, Chinese collaborators, research assistants and interpreters, local officials, drivers, and local residents. They will have individual interests that may differ from each other's and from your own. Your research will be smoother and more successful if you understand why everyone is there and can forge the various participants into a working team.

Academic administrators, often from the foreign affairs office of the sponsoring unit, are important to the success of your project. The best will be supportive of your work and active in bringing it to fruition. Many **foreign affairs officials** receive high marks from U.S. researchers, and it would be unfair not to recognize the great assistance so many have given. But some have been viewed as impediments to research. Many may have little interest in the substance of your work; many are busy with other things.

However, the breadth of authority of the foreign affairs office is wider than that of the individual scholars with whom you work; therefore, the academic administrator assigned to work with you is vital to your project. He is often responsible for making the local connections necessary to put you in the field, and his endeavors may require considerable expenditure of time and effort. Your way will be smoother if he understands and supports your project. You will be at an advantage if you can persuade him that your project is worthwhile.

Most American field researchers work with **Chinese collaborators,** although some social scientists prefer to work independently. Collaboration with Chinese colleagues has been one of the most rewarding aspects of the exchange relationship. Most Americans could not work in China without that collaboration, even when they approach the project with different motivations and methodologies. "I found her presence on many of the interviews a godsend," writes one researcher about her collaborator. "Her connections were clearly of immeasurable help to me. . . . I feel that my research access. . .[was] greatly facilitated through her."

In addition to carrying out joint research, your Chinese collaborators will also have their own interests. The concept of mutual benefit recognizes the need to work for your collaborators' interests as well. In one successful research project, local officials were happy to host the American fieldworker and her Chinese faculty collaborator because the town was trying to develop connections with the Chinese university. The young faculty member was happy to make the connections because her graduate students were looking for a place to do their fieldwork. Everyone's interests were served.

Similarly, institutions hosting projects with funding from the United States have a better chance of receiving additional funding from Beijing, and a collaborator able to bring in additional funds will gain both increased prestige and a financial bonus. Chinese scholars may expect collaboration to lead to a research opportunity in the United States. American funders, including the NSF, promote reciprocity and assume that collaborative projects will include the opportunity for members of the Chinese team to conduct research in the United States.

If you are individually funded and your home institution is not able to offer your collaborators direct financial support, they still might welcome a formal invitation from your institution to join you as a visiting scholar. A formal invitation may allow the Chinese scholar to receive approved leave from his own work unit and enhances his chances of receiving a U.S. visa.

Research assistants will be invaluable in implementing your research project. Many look forward to working with Americans as a way of gaining experience in the use of Western methodologies. The project they undertake with you may suggest new avenues of research as they pursue their graduate education. Many will also be looking forward to an opportunity to study in the United States. In some cases, research teams include research assistants from both the host and local institutions. The local assistant is likely to be much more familiar with the area and its people and can be an important source of information and help in becoming acquainted with the area. Research assistants from the host unit may be better trained academically but less conversant with local issues.

Interpreters are another vital part of the team. Researchers who have used Chinese interpreters report that an English-speaking scholar who is also part of the project, especially one who has studied in the West, is likely to be extremely effective. He will understand both the project and the specialized language, which "ordinary" interpreters might not.

You will, in any case, want to make certain your interpreter is able. You can facilitate the work of interpreters by providing outlines of questions ahead of time and perhaps making a glossary in Chinese to English for technical terms. Since he will also be interpreting during whatever negotiations you may have in the field, his position can be delicate. His English abilities will enable you to befriend him more quickly than non-English speaking members of the team, and his trust, friendship, insights, and information can be invaluable to your work.

While serving as your translator, the interpreter remains an employee of your host organization and is often junior to your Chinese collaborators. While you may become friends, his first responsibility is to his superiors in his own work unit. Your interpreter, too, may be looking for an opportunity to come to the United States and may want you to help.

Local officials who have been persuaded to accept you into their area are also vital to your research. Their continued cooperation is necessary for your success. Once you arrive, they are responsible not only for your food, housing, health, and safety, but also for assisting your research, which can be a heavy burden. Hospitality to foreigners is deeply ingrained in Chinese culture even as wariness toward them is pervasive. You will need good relations with your local hosts for the successful completion of your work, and it will be important to them to understand that your intentions are good. Representatives from your host institution may help you in the early stages of this relationship, serving, in effect, as middlemen in explaining who you are and what your project is about.

But if you spend lengthy periods in the field, you will want to develop good relations with your local hosts. Just as hospitality to foreigners is deeply ingrained in Chinese culture, so you will be expected to give your hosts face by reciprocating that hospitality. A generous banquet, where you publicly thank the hosts who have made your research possible, is one way of showing your appreciation. If you give one early in your stay and use it as an opportunity for your hosts to get to know you and win their trust, the foundations for further cooperation will be strengthened. In some cases, gifts are appropriate. Your interpreters and collaborators can advise you about the most appropriate ways of compensating your local hosts and showing your thanks.

Nonetheless, even scholars who welcome the opportunity for friendship sometimes complain that social demands can be overwhelming. Field researchers whose work requires traveling from place to place are often treated like VIPs. The presence of foreigners is an opportunity for local officials to throw an expensive banquet, and face is gained through concrete and longlasting evidence of the foreigner's visit in the form of numerous photographs. Local hosts may not understand the needs of a serious scientific researcher or a researcher's impatience over time-consuming banquets and photo opportunities. Your work schedule should allow for the exchange of hospitality, but you may need to remind your team members that time is limited, and obligations of hospitality and face ought not to overwhelm your work.

Your **driver** is the final member of your team, and he is especially important if your research requires travel to out-of-the-way places. Make sure that he is invited to banquets on the road (this is best done through a go-between) and carry cigarettes to present as occasional gifts. The article by John Olsen in Appendix O provides essential information on the types of vehicles you should use, the need for mechanical skills, and types of fuel available.

Because so few Chinese have private cars, drivers have a special status. Not only do many of them make far more money than their friends in factories, but the mobility afforded by a car gives them wide-ranging connections. They are likely to know their area well and to be a lively source of local lore.

But a number of researchers, particularly those who must travel long distances on crowded roads, have expressed concern about the speed and audacity of their drivers. While it is important to respect the driver's status and to make him part of the team, your safety—and the safety of others on the road—is paramount, and it is important to negotiate hard to ensure it. If you believe your driver is too reckless, a frank discussion with him and the Chinese members of your group may be necessary. The driver is responsible for your safety while you are in his vehicle, and it is a responsibility all drivers must take seriously.

THE RESEARCH SITE   If your field research is to be conducted in out-of-the-way places, basic urban amenities will be absent. Do not expect to be able to do any banking in small towns, regardless of what you are told, and do not expect that your hosts will know what an American Express card or travelers' check is. You will not be able to use them outside large urban areas. (See Appendix K for a list of places where American Express services are available.) Bring enough money to conduct all your transactions in cash. If you will stay several weeks or months in one place and have large amounts of cash, you should consider opening a local bank account for the deposit of *renminbi*.

Advanced medical facilities will also be unavailable. Many researchers suggest bringing along *Where There Is No Doctor*, and fieldworkers should follow the medical advice offered in Chapter 2. In addition, rabies is common in small animals in some areas of China; you are advised not to pet dogs in rural areas. The American doctor in Beijing recommends a rabies series (the embassy stores the serum) for anyone bitten by a small animal there. The first injection, administered intramuscularly, must begin within ten days after being bitten. You would either have to return to Beijing for the shots or have the frozen serum delivered to you on site to be administered by a local doctor.

Your hosts will attempt to house you in the best hotels or guest houses available. Some research stations have guest quarters and cooks on site. Most accommodations, while simple, are clean and adequate, though some will not have running hot water or modern plumbing. On the other hand, some researchers have described their housing as squalid. Fieldworkers with experience in developing countries recognize that difficult living conditions often come with the territory. If cleanliness is important to you and you are planning to stay any length of time in out-of-the-way places, you might want to bring your own bed sheets and strong bleach, cleansing powder, and rubber gloves to clean your room yourself.

Local people in out-of-the-way places may have little or no experience with foreigners. You may be the first to have visited in decades and hence the only foreigner most people in your area will have seen. Most researchers report that the people in remote areas are curious, friendly, and generous beyond their means. These researchers have greatly enjoyed the opportunity for interaction despite an occasional thirst for privacy.

You can expect banquets to be given in your honor. Alcohol consumption at rural banquets is high. Not only do the toasts, each drunk "bottoms up," escalate during the evening, but the liquor may be a rough-and-ready local brew. Some researchers believe that abstinence is ungracious and a barrier to potential friendships; some also report becoming very drunk and sick. Other researchers insist that scholarly decorum is best maintained by sticking to fruit juice and soda. Do what is most comfortable.

The quality of cooking on ordinary days varies widely in remote areas—from enormous quantities of tastily prepared fresh vegetables and meat to much less appetizing fare. Many researchers enjoy eating at the tiny independently run restaurants, while others note that sanitary conditions in such places may be inadequate and can cause digestive upset or worse. Of course, there will be no restaurants at all outside the towns and villages. If you have a favorite instant food that can be prepared by adding boiled water, or if you insist on morning coffee, bring some with you for times when you prefer a simple meal at home.

In recent years, many foreign scholars have conducted research in ethnic minority areas, and anthropological research may be easier to arrange there than in Han regions. Scholars contemplating research in ethnic minority areas should read the summer 1991 issue of *China Exchange News*, which is devoted to an examination of anthropology and ethnology in China. Many of the minority populations live in remote areas along China's borders that are more sensitive politically than the coastal areas with which most Westerners are familiar. Several researchers have had very successful visits to such areas (see, for example, Matthew Kapstein, "New Sources for Tibetan Buddhist History," *CEN*, Fall/Winter 1991), but others have had difficulty getting permission to conduct research in sensitive areas, even for such innocuous projects as data collection on minority languages. Relations between the dominant Han majority and China's national minorities have always been sensitive, most notably in Tibet and Xinjiang. With the breakup of the Soviet Union and growing ethnic nationalism everywhere, China's national minorities problem is even more delicate. U.S. field researchers are still conducting productive research in these areas, but conversations with colleagues who have preceded you may help to prepare you for the particular problems you might encounter.

EQUIPMENT AND SUPPLIES   The equipment and supplies you need depend very much on the nature of your research. You will want to consult extensively with both your American and Chinese colleagues for their recommendations.

A general rule of thumb for field researchers is to bring everything you will need. The following paragraphs are written by A.T. Steegman, a biological anthropologist at the University of Buffalo. The article by John Olsen, associate professor of anthropology at the University of Arizona and former director of the CSCC's Beijing office, in Appendix O, contains important recommendations, including how to purify water in the field, food and cooking equipment, and how to choose the best vehicle for your trip. The comments by Steegman and Olsen should be required reading for anyone conducting scientific fieldwork.

A.T. Steegman writes:

"A. If the Chinese have equipment to be used in the research, be sure it is of good quality, modern, and possible to calibrate independently. If you cannot test it on a preliminary visit, try to get manufacturers' specifications. The Chinese may be sensitive about the quality of their equipment, and it is easy to walk into a disaster.

B. Minor pieces of equipment are probably easiest to take through in personal luggage. Some people think you can take major and minor equipment through the "green line" at customs this way as part of your own gear. However, if customs stops it, there could be big problems.

C. If you are taking major equipment, try to send it early and get a "customs waiver without bond." Consult an import/export broker who does business in China.

D. Chinese customs is literally a law unto itself and is very powerful. It can ruin a research project by being slow and obstructive, especially if time is limited. The "bond" referred to above is a deposit worth one to two times the value of the equipment. It must be left with customs to get your containers unless it has been waived. Even then it can take days or weeks to clear, regardless of carrier.

E. If you ship air cargo, reserve space well ahead of time. Not all major U.S. carriers have competent offices in China.

F. Assume you will not be able to replace equipment. It is extremely hard to import equipment, nor are there facilities to repair high-tech equipment.

G. Take cameras as part of your personal baggage. It is nearly impossible to get them past customs as equipment.

Supplies: Take *everything* you will need. Much is not available in China or is of very poor quality. Here is a partial list:

A. Tools
B. Solder/soldering gun
C. Pencils/pens/sharpeners
D. Paper (all kinds)
E. Plastic tape/duct tape
F. Glue/fasteners
G. Lubrication (ex. WD-40)
H. Calibration equipment
I. Circuit testers
J. Film
K. Voltage transformers/surge protectors
L. Reference books
M. Tables/standards
N. Computers/software

SURVEY RESEARCH

Several research teams have been able to undertake systematic survey research with Chinese collaborators—in areas such as work and social life, the process of mate selection, the health and living status of elderly populations, occupations of urban residents, housing and community resources, the concept of modernity, epidemiology, and health and nutrition. Social survey work remains sensitive, and the experiences of researchers vary. For most of the 1980s, several projects were housed in universities under the administration of the SEDC, but following the Tiananmen Square tragedy of 1989, the SEDC banned collaborative social science survey research in universities under its jurisdiction. Several ongoing projects were suspended. As of this writing, negotiations to renew this type of research are nearing conclusion. Several other projects outside SEDC jurisdiction have continued.

Anyone contemplating survey research in China should read the articles in the spring 1993 edition of *China Exchange News*. Many of the scholars whose research is described there are happy to share their insights with others contemplating similar research. Some general advice follows, distilled largely from Gail Henderson's article, "Survival Guide to Survey Research in China."

The choice of affiliation and potential collaborators, and the contract agreed to by the participating parties, is key when contemplating survey research, just as for other types of research.

Henderson advises:

> Make sure that your collaborators can do what they promise and are interested in what you want to do. It sounds simple, but in the rush to get access to China, this step is often skipped. Talk to other people who have worked with your proposed collaborators. Look at work they have completed; don't let chance connections push you into a long-term relationship.[8]

In the case of survey research covering multiple locales, a national-level host institution is likely to be more effective in arranging access than a local one. Local-level institutions ordinarily do not have the connections necessary to arrange research in multiple settings. Some researchers, however, have been successful arranging to have multiple hosting institutions, carrying out, in effect, multiple projects under one large umbrella.

Researchers with experience in survey research in China also emphasize the complexities of designing questionnaires that will both measure what you are trying to learn and make sense to Chinese respon-

---

[8]Gail Henderson, "Survival Guide to Survey Research in China." *China Exchange News*, Spring 1993, pp. 23-25; 33.

dents. Plan to spend more time than you might think necessary to design the questionnaire and to pretest and revise it before the survey begins. An overly complex questionnaire, which might take several hours for respondents to answer, or one with unfamiliar concepts, is not likely to yield the desired data.

Training interviewers is also important. A few graduate students who have been persuaded to leave questionnaires with enterprise managers, for instance, have had mixed results at best. Few Chinese have had experience either administering or responding to questionnaires, and the result of insufficiently trained interviewers can be faulty data—even on so simple a matter as age, which the Chinese may calculate in terms of actual date of birth or *xu* and either the Western or the lunar calendar. Time spent in training is made up later in more accurately completed responses.

Researchers have also found that paying respondents after the interview is complete is more likely to produce better quality data than paying them before. Similarly, interviewers should be compensated for the quality of the data they collect rather than the speed with which they complete interviews.

LABORATORY RESEARCH

The advancement of science has been a major goal of China's modernization program, and U.S. scientists have been welcomed since the beginning of academic exchanges, especially in fields of high priority to the Chinese government.

Virtually all work conducted in the sciences is collaborative, and the NSF, which remains a primary funder of U.S. scientists in China, actively promotes cooperative research. Scientists who have done extensive work in Chinese laboratories describe facilities that range from "world class" to "tremendously inadequate." While generalizations are difficult, labs run by the CAS are often well-equipped, as are some in key universities. Those administered by provinces, cities, and localities, which have fewer funds, tend not to be as good, and some field stations are sorely lacking in basic equipment. Laboratories that have hosted foreign scholars—or have foreign scholars on their advisory boards—are often particularly well-equipped. Moreover, the experience of having hosted foreign scholars makes the integration of each succeeding foreign scholar easier.

Scientists are advised to visit several laboratories before deciding which to affiliate with. Sometimes basic equipment is not working for lack of a single part or necessary reagents are unavailable. If you can supply needed parts or reagents, your collaboration will be off to a good start. In any case, check again before returning for precise specifications on what is available and working, and plan to bring to China materials your lab does not have.

Scientists have several suggestions for ensuring successful research. First, your Chinese collaborator will be key to the success of your project. Find a collaborator who is genuinely interested in working with you, with whom you have an easy rapport, and who is both conversant with the scientific bureaucracy and able to work effectively within it. Personal connections are also important in scientific research. China's current emphasis is on applied research, and proposals in the applied sciences, such as materials science, biotechnology, natural resources, information science, chemistry, physics, and mathematics, are particularly welcome. These fields have been targeted as major recipients of Chinese government funds where international collaboration is encouraged.

Second, spell out the details of collaboration in your research agreement. Because the agreement must be approved by several bureaucratic layers, it will assume the force of law, though details can always be renegotiated. In addition to conducting research, your Chinese hosts will undoubtedly want you to lecture, and they will want to be introduced to new techniques. Many scientists spend several months conducting research at one site followed by short visits to other labs for collaborative exchanges, lectures, and training workshops.

Offer to arrange for Chinese collaborators to come to the United States for research and provide opportunities for graduate students to study. Spell out the precise financial arrangements for Chinese collaborators in the United States. Chinese scientists are often on very tight budgets, and most will need to be picked up at the airport and will need assistance finding reasonably priced housing. Occasionally, Chinese research institutes will try to send less-qualified researchers. The terms of the agreement should detail what their research obligations will be and what qualifications researchers in your own laboratory are expected to have. If your institution is able to provide equipment to the Chinese laboratory where you are working, offer to donate it. By providing opportunities for Chinese scientists in the United States and giving what equipment you can, you are in a better position to negotiate the terms and cost of your research in China.

Third, your research is likely to be more successful if you return for several visits during the course of the project. Successful research results are very difficult to obtain in one or two visits.

Fourth, share all data with your Chinese hosts and offer to publish jointly with them. Most welcome the opportunity to publish their research in international journals. If you are publishing independently, let Chinese collaborators comment on drafts. Be certain to send copies of all publications to your colleagues and to any other scientists and laboratories you have visited. Encourage your collaborators to do the same.

Fifth, communications between research institutes are often faulty. When traveling alone from one research site to another, ask your host to arrange for people at the next site to meet you when you arrive. If not, be prepared to get from the airport or train station to your hotel on your own. If you are paying your own way, costs can be cut if you make your own living arrangements and travel reservations until your research work actually begins. Many scientists spend several days in Beijing before proceeding to their research site. If that stay is arranged by your host unit, you could be charged US$200 to $300 a day. If you make arrangements on your own and stay in a relatively inexpensive hotel, you will save money.

SHORT-TERM ACADEMIC VISITS

Many people contemplating a longer-term research project in China find that a short-term visit to meet Chinese colleagues, visit different research institutes and universities, and, usually, to lecture is a necessary and valuable means of meeting potential collaborators and beginning to formulate a research plan. Short visits usually require stamina and flexibility because the pace can be intense. Although the short-term visitor does not develop firsthand experience with the inner workings of professional and personal life in China, you can expect frank conversations with Chinese colleagues and explorations into the potential of collaborative work. Moreover, the logistics of your visit will rest almost entirely in Chinese hands.

Timing during short trips is usually not under your control. Despite the best intentions of your Chinese hosts, and elaborate planning and scheduling by the U.S. sponsor, these scholarly visits almost always are marked by last-minute changes, unexpected developments, and missed opportunities.

When to go is an important consideration in planning a short-term academic visit. Work tends to slow down in the hottest summer months and during the Chinese New Year in January or February.

During the summer months, major Chinese cities are often crowded with other foreigners, who strain the resources of Chinese hosting organizations. Chinese scholars often use the vacation months to travel abroad. One visitor, disappointed that many Chinese scholars he hoped to meet were out of town, put it this way:

> The intellectual dimension of Deng's open door policy means that it has become much more difficult to meet Chinese in China. If no one travels, no one ever meets anyone from a different place. If everyone travels, however, no one also ever meets anyone from a different place except at conferences and in chance encounters at airports.

Internal travel in the heavy tourist season (May through October) creates headaches for Chinese hosts and guests alike. Several scholars complained that they were not met at airports nor informed ahead of time about schedules, hotel accommodations, or local travel arrangements. As is true anywhere during high-tourist season, long delays in airports owing to weather, mechanical failures, or overbooking of flights are not uncommon.

PREPARATIONS   In general, the most successful short-term visits are the result of careful arrangements with the hosting organization combined with communications with individual Chinese scholars. Itineraries, requests for meetings with colleagues, lecture formats, and collaborative arrangements must be worked out well in advance. Goals for the project, as well as meeting and site visit requests, must be presented clearly. If you are going to be lecturing, it is a good idea to ask your host unit for advance information about topics, the probable size and composition of classes, what students or colleagues expect to learn from the lectures, and what kind of interpretation will be provided.

If special equipment, such as audiovisual equipment, is necessary, be sure to inform your hosts well in advance. Visits to other organizations in China are difficult to arrange once the hosting organization assumes responsibility, and they are often too complex to arrange informally in a short time. Returned scholars therefore urge you to write ahead to arrange to meet organizations and individual scholars not associated with the hosting unit. In the words of one recent grantee:

> If I had it to do over again, I would invest a lot more time than I did before going to China in specifying exactly what I wanted on my schedule and, most importantly, corresponding directly with those institutions and individuals I wanted to visit, thus avoiding some of the lateral communications problems which existed despite the good intentions of my host.

This is particularly important if you are concerned that insufficient time may be devoted to substantive academic meetings. Be sure to give detailed guidance in advance about what meetings you desire.

Even with elaborate advance preparations, fine-tuning of the schedule will occur after your arrival, in consultation with colleagues from the host unit and the foreign affairs officer in charge of your visit. This is the time to point out any potential problems. If you will be lecturing, this is a good time to distribute abstracts or outlines, if this has not been done earlier, and to confer with interpreters.

If you have not worked closely with your hosts in planning your schedule, you may find that your travel schedule is lighter on academic time and heavier on touring. Many visitors are not aware of the time required and discomfort of travel in China. Some scholars have complained that during their visit they had little free time to meet people informally or simply to rest; others suffered from the lack of cultural stimulation. One scientist remarked:

> I had little opportunity to develop any sense of the Chinese people or their daily lives. This was all the more frustrating because I was aware that an incredible number of interesting opportunities existed beyond the walls of the hotel, but since I did not speak Chinese, I was reluctant to strike out on my own without a guide or interpreter.

Another scholar who does speak Chinese remarked that his visit was so intense and so richly rewarding personally and professionally that he lost 15 pounds, in spite of too many banquets, and returned home exhausted and elated. Most travelers report that at some point they politely declined to see one more site and instead took a day off to rest, write up notes, or prepare a lecture.

ACADEMIC CONFERENCES   China hosts many international academic conferences each year, providing excellent opportunities for Western and Chinese scholars to make new contacts and become more familiar with ongoing research in their fields. Scholars considering attending a conference in China should be clear on the following questions:

1. Who is paying for travel, lodging, and food? Find out if "conference fees" will be charged and how much they will be.

2. Is the conference a genuine attempt to gather serious scholars or a money-making scheme?

3. What is expected of participants? How long should one plan to allocate for a read paper? Will translation be provided? Will the entire text be translated? Do the translators need a written copy in advance?

4. What are the exact dates of the conference? When do the sessions actually begin and end?

5. Teaching

The Fall semester was the most rewarding academic experience that I have ever experienced. . . . I do not believe that I will ever have [another one] as rewarding and as enjoyable, writes one Fulbright lecturer.

I learned more in one year of the program. . .about life, politics, society, and the practice of journalism in China than from all the books I've read on the subject over the years. . ." writes another.

Adjusting to the teaching environment in China takes time. The fall semester the faculty member quoted above had begun with the discovery that his students were ill-prepared for the intermediate economics course he had planned to teach, the books he had ordered were inappropriate, his students were frightened because they did not understand market economics, and the dean of his college thought he should give up trying to teach them. But the Fulbright lecturer was determined to work with his students to teach them economics. He stuck with it, and so did the students, most of whom agreed that his course had been one of the best they had ever taken. Even the dean was pleased. While not all foreign faculty have similarly startling successes, most report great satisfaction with teaching in China. Many wish they could stay longer, and many do.

Most of the experiences described in this chapter have been taken from Fulbright reports and from meetings in China with Fulbright teachers and with foreign experts and teachers. The one consistent piece of advice they, like researchers and students, offer is to try to talk to someone who has recently taught in the school where you will be going. Every school is different, every locale has its own special characteristics, and China changes from week to week. The more you can learn from someone who has just had an experience similar to the one you are about to have, the better prepared you are likely to be. If employment is found while you are still in the United States, you should communicate with the Chinese side as soon as possible to find out about what courses you will teach, the language level and age of your students, and descriptions of their teaching materials and English-language library.

Bring as many of your own materials as possible, as most Chinese materials are poorly structured and do not stress class participation. Materials from Teaching English as a Second Language (TESL) programs in Taiwan and the United States should be helpful, as should your own dictionary, grammar book, novels, and videotapes. Ask if there is a photocopier and/or computer available.

Much is expected of teachers in China, both in the classroom and outside. Chinese faculty ordinarily assume responsibility not only for the intellectual growth of their students but for their personal development as well. Expertise is appreciated, as is good teaching. Students welcome opportunities for less formal interaction and may enjoy meeting with their foreign teacher in small groups. Some students visit their foreign teachers at home and invite them to participate in social activities. To give your students the best of your time and energy, you must be careful about accepting too much outside work, such as tutoring, editing, and proofreading.

By far the greatest demand in China is for teachers of English language and literature, but the range of subjects Americans are invited to teach is now much broader than in the early years of exchanges. Americans now teach American studies, American society and culture, U.S. history, economics, business management, international trade and investment, marketing, U.S. law (constitutional, criminal, and criminal procedure), environmental and natural resources law, library management, journalism, art, and music. American teachers are to be found in a wide variety of institutions and in all parts of China. Most believe they are making a significant contribution to China's educational process and to greater understanding between the two cultures. Most, like the journalist quoted above, believe they have learned as much as they have taught. One former teacher offered this advice:

> If you remember that you have gone to China to learn, to share knowledge and ideas and to enjoy the Chinese people and their culture, you will have an easier time "rolling with the punches." No one is going to change China during a year's teaching visit! Perhaps the most valuable characteristic a foreign expert can have is a healthy sense of humor.

THE BUREAUCRATIC STRUCTURE

The work unit or *danwei*, as explained earlier, is all-important in China, regardless of where you are employed. Teachers, more than researchers and students, depend on their work unit. It is their employer and pays their salaries, arranges their lodging, may help arrange schooling for their children and for travel to other parts of the country, and generally acts on their behalf with other bureaucratic offices in China.

As a foreign teacher, you will be responsible to one or more departments within your work unit. China's complex bureaucracy can be confusing, and many teachers do not know prior to arrival to whom they will be responsible. Most have a hard time understanding it clearly even after they arrive. Because this information is crucial to your work, it is important to clarify your place in the bureaucratic structure as soon as possible. Learning how to get things done within the system may require effort and patience for the newcomer. One teacher noted, "It took us almost two full months before we knew to whom to talk about what."

The two major offices with which a foreign expert or teacher will ordinarily have contact are the foreign affairs office (*waiban*) and the academic department. The duties of and relationships between these two offices vary from unit to unit. Some have excellent communication and work as a team. Others have little or no contact with each other. Generally, the foreign affairs office handles administrative details: hiring; conditions of employment; your contract; daily living concerns; issuance of necessary documents such as the university identification card, expert privileges card, alien residence card and library card; assistance with travel arrangements; and the like. The academic department is responsible for teaching matters: curriculum, course assignments, teaching schedules, class size, room assignments, class materials, and so on.

Before you make a commitment to teach, reach agreement with your *waiban* on the following: salary, living arrangements, class hours, in-country travel allowances, vacation time, library use, and a "white card" (actually orange), which allows you to buy travel tickets at Chinese prices[9]. Even if it appears that the school has a set arrangement for foreign teachers, more likely than not, there *is* plenty of negotiating room. Once an agreement is reached, hold them to it. Just as they will stick to principles at times during your stay, you must make clear that

---

[9]In early 1993, the Chinese government issued a new regulation barring foreign teachers from buying travel tickets at Chinese prices. The regulation is not consistently enforced, although its implementation appears to be stricter in the eastern urban areas.

you, too, have principles. If you ever break your side of the agreement, you might expect that they will feel at liberty to do so.

Some teachers have found the staff of the foreign affairs office to be extremely supportive; others feel they are not helpful at all; still others report they will only respond to specific questions. Relations with department personnel also vary considerably. It is therefore important to learn as quickly as possible how to get what you need. For example, one American teacher learned never to confront the director of the department about conditions of employment, as the answer would always be "no." But if he gathered all the official information about the situation and wrote a memo to the director outlining the regulations and stating his specific request, he always received an affirmative answer. Similarly, many find that information they felt should have been communicated to them was not. One teacher arrived in his regular classroom to find it empty. The room had been changed and no one had informed him. His students were waiting in the newly assigned classroom. Another teacher who had sent a box of books in care of his foreign affairs office was never informed that the books had arrived. Others, expecting to be informed by their departments of upcoming activities, such as a lecture by a visiting American scholar or the showing of a movie, often learn of the event only by accident and sometimes after the fact. Other foreign teachers at your own or neighboring schools will be a major asset in this regard. You probably share many of the same successes and frustrations. If several of you are at one school, you might select a "representative" to talk with the administration on everyone's behalf, even if a problem affects only one of you.

Many U.S. teachers speak little, if any, Chinese when they arrive, and official discussions between them and their departmental or institutional sponsors are in English (through an interpreter, if needed). Many teachers note that their departmental colleagues often speak far better English than do administrative cadres. However, while they indicate that language is not a key problem, most find that speaking some Chinese is extremely helpful.

The problems typically noted by U.S. teachers are cultural and social organization. "Americans are used to a high degree of independence and self-direction. The Chinese are not. There are a lot of banquets and other displays of friendship which cover up some very hard bargaining. One needs to go along with all the formalities and rituals and still be very assertive concerning one's own interests." Another teacher recommended that two important cultural characteristics be kept in mind:

(1) Chinese work through intermediaries. Americans like to talk things out face-to-face. This means that rather than talking over problems or concerns with the head of the department directly, you may have to work through a third person who will carry messages back and forth.

(2) Chinese prefer compromise. Chinese do a lot of horse-trading, bargaining, and exchanging of favors. In regard to classes, teaching loads, and academic responsibilities, this is an ongoing process.

WORKLOADS

Workloads and class size often vary substantially from one institution or program to another, but all teachers report that they do far more than teach assigned classes. Additional activities include work on special projects, such as helping to write or edit textbooks and dictionaries, editing university publications in English, giving informal English lessons to colleagues, conducting oral exams, overseeing thesis projects, and assisting students with writing papers. Teachers also may lecture to their unit and to other units about specific academic topics or about cultural and social aspects of the United States. English teachers may be asked to record tapes, and everyone may be asked to help students and faculty write applications to colleges and universities in the United States. Some teachers have even been offered bit parts in movies! Remember that it is easy to become overcommitted. Be very clear about what is required by your job and what is being asked as a favor. This will help in winnowing down the demands on your work time. As one teacher says, while it is important to be as helpful as possible, "How much work you do will depend on how much resistance you put up—you must not become chronically fatigued to the point of illness."

As a foreign teacher, the number of hours you spend in classroom teaching can vary from as few as six per week to as many as twenty. Teachers of English conversation often have particularly heavy class schedules. Additionally, you may spend several hours weekly holding "office hours"; perhaps five to six hours cutting tapes (if you are teaching English), and numerous hours preparing materials for class, correcting papers, having unscheduled or scheduled meetings with students and teachers, and doing editorial work. As one teacher put it, "No matter how many hours you are scheduled for, your actual work week will average between 45 and 50 hours." Another commented, "The work week is six days, and teachers can count on being busy almost all that time." As a rule of thumb, allow two to four hours of preparation time for one hour of class time.

Class sizes also vary radically. You might teach a seminar of only three or four students or give a lecture course to 75 students. The average class size seems to be between 20 and 35 students.

Some teachers report being told they will be teaching one course prior to their departure for China only to learn upon arrival that they are expected to teach something totally different. Others find that their host institution is not clear about what subject matter should be covered in a course or, alternatively, is adamant that what the American considers to be proper course content is not what the Chinese want at all. Still others may discover that they have been assigned to the wrong department to teach the wrong subject. For example, one economics professor was assigned to teach a course in international trade law. This is often the result of different nomenclature used by Chinese and Americans in titling courses.

STUDENTS

American teachers generally have found their Chinese students to be bright and able. They have also been surprised by how perceptive students have been in discussing a situation far removed from them in distance and experience. They have also been pleased that after overcoming an initial shyness, many students become active class participants, asking questions and presenting ideas for consideration. Many teachers described their Chinese students as extremely candid and friendly: "very friendly and a pleasure to work with"; the "brightest aspect of my experience in China"; "just about everything a teacher wants. . . . [they] make this assignment one to be envied and coveted; outstanding, extremely diligent, and highly motivated." One American wrote that he was "privileged to have students who are hungry to learn, who help themselves to knowledge the way harvest hands used to reach for mashed potatoes at my grandfather's table."

Other teachers have not been as enthusiastic.

About 60 percent of undergraduates had a good attitude, but they looked at their classes as a requirement to get a degree to graduate. They were not highly disciplined. They completed their assignments, but they didn't work up to their potential.

Chinese university students are not all hard working, disciplined, intelligent, and well prepared, which is the stereotype Americans bring to China.

Extensive demands are made on students that cause them at times to shift attention from class work to other things such as preparation for TOEFL [Test of English as a Foreign Language].

Students performed better than expected; it was difficult to get critical discussion in class as the students wanted to be told what they need to know; they like lectures.

Chinese students are mostly quite intelligent, but I was surprised by the lack of motivation of some; absenteeism is a big problem.

Recent reports from Fulbright faculty in China reveal several common problems Americans face teaching Chinese students and the creative ways Americans have found to overcome them. Several of the more frequently encountered problems and the means by which other U.S. faculty have coped are discussed below.

ENGLISH LANGUAGE ABILITY   Most Americans will be teaching in English without an interpreter, even in courses such as journalism, law, and economics. Faculty find that the aural comprehension of their students varies widely. Some will understand 90 percent of what the American says; some will understand only 50 percent. Most Americans have discovered that their students' reading ability is much better than their aural comprehension. One way to promote learning, then, is to make lectures available to read. Frequent handouts are useful, and faculty find themselves using the blackboard much more often in China than in the United States. Some begin class by writing a detailed outline of their lecture on the blackboard, making it easier for students to understand the lecture. Similarly, teachers have found it useful to use the blackboard while introducing new concepts.

Knowing that some students understand more easily than others, several U.S. faculty found it useful to take frequent breaks to encourage students to discuss the lecture among themselves. Students often gather together at the front of the classroom, speaking in Chinese and writing on the blackboard, and discussions became more and more animated as the students who had been having trouble understanding finally catch on. Faculty have thus found that encouraging cooperative learning and interaction among their students can be very productive, even when the teacher does not understand what the students were discussing. To encourage conversation during class, some teachers have recommended making the classes student-centered; that is, shifting the teacher's role from "instructor" to "facilitator." They note, "Giving the students more responsibility for the class' success will likely result in a better class for everyone."

In the early years of academic exchanges, teachers of courses other than English often relied on an interpreter. The widespread teaching of English in recent years has minimized the use of interpreters. But some teachers still rely on them and the experiences of these teachers have been mixed. One U.S. law professor reported that he had a regular interpreter through whom he did all his teaching, including dialogues with his students. He encouraged his students to speak English as much as possible. Without a good interpreter, however, teaching the course would have been impossible. Others have found themselves with an interpreter who speaks less English than some of the students and who sometimes challenged the U.S. teacher even though the interpreter knew little about the subject.

Grading papers is also difficult when courses are taught through an interpreter. Because the exams are written in Chinese, the teacher must depend on the interpreter to understand what the students write. Teachers have handled such problems in various ways. One began using an interpreter who proved less than satisfactory and later tried teaching the course without the interpreter. Although comprehension was sometimes difficult, he found that both he and his students were happier. In this case the students discussed particularly difficult topics in Chinese and then reiterated their understanding to the teacher in English.

Other teachers have tried using simpler materials—switching from complicated texts to short articles. Others provided outlines of lectures that could be followed while the lecture was being given—a time-consuming effort but one that had worthwhile effects. Some found it essential to spend time outside of class with the students to give them enough exposure to a foreigner speaking and to overcome typical language problems such as lack of confidence, shyness, misuse of verb tenses, and omission of pronouns and articles. The teachers found that once the students gained confidence, their rate of learning increased dramatically.

CLASS PARTICIPATION   The U.S. style of teaching tends to be much more interactive than the Chinese style, and many Americans encounter difficulties encouraging their students to speak up in class. Not only do most courses in Chinese universities tend to be lectures, but the voice of the teacher is the voice of authority, and most students work on the premise that there is only one right answer to any question. Students thus are accustomed to memorizing but not to discussing and debating.

Some foreign teachers report real fear on the part of their students when they were called on in class and asked to discuss, debate, or dissent. Some foreign teachers, faced with such reluctance, finally opt to give lectures. Others find ways to draw their students out. One professor begins his courses by asking each student to write a short autobiographical introduction and include a picture and brief statement about why they are taking the course. This teaching helps the professor link names and faces so he can call on students individually in class, allows him to get to learn something about the students' backgrounds and their written language ability, and gives the students an opportunity to introduce themselves to their teacher while maintaining a degree of anonymity. Then the faculty member meets the students, first individually and then in small groups, again drawing them out and hearing their views in a relaxed, nonthreatening atmosphere. Finally, after explaining his teaching style and his belief in competing interpretations of the subject matter, he begins encouraging his students to speak out in class, calling on them when necessary.

Other faculty set up debates and panel discussions where students are asked to play roles and take sides, expressing opinions that may not be their own—thus relieving students of the burden of presenting the "wrong" answer. One teacher, for instance, had her students stage a congressional hearing and a mock news conference, both based on real issues, with great success. Many teachers report that as the semester progresses, their students become more and more comfortable with class participation, and some students even come to relish it.

STUDENTS' PRIOR BACKGROUND   Some teachers find their students do not have the necessary background to understand the subject matter they were planning to teach. As a result, what was planned as an intermediate or advanced course may become an introductory one. Others have been amazed at how well trained their students are. There is almost no way to know how well prepared your students will be, but U.S. faculty should be prepared to spend time early in the semester readying their students for more advanced work.

HOMEWORK AND WORKLOADS   American teachers report that their students do not expect to do homework and complain about extra reading and assignments outside of class. There are several reasons for this. Chinese students may be taking more than five courses a semester and spending more than 25 hours a week in class. Time for homework is limited. Moreover, the use of library books is restricted. Often, books that the American teacher wants to assign students are not available. No one has suggested eliminating out-of-class assignments altogether, but Americans need to get a sense of their students' schedules before deciding how much outside work is appropriate.

In fact, after initial complaints, many Chinese students have been proud to have studied with "strict" American faculty.

THE CLASS MONITOR AND GROUP PRESSURE   Some faculty report that while their students are quiet in class, they are often quite effective making group requests to the teacher, sometimes in the form of communications through small groups of representatives or the class monitor, who is responsible for representing the students and conveying communications from the administration to the students. Often these communications are complaints about too many tests or too much work, and some teachers have complained that such group organization seems manipulative. Students on the verge of graduation seem to have a greater tendency to organize themselves. American teachers must find the right balance between accommodation to the realities of their students' limited time, the requirements of the course, and the other responsibilities of their students.

STUDENT-TEACHER RELATIONSHIPS   Teachers often receive visits from their students, not only at the office but also in their homes, and sometimes three or four students will arrive together unexpectedly. These informal exchanges are a good way for both the teacher and students to learn more about one another. If informality and close relationships with your students are important, one way to break the ice is to throw a party for them early on. Teachers report that a good party can be held very inexpensively—some beer and soft drinks and a few bowls of peanuts are sufficient. Bicycle or bus outings with students (the whole class or a group of friends) to a park or scenic site are welcome. Teachers also learn to make it clear that "friendship" is no substitute for hard work and cannot be the basis for the students' final grades.

PLAGIARISM AND "CHEATING"   A few faculty have found that papers submitted by their students contain long passages copied verbatim from published texts without attribution. While the initial reaction of some teachers is to treat this as plagiarism and hence to discipline the student, others recognize that Chinese students have usually not been taught the same academic codes as Americans. With so much emphasis on memorization and the "one right answer," copying from books may be seen as simply getting the right answer. Both the rules on plagiarism and on copying during exams need to be spelled out early. Some U.S. faculty have found success by encouraging group learning and interaction among students until they write their papers or take their exams.

Designing writing assignments and questions for which the students must create an answer based on the material learned can often prevent this problem. While an assignment to write a fable may produce many familiar tales, an assignment to write about a childhood memory will not. Dreams are a fascinating topic.

WORKING CONDITIONS

Most school buildings are austere, unpainted, damp, and virtually unheated, which is why dressing in many layers is so important in winter. Usually they are also relatively clean and supplied with adequate lighting, blackboards, chalk, and standard classroom furniture. In some locations, electricity is erratic. Classes are occasionally rescheduled because of the lack of electricity. Upkeep on some buildings may not be adequate, and broken doors or windows may not be repaired promptly, allowing cold air to enter classrooms in the winter. Most classroom buildings are not air conditioned in the summer, but in some places electric fans are used during the hottest months.

Some institutions assign private offices to their foreign teachers; in others, foreigners share a single work room. Offices are "not Madison

Avenue plush, but they are embarrassingly spacious compared with those of our Chinese colleagues." Some teachers discover that many of their Chinese coworkers must give up their own work space to make room for a foreign expert.

Availability of books and teaching materials in China is also a problem. Fulbright faculty are given a generous allowance to purchase books for their classes. Most foreign experts and teachers suggest bringing your own teaching materials, although in some English-language classes the course material is dictated by the school. Check with your department before arriving about whether you will be using materials provided by your school, what materials are available, and whether you will be able to duplicate materials you bring. (See Chapter 2 for some advice on types of teaching materials.) Explore your town for alternative sources of materials and technology, such as the Foreign Language Bookstore, private copy shops, and stationery stores. Check in advance about whether other teaching aids—like video equipment and overhead projectors—will be available for your use. Many schools do have equipment, but others do not. Also, check into the type of video equipment. Most Chinese videos use the PAL system. Bear in mind, however, that you should not *rely* on slides, video, or any other equipment for a lesson plan; even if the equipment is there, you may encounter a power blackout. Always have a low-tech backup lesson plan.

Despite the austerity of their physical surroundings, most foreign teachers adjust. Not only does the foreign teacher live and work in better conditions than his students and colleagues, the rewards of teaching ordinarily far outweigh the physical discomfort.

PROFESSIONAL RELATIONSHIPS

Most Americans report remarkably little interference in the content or method of their teaching. "I have been given complete freedom regarding methods of instruction," writes one. "While the dean, Chinese faculty, and students did not agree with all my views, I was given complete academic freedom," he says. A few incidents have occurred, but most Americans, while being polite and sensitive to different cultural and political views, attempt to teach and conduct themselves "American style," recognizing that there are different points of view and encouraging those different views to be aired.

American teachers report a range of relationships with Chinese faculty members and administrators. Some had excellent relationships with faculty in their departments and became good friends. There were visits by Chinese faculty to classes conducted by U.S. teachers and vice versa.

Relationships with all administrators, faculty, and students were thoroughly professional and friendly; assistance was given and returned freely. . . . Contact with Chinese faculty was abundant, frequent, and very cordial. I only wished I had spoken more Chinese, as collegiality was limited only by the language barrier.

Other U.S. teachers, however, report constraints on interactions with their colleagues.

All relations with officials. . .have been cordial, helpful, and distant. I am regularly invited to department social functions. However, any professional discussions about collaboration and exchange of research very quickly run into barriers. This is frustrating. Just when you meet someone who has similar professional interests, the relation cools. I have had some private conversations that reveal the constraints imposed from above. It is simply not in their interest to collaborate with you.

Another American teacher, who had very good rapport with his students and a very successful teaching experience still lamented the absence of professional contact:

I have no professional contacts with anyone in the department. For a generally outgoing and friendly person, this has been a serious personal disappointment. I have been here for more than four months, and to date no one in the department has asked me a single question about American studies, no one has asked me a single question about American culture, no one has asked me a single question about American literature, no one has asked me a single question about my own work, and no one has asked me a single question about why I came to China.

Explanations for the failure of professional contact are varied. Many Chinese faculty have heavy teaching loads and teach extra classes to earn more money. With the new pressure on universities to earn their own way, faculty also are being called on to contribute to these efforts. Many have significant family responsibilities. But many feel constrained to minimize contact with foreigners.

SOCIAL RELATIONSHIPS

Many teachers develop rewarding informal relationships with colleagues and students. Just as a professor in China is expected to take an interest not only in his students' class work but in their overall development as well, so students' obligations to their teachers extend beyond the classroom. Your students may well offer assistance in dealing with difficult mundane chores—by introducing you to local shops and markets, making sure you see points of interest, serving as an interpreter on occasion, and keeping you informed of activities that might be of interest—lectures, movies, band concerts, basketball games, and plays.

Some teachers eat with their students periodically and are often invited to participate in activities such as dances—where the tango and waltz are as popular as disco and other contemporary steps. Teachers also suggest bringing along books of American folk songs and Christmas carols. Social student gatherings often require the participants to perform, and you may want to use the occasion to teach your students and friends some American songs.

Many find their students visiting their homes for help with English or schoolwork—or to visit the American toddler who lives there, too. Occasionally, teachers are invited to visit their students' homes.

A few teachers noted, however, that their students seemed hesitant to have informal contact with them. These teachers believe it is best to let Chinese students take the initiative in establishing relationships outside the classroom, and a student's offer of help should be accepted with a certain parsimony. "The teacher's pet" may face problems with his or her peers, and the teacher who takes too much advantage of helpful offers also runs the risk of being seen as exploitative.

Similarly, many students and some faculty are eager to attend schools in the United States and many teachers find themselves called on for advice and help about how to get to the United States. Students want to know more about the U.S. educational system and may ask for letters of recommendation. Most teachers are delighted to write letters of recommendation and advise other Americans planning to teach in China to be prepared to serve as an adviser. However, they also caution against making overly optimistic comments about the possible assistance they or their home institution can give to Chinese students.

Many students have an exaggerated notion of what "help" their foreign teacher can provide, sometimes assuming that their teacher will have the power to place them in the right school. Offhand encouragement may inspire unrealistic hopes for acceptance and funding. Teachers also caution newcomers in becoming involved with the selection of students being sent abroad by the work unit, as the word of a foreign expert or teacher may be given a great deal of weight.

Relationships with Chinese colleagues are generally cordial but a bit formal by U.S. standards. Contact outside working hours may be limited to special ceremonial occasions, banquets, and outings planned by the host unit or department. Some foreign teachers have developed close relationships with Chinese colleagues, frequently visiting their homes for meals and evenings of discussion or inviting their colleagues to their own homes. If the foreigner speaks Chinese, relationships tend to develop fairly easily: "knowing the language opens up an entirely different realm in relationships with Chinese people." Conversely, those who do not speak Chinese may interact most frequently with their English-speaking colleagues.

CHINESE LANGUAGE LESSONS

Many teachers in China use the opportunity to learn or improve their Chinese language proficiency. As one Fulbright scholar writes, "I would *strongly* urge all Fulbrighters to work hard to learn the language. My wife's success at becoming conversant demonstrates that a lot can be accomplished with a tutor and determination, and believe me, your whole perspective, your relationships, everything will be different if you can communicate in the native language."

Many people, though, find that learning Chinese requires enormous discipline and determination. Teaching obligations can take up all your time. Most work units, however, will help you find a language tutor upon request. The American pays the teacher's fee. Most people recommend bringing your own teaching materials and tapes from the United States, since many tutors may not be language teachers and good teaching materials may be hard to find. You can set your own pace, but meeting several times a week, either in your apartment or in the departmental office, will speed your learning.

People caution the student of Chinese to make certain the tutor speaks standard Mandarin. There are many dialects and accents in China, and most people want to approximate the "standard spoken language."

Many warn that "trading" English lessons for Chinese can be tricky and is usually not worth the effort—a tutor is inexpensive, but tutoring is costly in time and effort. Many "traders" end up in an unbalanced relationship.

GENERAL ADJUSTMENT ADVICE

Every teacher encounters problems in adjusting to life in China, but the individuals who provided information for this book believe the satisfactions of working with intensely dedicated students, participating in Chinese life, making a contribution to the quality of Chinese education, and feeling their way through the subtle nuances of friendships with Chinese people outweigh the negative aspects. Some general pieces of advice offered to future Americans going to teach in China include the following:

> Get a good English-language map of the city you're in, and explore the city early and often. It quickly makes a very alien-seeming place begin to feel comfortable, and the feeling of ease helps immeasurably with the inevitable major cultural transition.

> Perhaps the greatest adjustment problem was having to learn Chinese-style decision making through consensus reached in informal discussions conducted before a formal meeting. Also, information and ideas came to

me indirectly through the class monitor rather than directly from students. Everything happens slowly in China, so I had to learn to be more patient after making a request. And, although I had an apartment to myself, I had to learn to expect visits from students, colleagues, and the department chairman as early as 7 a.m. and as late as 10 or 11 p.m.; American-style privacy is nonexistent in China!

Be as open and informal as your personality allows. Learn about and be sensitive to cultural differences. Spend as much time as possible with Chinese people.

One U.S. teacher's summary of the experience of living and working in China seems particularly appropriate: "Go planning to learn more than you teach, expect a challenge, and above all, expect to enjoy China and its people—you won't be disappointed!"

6. Study

The largest number of Americans in China are students, and most of them are studying Chinese. Many types of programs are available; some are noted in Appendix B. In general, there are three types of options: programs organized by U.S. universities or other educational institutions where Americans study together as a group; programs at Chinese-language training schools where Americans study with students from all over the world; and attendance at a Chinese university together with Chinese students. (Possibilities for advanced graduate students to do dissertation-level research are discussed in Chapter 4.)

There is some debate over where Chinese language study is best undertaken. Many former students and language instructors in the United States would argue that if learning Chinese is your primary goal, the quality of language teaching on Taiwan will better serve most students' needs. Others would argue that introductory Chinese is best studied in the United States and that students should go to Taiwan or the PRC only after getting a solid foundation. Many language students in China, however, are there not only to improve their Chinese but to get firsthand experience of the country as well. If these are your goals, there are numerous programs available in the People's Republic, each with its advantages and drawbacks.

AMERICAN-SPONSORED PROGRAMS

Many universities offer summer, semester, or year-long programs in the People's Republic. The quality (and longevity) of these programs varies considerably, but some are now well established and quite good. Of special note is the new Princeton-in-Asia program, based at Beijing

Normal University, which offers intensive Chinese training using the "total immersion" method. Your Chinese-language instructor or other knowledgeable China specialist at your university can help you decide which program would be best for you. In some programs, an American adviser, who is often a faculty member from the sponsoring university, stays with the students to supervise language training and other activities. You may want to call the program instructor with specific questions. Many programs include, in addition to language training, courses in Chinese culture and history taught in English by either American or Chinese faculty. Many also include excursions to nearby sights of historic and cultural interest and a tour to other parts of China.

The advantages of such a program (when it is well managed) include a structured, well-supervised program, the mutual support of fellow students, substantive courses in English, and a supervisor who both helps with problems students might have and works directly with the Chinese university administrators and teachers. Language instruction tends to be more suited to American needs as well, since course content may be jointly decided between Chinese and U.S. faculty, and more participatory styles of U.S. instruction may be employed. The style of a well-run program thus retains a certain "American" flavor despite the Chinese setting, and the supervisor can serve as a buffer and mediator between the Chinese *liuban* and the students. Students experiencing their first taste of China, and perhaps abroad for the first time, often have difficulty knowing how to negotiate the Chinese academic bureaucracy. Moreover, U.S-sponsored programs can work out rules governing dormitory behavior, including late-night noise levels, that less-structured programs cannot, allowing students more quiet time for study in the dorm.

U.S.-sponsored programs tend to be more expensive than enrolling directly in a Chinese school. You will want to inquire about what the package includes—international airfare and travel within China, for instance. Inquire whether course credit is given and whether your university will accept the credits. Find out as much as you can about who will be teaching, how the courses will be structured, and what materials will be used. You might then ask your own language instructor's guidance on whether the materials are suitable for your goals.

The main disadvantage of most U.S-sponsored programs is that while language instruction may be good, many of the potential benefits of absorbing a language through constant exposure are lost. Most interaction outside of class will be with fellow Americans, and unless students have pledged to speak only Chinese (which a few programs require), the medium of communication will be English. Students in such programs tend to be so isolated from the mainstream of Chinese life that interaction with Chinese students and administration is limited.

Unless you make a concerted effort to make Chinese friends and experience Chinese life, you will see China largely "from the outside in." Moreover, the level of language competence of students in the same class may be markedly different, making both teaching and learning difficult.

Such programs are probably best for undergraduates who want a structured and supportive environment that allows them to explore on their own if they want, knowing that a more experienced "China hand" will be available for guidance and help. For students who do not yet know how far their commitment to China studies might go, it is a way to test the waters and decide whether to take the plunge.

CHINESE-LANGUAGE INSTITUTES

As a student at a Chinese-language institute, you make your own arrangements directly by obtaining application forms from the education section of the Chinese embassy or a consulate and then submitting your application directly to the school. Students are not necessarily guaranteed admittance to the school to which they apply. Once in China you will negotiate your living, study, and payments directly with officials at your school—a frustrating experience if your language skills are not yet sufficient for the task. Then you will become part of a class with students from all over the world who will have varying degrees of fluency in the language. The advantages of direct enrollment in a Chinese university are that tuition is much cheaper than most U.S.-sponsored programs, you are permitted considerable independence, you meet new people from far-flung parts of the globe, and school administrators often have decades of experience dealing with foreign students.

Reports on the quality of language instruction differ among schools and teachers. In the early years of exchanges, U.S. students (and their language teachers in the United States) were often disappointed in the quality of language instruction. Texts were uninteresting, vocabulary was often inappropriate for daily use, emphasis was on memorization, and learning was often passive. The quality of instruction in many places has improved considerably since then, but language instruction is still likely to be less participatory than that in the United States.

Moreover, while the international environment provides the opportunity to make many new friends, fellow students will not be Chinese, and making Chinese friends can be difficult. Some language schools have no Chinese students. Some students find that adjusting to the multinational foreign student community is more difficult than adapting to China. Many students discover that English is still the medium of communication outside the classroom, and some students serve unofficially as English-language tutors to students from other countries. Chinese friends hoping to study in the United States may call on you to help with everything from writing away for catalogues to filling out application forms. Students in language institutes face similar problems of isolation from China as the U.S.-sponsored programs.

Moreover, with no adviser and no rules governing dorm life, some dormitories are livelier than serious students prefer. Noise from late-night parties is a frequent complaint, and occasional quarrels break out when cultures and values collide. Serious students complain that too many of their colleagues are there for fun rather than study. Conditions for study in dormitories are less than ideal, and libraries can be noisy and crowded, too. Moreover, the long-term experience of the *liuban* with fun-seeking foreign students can work to the disadvantage of the serious student.

If the perception of university administrators and teachers is that most foreign students are not really there to study, perseverance and hard work will be necessary for the serious student to convince them otherwise. This and the inevitably lower status of students can be a difficult burden for the hardworking student to shoulder.

But the difficulties of coping on your own may also be to your benefit. By learning to work with Chinese administrators and to negotiate your own way through China, you will learn much about the Chinese "system" and can apply that knowledge to many other situations in China. You will have had the opportunity to experience not only China but other cultures, too. And the experience may lead you to further study of the Chinese language and culture.

ATTENDING A CHINESE UNIVERSITY

The student with sufficient language skills can also enroll directly in a Chinese university. Some students who begin in language programs and become committed to the serious, long-term study of China find this a useful way to become more integrated into Chinese student life and to learn something of the academic environment in a Chinese university. Most such students continue to live in foreign student dormitories, but they are able to develop a life outside.

This type of program is an excellent route to "total immersion." But it has two major drawbacks. First, unless your Chinese is fluent (and many students do have fluency in Chinese), language can continue to be an impediment to full participation. As one student lamented in the last edition of *China Bound*, teaching is in "rapid, unadulterated Mandarin," and some teachers have heavy, almost incomprehensible, accents. Note-taking in class can be a challenge.

Second, course content, style of instruction, and approach remain very different from those in the United States. Some courses do not even have texts. As one recently returned student points out, it is a mistake, despite recent press descriptions of China, to think that China is a capitalist society. Chinese values and perspectives are still very different from our own and those differences are reflected in the classroom. The graduate student steeped in Western theory and methodology often discovers that the motivating impetus of research in China is different. If you understand this, however, and take as your goal learning how your subject is taught in China, studying in a Chinese university can be an extremely valuable experience.

Unlike Chinese students, who usually take courses only in their major, foreign students are often allowed to take courses from other departments. You will want to choose your major carefully, however. Some specialties, such as anthropology, are available only at a handful of universities, and course content may be very different from what you have come to expect in your American university. Course catalogues are not widely available, so finding out what courses are being taught may take some probing of your *liuban*, your professors, and other students. Look on your department's bulletin board, too.

You may want special, more directed help as a student in a Chinese university, which can be difficult to obtain. Only advanced, dissertation-level graduate students are ordinarily assigned advisers. You must first prove yourself worthy of extra help from your professors, and this will take perseverance and dedication. Once you have made a commitment to a particular course, class attendance becomes mandatory because your professor may take personal offense if you do not attend. In time, diligence and devotion to your studies is likely to be rewarded with special attention from professors. Many are openly moved to discover a foreign student who has taken the time and trouble to learn their language, traveled so far to study, and remains diligent despite the obvious difficulties.

Thus, enrollment in a Chinese university is only for the serious and independent student who is willing to interact with the Chinese academic bureaucracy and with Chinese faculty with little outside help. The long-term advantages to such total immersion are tremendous. You will have experienced China as few foreigners have; the language skills you develop will serve you the rest of your life; and you will be able to return to China year after year comfortable in the knowledge that you will know how to behave and get things done with ease and understanding. And you are likely to have made several good, lifelong Chinese friends in the process.

STUDENT LIFE

As a foreign student, your daily life is likely to revolve around a small group of foreign friends and classmates, a few *liuban* personnel, teachers, and, if your efforts have been successful, a few Chinese friends, too. Your dormitory is apt to be rather spartan, and at first sight, after a long and exhausting plane trip, may initially strike you as dismal. You may chafe at Chinese expectations of conformity just as you have broken with your friends and peers back home to take the daring step of coming to China for the first time. The top-down decision making of Chinese universities may not sit well.

The Chinese you learned in the United States may suddenly seem hopelessly inadequate, and what you are learning in the classroom may not meet your immediate communications needs. You may find the single telephone on your floor difficult to use and discover that when you finally connect with the number you are calling you don't know what to say or how to say it. You may be humiliated when the person on the other end of the line hangs up. Living with foreigners when you really want a Chinese roommate can be disappointing. The rules that require Chinese guests to register at the door, giving their names and *danwei*, can be irritating, and doubly so if visiting hours are limited. The food in the dining hall will not be the same as in your favorite Chinese restaurant back home. If you ordinarily take a shower at the beginning or end of your day, you may have difficulty adjusting your schedule if the hot water in your dorm is on for only two hours after dinner. The absence of your usual newspapers or television programs can magnify the feeling of isolation.

In short, expect to experience the normal signs of culture shock for the first few weeks of your stay. It may help to remember what is a nearly universal phenomenon—that the most difficult experiences usually prove to have been the most interesting and instructive.

Students can find rewarding ways of breaking out of what initially may seem to be the too restrictive confines of dormitory and classroom. You may not have a Chinese roommate, but most universities will let you participate in team sports. Even if you are not athletically inclined, every Chinese university has plenty of ping pong tables, and no skill is required to play. You will be beaten, of course, but you might make a friend or two in the process. If your sport is solitary, like running, try using the university track. You will quickly meet someone there. Or join an impromptu game of basketball.

If you play a musical instrument, go to your local music conservatory and see if you can participate in some of their activities. If you play the guitar, offer to teach. Find out if someone can teach you to play one of the ancient Chinese instruments, like the *qin*. The *pipa* is a nice instrument for people with guitar experience and teachers are easy to find in the Jiangnan area. Or just listen to practice sessions. Organize a singing group of fellow students and offer to perform for your Chinese schoolmates.

You can network, too. Before you go to China, ask friends in the United States to give you names and addresses of their Chinese friends. Find out if your hometown has a sister-city relationship in China, and see if you can do something to further it. Or offer to help establish a sister-city relationship. Contact the international trade division in your state, and find out about possible business contacts or other types of exchanges. If Chinese have studied at your university, find out their names and addresses and contact them in China. You are *tongxue*—schoolmates—which creates an automatic bond. If any of your American friends in China have Chinese friends, ask to be introduced or join them when they meet.

Go to church and stay after the service is over. One or two people will almost always come up and introduce themselves. Go to parks early in the morning and participate in exercise activities there. The same people return every day. Take a group course in *taijiquan*. Offer to teach English. Go to the town's "English Corner."

Find out about volunteer work. One group of students began volunteer work at a local orphanage. After several months, they put on a concert to help raise money for the orphanage and were able to contribute more than Y10,000. The concert was attended by local officials and broadcast over local television, and as a result the students have made many new friends. Writes one of them, "Volunteering at the orphanage has given me the feeling that I'm doing something real here in China, that I'm in some small part contributing to this society instead of just observing it and wondering about it from a distance."

Read the newspaper for announcements of upcoming events. Find out about the latest rock stars and go to their concerts. Bring a short-wave radio to stay abreast of news outside. Give your old *Time* and *Newsweek* to Chinese friends.

Travel. Take weekend bicycle excursions to local scenic sites. Invite your Chinese friends, and take a picnic lunch. Over longer Chinese holidays, travel by train alone or with a friend. Visit an ethnic minority area and try staying off the beaten path. Many students report that travel provided both the most difficult and rewarding experiences of their stay.

CLASSES

What you study and how many hours you spend in the classroom each week will depend on the program you choose. Most intensive language programs involve four hours in class a day, from 8:00 am until noon, Monday through Saturday. Afternoons are set aside for occasional excursions and provide time for special tutoring (*fudao*). While Chinese tutors may not be trained in teaching Chinese to foreigners, these private sessions can provide an opportunity for more active involvement in learning the language. Make the best of the opportunity by bringing along your own textbooks and tapes (consult with your language instructor in the States before leaving) and asking to use them as the basis for your special instruction. If you are weak in conversation skills, ask to practice dialogues. Or practice writing or learn to read cursive Chinese handwriting. Be clear about your own language goals, and explain them clearly to your tutor. If your language is good enough and you want to work on translations, bring along your texts or explain what materials interest you most and ask the tutor to help find them. Prove your devotion to studies by regular attendance in class.

You are likely to find student-teacher relations to be different in China. They are more hierarchical, and students are not expected to disagree with or challenge their professor. Your teachers' interest in you is likely to extend beyond the classroom into aspects of your life that you may regard as personal. A visit from a teacher to your dormitory is not uncommon, and they will be concerned if you are obviously unhappy or ill, or if you are having problems in class. Some Americans find this attention suffocating, but by understanding that the concern is genuine and well-meant, most come to feel affection and respect for their dedicated, hardworking Chinese instructors.

7. Services Available

THE U.S. EMBASSY AND CONSULATES

You should register with your local consulate after you arrive in China and each time you change your address. They will keep an emergency locator card on file in case relatives need to reach you quickly. The card is also useful if you lose your passport, develop a serious illness, or have other problems. If you live in a city where there is a consulate, you can also expect to be invited to functions hosted by the consulate—dances, movies, Friday afternoon happy hours, Christmas parties, and the annual Fourth of July gathering. Bring your passport with you to register and whenever you visit, because entry is granted only to U.S. citizens. In fact, many people advise carrying your passport with you at all times. You will need it for routine banking, for currency exchange, and internal travel. Anyone wandering off the beaten track will find it particularly useful to have proof of U.S. citizenship.

The staffs of the U.S. Embassy in Beijing and the U.S. Consulates in Chengdu, Guangzhou, Shanghai, and Shenyang can help in case of medical or financial emergency, difficulties with the police, or the death of a friend or relative in China. You should contact them for advice and assistance. They can get plane tickets out of the country fast. In a medical emergency, they can arrange for a plane or helicopter to take you to Hong Kong or Japan. The telephone number of the Cultural Affairs Officer in the U.S. Embassy in Beijing is 532-1161.

For more information on consular services, consult *Tips for Travelers to the People's Republic of China*, available for $1.00 from:

The Superintendent of Documents
U.S. Government Printing Office
Washington, D.C. 20402

The U.S. Embassy in Beijing is housed in three compounds near Ritan Park. The ambassador's residence and the offices of the press and cultural section (the U.S. Information Service office in Beijing) are located at 17 Guanghua Lu. The Bruce Building, located at 2 Xiushui Dong Jie, is a few blocks away and houses the consular section (where U.S. citizens register) and the administrative section. The main compound houses the embassy's executive offices and the offices of the political, science and technology, and economic sections as well as the Foreign Commercial Service and the Foreign Agricultural Service.

The following list of U.S. Embassy and consulate addresses and personnel was current as of February 1994. Area codes are provided for your reference but do not need to be dialed if you are calling from within the same city. When calling within China, the city area code is preceded by a "0."

U.S. Embassy/Beijing
Xiushui Bei Jie #3
Beijing 100600, PRC
Telephone: 1-532-3831
FAX: 1-532-3178

Ambassador	J. Stapleton Roy
Deputy Chief of Mission	Scott Hallford
Political Counselor	Neil Silver
Economic Counselor	Christopher Szymanski
Commercial Counselor	Melvin Searls
Agricultural Attache	William Brant
Science/Technology Attache	Marco DiCapua

U.S. Information Service (USIS)
Telephone: 1-532-1161
FAX: 1-532-2039

Public Affairs Officer	Frank Scotton
Deputy Public Affairs Officer	Larry Daks
Cultural Affairs Officer	Eugene Nojek
Information Officer	Lorraine Toly
Education Officer	Elizabeth Kauffman

U.S. Consulate General/Chengdu
No. 4 Ling Shi Lu
Renmin Nan Lu, Section 4
Chengdu 610041
Sichuan Province, PRC
Telephone: 28-558-3992
FAX: 28-558-3520

Consul General	Donald Camp
Branch Public Affairs Officer (USIS)	Frank Neville

U.S. Consulate General/Guangzhou (Canton)
White Swan Hotel
Guangzhou 510133
Guangdong Province, PRC
Telephone: 20-888-8911
FAX: 20-886-2341

Consul General	Eugene Martin
Branch Public Affairs Officer (USIS)	Phillip Wright

U.S. Consulate General/Shanghai
1469 Huaihai Zhong Lu
Shanghai 200031, PRC
Telephone: 21-433-6880
FAX: 21-433-4122

Consul General	Jerome Ogden
Branch Public Affairs Officer (USIS)	M. Lynne Martin

U.S. Consulate General/Shenyang
No. 52, 14 Wei Lu
Heping District
Shenyang 110003
Liaoning, PRC
Telephone: 24-282-0068
FAX: 24-282-0074

Consul General	Gerald Pascua
Branch Public Affairs Officer (USIS)	Valerie Crites

POSTAL SERVICES

Every university campus and most hotels and neighborhood shopping areas have post offices or counters that provide basic postal services; in many cases, this includes international registered mail. Some of the smaller counters sell only cards, letters, and stamps. International parcel post and other special services are usually offered in specified post offices—in Beijing, at the Friendship Hotel and the International Post Office, located in Jianguomenwai, near the diplomatic quarter.

In February 1994, airmail rates from China to the United States were Y2 for a letter and Y1.60 for a postcard. Internal airmail costs Y0.30 or Y0.40 if more than 10g. Internal surface rates are still inexpensive at Y0.20 outside the city and Y0.10 within any urban area. Sea-mail shipment of printed matter is Y26.10 for a 2-kilogram package and Y11 for each additional kilogram. A supply of book mailers can be useful for easy shipment of small parcels. Sea-mail rates for other materials aver-

age about Y20.90 per kilogram. Packages must be opened and inspected
at the post office, which also provides customs forms. Some post offices
sell the paper and string for sealing the package. Many Chinese customers prefer to sew cloth bags or build wooden crates for their fragile
parcels. Film can be mailed out in special containers sold in the major
post offices. Books can be mailed from any postal counter. Express
mail is now available from Chinese post offices in major cities for about
the same cost as similar services in the United States; it takes from four
days to one week to reach most U.S. destinations. Air freight is handled
through the Friendship Stores and the airlines. DHL Worldwide Express has service from Beijing, Shanghai, and Guangzhou. Delivery to
the United States takes three to four working days. Larger packages
can be shipped through special arrangement.

Mail delivery in larger cities is usually quite reliable. Letters from
the United States to Beijing take about seven to twelve days and from
Beijing to major U.S. cities, from four to seven days. You should add a
few days for mail that must reach smaller cities on either side. Mail in
China sometimes shows evidence of tampering, but rarely goes perma-
nently astray. Since mail at work units is often put into boxes for one or
more persons or just laid out on a table or in a hallway, mail is lost
usually between this point and the intended recipient. One solution is
to make a point of meeting the person who distributes the mail and get
to know him personally. For important documents, registered mail is
safest. The post office will send a notice for the addressee to pick up the
package at the post office, and identification is required. If you move
within China, mail will not be forwarded. Notify your correspondents
of your new address. In the meantime, you or a friend must return to
your original address to pick up mail.

Mail delivery from the United States can be expedited by asking
relatives and friends to stamp letters and packages clearly as airmail
and address them to you in the People's Republic of China. If you are
literate in Chinese, or have a friend who is, write out the address in
characters on a label that can be left at home and photocopied for multiple use. If not, use Pinyin[10] romanization for the name of your city.
Not all postal clerks are familiar with Pinyin, however, and delivery
can be slowed while the mail is referred to someone who is. As noted
earlier, Chinese postal regulations prohibit mailing large amounts of

---

[10]Pinyin, the system of romanization now used in China, has replaced the Wade-
Giles romanization system used prior to 1979. The Pinyin system more accurately
reflects standard Mandarin names and pronunciations. Thus, Peking is now cor-
rectly rendered as Beijing, Canton is referred to by its Mandarin pronunciation—
Guangzhou—and so forth. Maps and atlases published after 1979 should list the
Pinyin romanizations of Chinese cities and provinces.

used clothing into the country for other than personal use, and medicines of any kind may not be mailed to China except with special permission in emergency situations. Americans who are not members of the diplomatic community may not ordinarily use the diplomatic pouch.

CURRENCY AND BANKING

The Chinese currency (*renminbi* or RMB) is based on a decimal system. The basic unit is the *yuan* (or Chinese dollar), referred to colloquially as the *kuai*. The *yuan* is subdivided into 10 *jiao* (more commonly called *mao*, the Chinese dime) and 100 *fen* (penny). The largest paper RMB amount is the 100-*yuan* note (Y100). There are also notes in amounts of Y50, Y10, Y5, Y2, Y1, and 1, 2, and 5 *jiao* and *fen*. Coins come in denominations of Y1 and smaller. The official rate of exchange in February 1994 was Y8.7 to US$ 1.00. It is now legal to take up to Y6,000 of RMB in and out of the country, and RMB can be legally bought and sold in Hong Kong, at the Po Sang Bank on Queen's Road Central.

Prior to January 1, 1994, the Chinese government also issued a special scrip called foreign exchange certificates (FEC) in exchange for foreign currency. FEC can still be used as currency, at a value and in a manner equivalent to RMB, but it is no longer issued by the bank. The bills are gradually being withdrawn from circulation. No transactions now require FEC payment. When foreign currency or traveler's checks are exchanged at a bank, only RMB is given in return. As of February 1994, FEC can still be converted back into foreign currencies at the Bank of China, at the rate valid on December 31, 1993 (approximately Y5.8 = US$1.00). Exchange memos documenting previous exchange transactions from foreign currencies into FEC may be required for this transaction. This reconversion privilege is subject to revision at any time, so readers are encouraged to check with the Chinese Embassy, the nearest consulate, or the Bank of China about current practice.

U.S. dollars remain in high demand. Some universities and research institutes have asked that tuition or affiliation fees be paid in dollars. Prices at joint venture hotels are often quoted in dollars.

Ask your host unit to direct you to the nearest Bank of China branch with full services for foreigners. In Beijing, most Americans frequent either the office on Dengshikou Xijie just north of Wangfujing Dajie or the bank on the ground floor of the CITIC building in the Jianguomenwai area. You can open a bank account (a savings account that pays a low rate of interest) easily, in U.S. dollars or RMB, and withdrawals can be made at any time. If your account is opened as a U.S. dollar account, you can withdraw funds in either U.S. dollars or RMB; but if it is opened using RMB, you can make withdrawals only in

RMB. All transactions are recorded in a passbook that must be surrendered when you leave the country. Bank drafts drawn on the Bank of China and issued in foreign currency may be sent out of the country, and no problems in cashing them have been reported in the United States. Wire transfers carry a minimal fee and usually go smoothly. As noted earlier, it is important that your U.S. bank have correspondent relations with the Bank of China.

Banking can be time-consuming, especially if you live far from a branch that handles foreign exchange. Some people choose to keep traveler's checks on hand since they can be converted at the exchange counter of any hotel or store that serves foreigners. In some hotels these counters are open only a few hours each day. Even in hotels where the counters are staffed seven days a week, some close for two hours at lunchtime. The counters at joint-venture hotels, however, are usually open from early morning until late in the evening.

ELECTRONIC MAIL, FAX, AND TELEX FACILITIES

For information on bringing your own fax machine to China, see Chapter 2. While telex facilities are widely available at major hotels, the telex is now rarely used except in the most remote locations. Faxes have become more common for business communication. Most large work units in urban areas have a fax machine or access to one. Be aware, however, that while business communications will be free of charge to the recipient, some Chinese may be charged for both sending and receiving of personal faxes. Because the charges are usually too expensive for ordinary Chinese, faxes are not typically used as a means of communicating with friends. Charges to send faxes from joint-venture hotels can be $10 to $12 for two pages. At one university, the cost was Y66 per page to send to the United States. You will receive an incoming fax more quickly if it includes your name and address in Chinese. In general, it is wise to check with the office housing the fax if you are expecting to receive one. However, be warned that many offices turn off their fax machines outside working hours, which is when most faxes are sent from North America.

Electronic mail (e-mail) is being introduced into some universities and research institutes, and businesses with their own telephone lines may be able to communicate by e-mail. At this writing, the two primary e-mail services available for use in China are AT&T E-mail and CHINAPAC, China's national packet switching data network, which is supported by the Chinese Ministry of Posts and Telecommunications. (The telephone number for the CHINAPAC office in Beijing is 1-601-0861 or 601-1376.) CompuServe connections are possible from Beijing but require a long-distance connection. Electronic mail is so new and rare that, at present, individual U.S. scholars, students, and teachers cannot rely on the system for communicating with the United States. This situation is likely to change soon, however, and if you are accustomed to communication by e-mail, you will want to keep up with the latest developments in China.

THE TELEPHONE

While major efforts are under way to modernize the Chinese communications system, most individuals still do not have private telephones, and many have no phones at all. In some cases, people can be reached by a phone housed in a local residence committee office. The person answering the phone will then have to fetch the person being called. Some people, however, have phones in their apartments that go through a central switchboard in their work unit. Incoming calls go through the switchboard and are connected through an extension number. Outgoing calls are made either by going back through the central switchboard or by dialing "9" or "0." Some teachers living in apartments and most researchers in hotels have phones in their rooms that are hooked up to a central switchboard.

Most student dormitories, however, only have one phone per floor. Incoming calls are received by a worker in the dormitory office who then announces the call by loudspeaker. Since these workers do not know English, callers must know your Chinese name. Placing a call from a dormitory can take time. Demand for the phone can be high, and many institutions have only one outside line. Local calls within any city in China are generally free, although public pay phones are coming into use in larger cities like Beijing. The cost is a few *fen* per call.

Connections on both local and long-distance calls within China continue to be poor, but telephone lines are constantly being improved. Long-distance calls within China placed through an operator can take considerable time to connect—from ten minutes to a couple of hours— particularly during peak business hours, because the phone lines are often overloaded. Some cities now have domestic direct dial (DDD) calls, which go through immediately and are quite clear. International calls, transmitted by satellite, are always clear, and major hotels and office buildings now have international direct dial (IDD). IDD service is now being introduced to many buildings housing foreign teachers and students.

Collect calls or calls from the United States to China are much cheaper than calls from China to the United States. Major U.S. telephone companies now have money-saving plans for frequent callers from China and other parts of Asia. For a small monthly service charge, phone calls to and from the United States are considerably cheaper than the standard rate.

International calls to the United States are possible from phones without IDD hook-ups by dialing 10811, which will connect you with an AT&T English-speaking operator. English-speaking operators for other international calling companies, such as MCI and Sprint, can be accessed by dialing 10812, 10813, etc.

While these calls can take some time to place, the introduction of IDD lines has greatly reduced the demand on these lines, and most calls will go through in 10 to 30 minutes, particularly if they are made in off-business hours. After your conversation is completed, the operator will call back to verify the time. The bill is usually paid at a service desk.

If you are staying in a Chinese hotel, let friends and family know your room number if you are expecting them to call. Foreigners are typically identified by room number rather than by name. Joint-venture hotels, however, do keep a central registry with the names and room numbers of their guests.

All of China operates on one time zone: 13 hours ahead of U.S. Eastern standard time and 16 hours ahead of Pacific standard time (even though, geographically, the country covers the equivalent of several time zones). As of this writing, China is not using daylight savings time.

Telephone books can be purchased in China, but they contain only business numbers. Especially recommended are two directories that contain addresses and telephone numbers of various work units, including foreign firms. The first, *The China Phone Book and Business Directory*, can be ordered from:

The China Phone Book Company
G.P.O. Box 11581
Hong Kong
Telephone: 852-508-4448

The second, *China Telephone Directory*, is published annually by the Beijing Telecommunications Equipment Plant (telephone: 1-513-7878). Many bookstores in China also sell telephone directories. Since private telephones are not publicly listed, be sure to give your phone number to Chinese friends and colleagues and ask for theirs (if they have a phone) as well. Most business cards also contain a number where the person can be reached.

MEDICAL CARE

If the host unit will be responsible for your medical care, you will be issued a medical insurance card specifying which hospitals will provide treatment. If home remedies do not work and you are ill with a common complaint, such as a bad cold or stomach upset, your work unit's medical clinic may be able to prescribe medication. Health care staff there will be trained in basic medicine, although most will not speak English. There is a tendency to over-medicate, however, by prescribing a combination of large doses of antibiotics and traditional Chinese medicine. Injections with large needles are common. Chinese medicine is effective for a wide range of illnesses and is especially useful for the colds and diarrhea that often trouble foreigners. If you are seriously ill or if you feel a diagnosis is needed, you have several options. If you are covered by the SOS Assistance Plan, you may want first to call the SOS doctor or your own doctor in the United States. Either of them may be able to make a preliminary diagnosis and suggest what medication you might need and what further medical help you should get. You could also go immediately to one of the hospitals in your city that offers outpatient care to foreigners. In Beijing, the Peking Union Medical College is generally considered the best, but the Sino-Japanese Hospital and the Friendship Hospital are also good. There is also the International Medical Center, in the Beijing Lufthansa Center, Rm. S106, No. 50 Liangmaqiao Road.

If you prefer Chinese medicine, the hospital associated with the Chinese Academy of Traditional Medicine is good, particularly for people with back problems seeking a good therapeutic massage. The Worker's Hospital in Nanjing and the Huadong Hospital, the Huashan Hospital, and the Number One People's Hospital in Shanghai have a special wing for foreigners and usually have at least one English-speaking physician on duty. The Wuhan University Hospital is also good. Speak with other foreigners in your city to find out which hospitals serve foreigners.

If you or one of your family members or friends have a medical emergency, a taxi is ordinarily the quickest way to get to the hospital. Ambulances are in short supply and do not ordinarily have medical equipment. If you are diabetic, or if you have asthma or severe allergies, let your close neighbors and friends know, since they are likely to be available and can help if you have an attack. Wear a medical identification bracelet if you are allergic to any medications or if you have Rh-negative blood. Chinese do not have Rh-negative blood and thus do not stock it in their blood banks. Therefore, it is extremely important that anyone with Rh-negative blood register at the U.S. Embassy so that blood can be located quickly from the foreign community in case of emergency. The embassy launches periodic blood drives and encourages all Americans to participate.

Medical service at the U.S. Embassy is confined to the staff except in extraordinary, life-threatening situations. The Japanese, Australian, French, and British embassies usually have a physician on staff who will see other foreign nationals, and they sometimes stock medications not available in Chinese facilities. You can call the general information number at these embassies to obtain telephone numbers of their staff physicians.

If you will be relying on your own medical insurance, the cost of a recent hospitalization in the Peking Union Medical College is instructive. In 1992, a two-week hospital stay, including all tests and doctors' fees, was US$3,000. Emergency treatment, including medications, may be as little as Y100.

URBAN TRANSPORTATION

There are many means of transportation to get around—bus, minibus, taxi, bicycle, and by foot. Buses are slow and often crowded, particularly at rush hour, but they are cheap and monthly bus passes cut the price still further. Ask your work unit to help you apply for a bus pass.

Most universities are located in the suburbs. A bus ride into the city can be long, although buses typically run frequently. In Beijing, the bus from Peking University to the center of the city takes at least one hour. In Shanghai, the ride from Fudan University to downtown can take up to an hour and a half. In some cities, the buses stop running early in the evening. Check your bus route for the times of operation.

Some cities now have minibuses that are usually less crowded. Ask people in your work unit about the routes. Minibuses (or *mianbaoche*— "bread trucks," because they are shaped like a loaf of bread) can also be rented by the day or half-day for group outings. Most cities now have an ample supply of taxis. Every hotel will have a line of waiting cabs, and in most places they can also be hailed in the street. Some campuses also have a taxi stand. If not, call the nearest taxi company and wait for the car to arrive. The cost of taxis ranges from Y1 to Y2 per kilometer, depending on the model of the car. Taxis in some cities charge a set fee for initial flagfall; in Shanghai this can range from Y10 to Y15. Be certain to check the mileage costs *before* engaging a car. Most taxis are metered, and all should have a sticker or information card that cites fares per kilometer. Beware of unregistered taxis and broken meters. Beijing now has yellow minivan taxis (*miandi*) that cost about one-fourth the price of regular taxis and can be hailed on the street.

If you need a taxi to visit places where return cars are not available, you can ask the driver to wait. Waiting costs are calculated at five-minute intervals—five minutes equals one kilometer. You can also hire a taxi by the day or half-day. Rates vary depending on the city, company, and the make of the car. In Beijing, for example, daily rates start at Y200 with a distance limit of one hundred kilometers.

Most foreigners in China purchase bicycles. They are often the quickest and most efficient means of going short distances and are fun to use on an all-day outing. Most cities have bicycle lanes, but riding a bicycle still takes getting used to. Traffic in China's cities is heavy and can be chaotic, and accidents are on the rise. Women should be careful riding alone at night as some have been harassed. Bicycle repair shops are plentiful but usually open only during daylight hours.

The best way to see any Chinese city is still on foot; and much of the fun of living in China is getting to know the place where you live. Taking a bus or taxi, or riding your bicycle into the heart of the city, and then setting out by foot will give you a taste of the local flavor. Buy a map of the city and set out to explore its various parts.

RECREATION AND ENTERTAINMENT

There is no reason to be bored in China. For sports enthusiasts, most university campuses have basketball and volleyball courts, track and soccer fields, and horizontal and parallel bars. Some have tennis courts and swimming pools. On most campuses, foreigners are welcome to participate in team sports, which is a good way to make new Chinese friends.

Every city has at least one park, where people go early in the morning for different forms of exercise—*taijiquan*, ballroom and disco dancing, as well as *qigong*, Beijing opera, chess, and the daily "exercising" of pet birds. Foreigners are usually welcome as spectators or participants, and early morning visits to the local park are a good way to get to know city residents. Many parks are also large enough for a morning or afternoon run.

Many activities have been organized especially for the foreign fitness buff. In Beijing, the International Club downtown and the Friendship Hotel in the university section of the suburbs each have a 50-meter pool and tennis courts. Most of the joint-venture hotels have exercise rooms and swimming pools. The International Club and Friendship Hotel pools offer monthly and daily passes. The Friendship Hotel requires a minimal physical examination for a monthly pass, given at the hotel's own clinic. No physical exam is necessary for a day pass, which is Y20. Most joint-venture hotels also have monthly memberships for their health club facilities.

Most dormitories have communal television lounges, and almost all hotels have color televisions in each room. Many now have satellite dishes, so CNN, BBC, and many Hong Kong-based programs are also available. Universities often show movies, and every city has many movie theaters. Joint-venture hotels, such as the Great Wall Sheraton in Beijing, also sometimes show foreign movies. Some theater and opera tickets can be ordered by phone, but you must stand in line early in the day to buy tickets for popular performances. Tickets for performances at popular concert halls are often difficult to obtain, but some work units are willing to help foreign guests obtain tickets for special shows. Students are often given tickets for a variety of events by their foreign affairs officials who also arrange for group transportation to the event.

Many new forms of entertainment are now being introduced into China. Coffee shops and evening beer halls have become popular, along with the night food markets. Discotheques and karaoke bars are packed. Eating out is a favorite form of entertainment, and you will want to explore local restaurants. New, privately run restaurants are springing up all over China, and you should consult with both Western and Chinese friends about which are the best in your area. Every city also has a few old and famous restaurants that you will want to visit a few times during your stay. In Beijing, the Sichuan Restaurant, located in a "four-cornered courtyard" complex that once belonged to the Qing general Yuan Shikai, is still a charming spot to eat hot and spicy Sichuan food, and the restaurant in Ritan Park, long famous for its dumplings and now refurbished with outdoor tables in warmer weather, is still popular for anyone visiting the Jianguomenwai area. Excellent Chinese food is found in some of the joint-venture hotels. The two Chinese restaurants in the Palace Hotel—one Sichuanese and the other Cantonese—are among the best in the city, as is the Jinglun's Tao Li Cantonese Restaurant. All joint-venture hotels also have Western food, and many have lunch or evening buffets, complete with salad bars. McDonald's, Kentucky Fried Chicken, and Pizza Hut also have restaurants in Beijing.

Other large cities have similarly good restaurants well worth exploring. Check your guidebook and talk to friends about which are best. The names of Beijing restaurants are given here only because most people pass through Beijing for a few days during their time in China.

Finally, almost every city has a few spots that are fascinating to explore but off the usual tourist routes. In Beijing, walks around the walls of the Forbidden City and a climb up Coal Hill, or walks through the tiny alleyways of Dashalan behind Qianmen, are always interesting. Taking a picnic lunch for a day to explore the unrestored Ming tombs will be a memorable experience. The huge Summer Palace complex has many areas where few tourists venture and which are best explored very late in the afternoon when most of the tourists have left.

INTERNAL TRAVEL

The possibilities for travel in China today are so rich and varied that only general guidelines can be suggested, especially since guidebooks, newspapers, and magazines provide such a wealth of travel lore and advice. Hundreds of cities and towns are open to foreign travelers now and can be visited without special travel permits. Areas that are still not open can be visited only with a travel permit issued by the Public Security Bureau (*gonganju*). Foreign affairs officials should be asked to help secure these permits. Travelers willing to explore on their own can consult the guidebooks noted on page 40.

Inexpensive casual travel is no longer limited to students. Many hardy travelers with no Chinese-language expertise are striking out through China on their own. One such traveler reports, "It was exhilarating to plan my own itinerary, to leave the beaten path and stir up a town with my presence, to eat and travel and suffer with the average Chinese. But it was also aggravating to cope with the lines and the language barrier while buying food or train tickets, and there were times when I was exhausted by 'hard class' trains and spitting passengers and lying hotel staff who insisted that there was no room at the inn."

A strong sense of adventure is essential for this type of travel, but almost all who have struck out on their own discover that the warmth and hospitality they received along the way far outweighed the frustrations. For many, travel Chinese-style remains one of the most memorable parts of their stay.

The first step in arranging travel is to purchase train tickets at the local train station or airline tickets at one of the airline offices. As soon as you know when you will leave, it is a good idea to make hotel reservations, especially during busy tourist times (May through October) in popular tourist sites. Remember, too, that Chinese people are traveling more these days; trains will be packed during national holidays and plane reservations will be more difficult to secure.

While the Civil Aviation Administration of China (CAAC) has been decentralized and there are now many regionally based airlines, most domestic airline tickets can still be purchased at a central office. Prices have gone up in recent years, but domestic air travel in China remains inexpensive by international travel standards. Air cargo, air freight, and excess baggage costs are also going up. Round-trip air tickets can be purchased, but only for unbroken routing which returns to the city of origin. Otherwise, you must purchase separate tickets for your next destination at each stop. If you need help, consult the local China Travel Service (*luxingshe*) counter at your hotel and be prepared to wait a day or two for your reservation.

In nearly all cases, only one-way train tickets can be bought. If you buy tickets at the train station, you can sometimes avoid the tourist surcharge, but if you do not speak Chinese, the process can be confusing. Few service personnel speak English, and the demand for tickets is high. Timing must be carefully orchestrated, since train tickets can be purchased only a few days before departure.

Train accommodations are of two types: soft and hard class. Within each, you can choose seats or sleeping berths. For long or overnight journeys, soft-class sleeping compartments have four berths with comfortable padded mattresses, a small table, doilies, pillows, a thermos of hot water, an overhead fan, and an overhead luggage compartment. Your traveling companions are likely to be Chinese officials on business, Chinese entrepreneurs, or other visiting foreigners. Many people from Taiwan are now visiting China and traveling by train.

Hard-class compartments have wooden benches for seats and thinly padded berths for sleepers. The berths are not enclosed and are stacked three high. Prices for berths depend on the level, with the lowest berth being the most expensive. Hard-class tickets do not guarantee a seat, and many a traveler has sat out a long journey in the dining car—or stood for lack of a seat. Some foreigners enjoy the lively atmosphere of the hard-class sections, where they are often the main amusement for their fellow travelers; others prefer a more sedate ride.

Train food varies in quality. About two hours before mealtime, a service person will ask each foreign traveler about their dinner plans and will offer two or more grades (*biaozhun*) of food starting at about Y20 for four or five dishes. Experienced travelers say that there is no discernible difference in the amount or quality of the food in different grades and suggest taking the lowest *biaozhun*. If you are on a route with less palatable food, you can still eat reasonably well by mixing a vegetable dish together with rice for improvised "fried rice." Or you can skip the arranged fare altogether and order a noodle dish for half the price or even the cheaper boxes of hot rice and vegetables that Chinese passengers often favor. Another option is to purchase food from platform vendors at scheduled train stops. Most passengers carry a wide assortment of food (from watermelons to peanuts) to be consumed along the way. Tea bags can be purchased on the train. Often there will be no English-speaking personnel, which can be a problem for foreigners when ordering dinner. If you do not speak Chinese, you might want to take a supply of nonperishable foods.

Plan to carry your luggage with you on the train and make certain that your bags are locked. A number of travelers have reported items missing from outside pockets of luggage upon arrival at their destination. On some train routes (especially hard berth sections) security personnel may quietly ask foreigners not to associate closely with certain people they believe are undesirable; some foreigners have been set up by con men (and women) on trains.

Teachers and research scholars (or anyone of senior status) are expected to travel as tourists and pay tourist prices. Some U.S. researchers who speak Chinese and can negotiate on their own have traveled hard class and dispensed with guides.

Some hosts are willing to help arrange trips within China, particularly for researchers with no Chinese. Many charge relatively high service fees for such assistance and encourage the traveler to stay in more expensive hotels. While some foreign affairs offices are also willing to help teachers, many report that the *waiban* officials are now so busy that they cannot afford the time. Your students can sometimes be called on to assist you if you are making arrangements yourself.

Host units often sponsor special tours for their foreign students that usually include visits to five or more cities in three weeks. Because students often stay in dormitories, these tours are considerably cheaper than ordinary tourist rates. What they lack in spontaneity and comfort is compensated for in lower costs and opportunities to see sites not always accessible to tourists. In some universities and colleges, researchers and teachers and their families have also been invited to go along on these trips.

Whatever the style or itinerary, try to travel at every opportunity. There is no better way to learn about China and to meet the *laobaixing* ("old hundred names"), meaning ordinary Chinese people.

8. Leaving China

As the time for departure approaches, you will need to decide how to ship belongings back to the United States, particularly if you have accumulated much more than you arrived with. You have several options. Parcel post is one. Air freight is another, although it can be expensive. Check with international airline offices in your city. Sea freight is a much less expensive alternative, although you should count on the shipment taking about three months. The Friendship Store in Beijing will crate and ship your belongings, and so will several other companies. Check with the U.S. Consulate in your area to find out which companies they recommend for their diplomatic personnel or check with foreign affairs personnel at your host institution.

If you are returning during the busy tourist season (May through October), plan on booking your return ticket early (about six weeks before departure). This is especially important if you are exiting through Hong Kong, since eastbound flights from Hong Kong tend to be booked well in advance. Remember that most airline tickets are good for one year after issuance. Confirm your flight directly through your airline or, if there is no office in your city, through CAAC. Bring your passport with you when making reservations. If you have any doubts about your ticket, fax your travel agent in the United States to confirm you are properly booked, and be certain to reconfirm your ticket three days before the flight. If there are things you want to leave behind, consider donating them to your school, giving them away to friends, or selling them to newly arrived foreign colleagues.

Do not wait until the last minute to pack. Just as China has rituals for greeting foreign guests, so there are rituals for departing. Friends and colleagues will come to say goodbye, and some may bring small farewell gifts. You, too, may want to present them with small tokens of your friendship—books and tapes, for instance, or that old manual typewriter you are not likely to use again. You may want to treat friends and officials to farewell dinners, and they may want to do the same for you. You may be asked to speak to colleagues and research collaborators about the fruits of your stay. And the interview you awaited for months may finally come through. Your last week or so in China is likely to be hectic.

If you are concerned about exiting China, or have more luggage than you can manage, ask a friend or officials from the host institution to accompany you to the airport and plan to arrive two hours before your flight departs. Be prepared for a very busy airport. The people who have come to see you off will be able to accompany you only to the customs checkpoint. After that, you are on your own. Most customs officials will simply wave you through with no questions asked, but you must put your checked baggage on a conveyer belt for a security check. A sticker will then be placed on your luggage. You must pay a departure tax, which in the summer of 1993 was Y60. After paying the tax and going through the security check, proceed to check-in at the airline counter servicing the flight. After check-in, you will go through exit formalities, presenting your passport and boarding pass to Chinese officials. After your passport is stamped, you will be in the departure area, where you can exchange your Chinese currency for U.S. dollars. It is safest to have exchange memos equal to the amount you want to exchange, although few clerks ask for them anymore. You have a chance to purchase a few last-minute duty-free items before proceeding through the final security check, where your carry-on luggage is examined, and on to the gate where your plane will depart.

Yilu ping'an, "have a pleasant journey"—and welcome home!

Glossary of Chinese Terms

The following Chinese terms, used in *China Bound*, are listed below for quick reference.

Chinese word (pinyin)	Meaning
ayi	female helper
biaozhun	grade or standard
cesuo	toilet
chunjie	"Spring Festival," or Lunar New Year, which symbolically marks the end of winter
danwei	Chinese work unit
dong chuang	chilblains
fen	local currency (the Chinese penny)
fudao	private tutoring
fuwufei	service fees (in research)
fuwuyuan	service personnel
gaoji jinxiusheng	senior advanced student
getihu	"privately owned" (restaurants, etc.)
gonganju	Public Security Bureau
guanlifei	administrative costs (in field research)
guanxi	personal connection, relationship
jiao	local currency (the Chinese dime)
jiating	family
juan	fascicles (of research material)
kuai	Chinese dollar (colloquial)
laobaixing	ordinary Chinese people (literally, "old hundred names")

laowufei	work compensation fees (in field research)
liuxuesheng bangongshi/liuban	The Foreign Student Affairs Office
luxingshe	China Travel Service
mao	Chinese dime (colloquial)
maotai	a strong Chinese liquor
mian'ao	cotton padded jacket (same as *mianyi*)
mianbaoche	mini-buses (literally, "bread trucks," named for their shape)
miandi	yellow minivan taxis
neibu	"internal" or classified materials that cannot leave the country
neiwai youbie	difference between "insiders" and "outsiders" and the treatment thereof
paidui	to line up
pipa	a Chinese guitar-like musical instrument
renminbi	local currency, Chinese dollar (same denomination as *yuan*)
shaobing	sesame-seed cake
shifu	term of address used for Chinese service personnel
suibian	casual
taijiquan	a kind of traditional Chinese shadowboxing
tiaojie jia	the "adjusted rate" of monetary exchange, higher than the official rate available at the Bank of China
tongxue	schoolmates
waihuijuan	Foreign Exchange Certificates (FEC) (no longer printed)
waishi banshichu/waiban	The Foreign Affairs Office
wen ya dian yuan	surge protector
xian	county
xiang	township
xiuxi	rest, as in the rest period from noon until 1:30 or 2:00 p.m.
xitong	the larger system of which the *danwei* is a component, such as the CAS, CASS, or SEDC
youtiao	fried dough sticks, most often eaten with *shaobing* and/or *doujiang* (soybean milk) for breakfast in North China
yuan	local currency, Chinese dollar (same denomination as *renminbi*)

APPENDIXES

APPENDIX A

Funding for Graduate and Postdoctoral Research in China

Most of the organizations listed below award fellowships to scholars across disciplines in the sciences, social sciences, and humanities. Organizations are listed alphabetically, but disciplines awarded under each are highlighted in the text to facilitate searching. Programs listed below make awards to individuals rather than to institutions. Contact program offices for application deadlines.

American Council of Learned Societies
228 East 45th Street
New York, NY 10017-3398
Telephone: 212-697-1505

Description: The American Council of Learned Societies (ACLS) administers a general humanities postdoctoral fellowship program and a pre- and postdoctoral fellowship program for scholars in the **humanities and social sciences** for research on China. These programs, however, are not intended specifically for research *in* China. Individual programs are described below.

Application materials are available from the ACLS Office of Fellowships and Grants. Requests for applications must be submitted in writing by U.S. mail (no inquiries or applications will be accepted by fax) and must include the following information: highest degree held and date received; country of citizenship or permanent legal residence; academic or other position; field of specialization; proposed subject of research or study, proposed date for beginning tenure of the award and duration requested; and specific award program for which application is requested. Graduate students should include their current level of

159

graduate study; department and institution where enrolled; and where the planned work would be conducted.

Funding may also be available for support of conferences, workshops, and planning projects. Inquiries regarding these activities should be directed to the ACLS China Program Office.

Fellowship Program: The ACLS Fellowship Program supports postdoctoral research in the humanities. Interdisciplinary and cross-disciplinary projects are also welcome. Research in the social sciences with a predominantly humanistic emphasis may also be considered. The Fellowship Program seeks to enable scholars to devote a summer or six to twelve continuous months to full-time research by supplementing primary salary. To that end, scholars may apply for one of two types of grants: summer fellowships, for a minimum of two consecutive summer months, or six- to twelve-month fellowships.

Typical grant size: $5,000 to $20,000

Requirements: Applicants must be U.S. citizens or permanent residents who have held a Ph.D. for at least two years prior to application. Established scholars who can demonstrate the equivalent of the Ph.D. in publications and professional experience may also qualify. Scholars enrolled in any kind of degree program are ineligible. Scholars may not accept both an ACLS fellowship and an ACLS/Social Science Research Council Joint Area Studies award in a single competitive cycle. Other restrictions apply; see application materials for details.

Chiang Ching-kuo Foundation/JCCS Fellowships for Postdoctoral Research: Support is available for six to twelve months of full-time original research on Chinese culture or society, including synthesis or reinterpretation of the applicant's previous research. These fellowships are intended to support research or writing outside the People's Republic of China, although short visits to the PRC may be supported as part of a coherent program carried out primarily elsewhere.

Typical grant size: Up to $25,000. Normally, the cost of travel to Asia for less than six months of research cannot be covered.

Requirements: No citizenship requirements apply. Foreign nationals must have resided in the United States for at least two consecutive years at the time of application. Applicants must hold a Ph.D. or its equivalent at the time of application.

Chiang Ching-kuo Foundation/JCCS Fellowships for Dissertation Research Abroad. These fellowships enable Ph.D. candidates to carry out six to twelve months of dissertation research in any country outside the

U.S. and the PRC. Support is limited to the social sciences and humanities, or interdisciplinary research. The dissertation must be related to China, although it may be comparative in nature.

Typical grant size: Up to $20,000

Requirements: No citizenship restrictions apply; however, foreign nationals must be enrolled as full-time Ph.D. candidates in U.S. institutions. Additional requirements apply. See application materials for details.

Asian Cultural Council
Awards in the Visual and Performing Arts
1290 Avenue of the Americas
New York, NY 10104
Telephone: 212-373-4300
FAX: 212-315-0996

Description: The Asian Cultural Council (ACC) supports cultural exchange between Asia and the United States in the **visual and performing arts.** The emphasis of the ACC's program is on providing opportunities for Asian artists; however, the ACC also awards grants to American artists, scholars, students, and specialists to study, conduct research, and travel in Asia. Projects of significance to Asian-American cultural exchange by arts organizations and educational institutions are also eligible. Grants are made in the following fields: archaeology, architecture, art history, conservation, crafts, dance, design, film and video, museology, music, painting, photography, printmaking, sculpture, and theater.

Asian Art Fellowships: The Council provides fellowship support for American scholars, curators, and conservators of Asian art to conduct research and travel in China, Taiwan, and Hong Kong (among other Asian regions). Individual research projects, visits to Asian institutions in connection with proposed exhibitions of Asian art in the United States, and observation tours to collections, sites, and conservation facilities in Asia will be considered for support. Grants range in duration from one to three months.

Asian Art and Religion Fellowships: American scholars, specialists, and artists wishing to conduct research and undertake projects in South, Southeast, and East Asia involving interdisciplinary study of Asian arts and religion may apply for support through this program. Awards include research fellowships, visiting professorships, and travel grants.

Asian Art and Religion Fellowships range in duration from one to six months.

Humanities Fellowships: This program assists American scholars, doctoral students, and specialists in the humanities undertaking research, training, and study in South, Southeast, and East Asia in the following fields: archaeology; conservation; museology; and the theory, history, and criticism of architecture, art, dance, design, film, music, photography, and theater. It also supports American and Asian scholars participating in conferences and exhibitions, and visiting professorships. Grants range in duration from one to twelve months.

Typical grant size: Full fellowships provide round-trip international air transportation; per diem, domestic travel, and medical insurance allowances; and a miscellaneous expense allocation for books, supplies, and other grant-related costs. The Council also awards partial fellowships.

Requirements: Projects must fall within the field of visual and performing arts. The Council will not consider requests for support of lecture programs, personal exhibitions, individual performance tours, undergraduate study, activities conducted by individuals in their home countries, publications, capital campaigns, or general program and administrative costs.

The Center for Field Research
Earthwatch Grants for Fieldwork
680 Mount Auburn Street
P.O. Box 403
Watertown, MA 02272
Telephone: 617-926-8200
FAX: 617-926-8532

Description: The Center for Field Research (CFR) supports **field research by scientists and humanists** working to investigate and/or preserve our physical, biological, and cultural heritage. CFR considers a broad range of basic and applied field research initiatives, giving particular attention to those of a multi-disciplinary nature or involving international collaboration. CFR encourages the inclusion of host-country nationals as research staff in developing countries. A typical project employs 18 to 50 volunteers, with 5 to 12 volunteers each on three to five sequential teams. Teams normally spend 10 to 20 days in the field. Longer-term research projects are encouraged.

Typical grant size: Awards are calculated on a per capita basis. Per capita grants range from $250 to $1,000, and project grants range from $10,000 to $150,000. The financial and volunteer structure of each grant should be discussed with the appropriate CFR program staff member at the preliminary proposal stage, before a full proposal is submitted.

Earthwatch does not normally provide funds for capital equipment, principal investigator (PI) salaries, university overhead or indirect costs, data analysis, or preparation of results for publication.

Applicants may present preliminary proposals by telephone, fax, or two-page letter to the director at any time. The preliminary proposal should describe the project, its research discipline, objectives, scholarly significance, and the composition and qualifications of the research staff. The preliminary proposal should also specify the number and use of volunteers, field dates, location, and approximate budget. CFR staff responds to preliminary proposals within 30 days of receipt.

If CFR determines that the project is consistent with Earthwatch's interests, the staff will invite a full proposal, due approximately 12 months before the scheduled start date of the fieldwork.

Requirements: Application is open to scholars of any nationality. Earthwatch primarily supports post-doctoral scholarship, although it occasionally funds exceptional initiatives by younger scholars and seasoned graduate students. CFR also welcomes proposals from advanced scholars. Projects must present field research in the sciences and humanities that deals directly with natural, cultural, and, occasionally, archival primary resources in any geographic region worldwide. Proposals from the full range of field disciplines will be considered. The research design must integrate non-specialists into the project.

Chiang Ching-kuo Senior Scholar Awards
Chiang Ching-kuo Foundation for International Scholarly Exchange
Suite 131, Van Ness Center
4301 Connecticut Avenue, NW
Washington, DC 20008
Telephone: 202-362-2914
FAX: 202-362-2935

Description: Chiang Ching-kuo (CCK) Foundation grants support work in Chinese studies only in the **humanities and social sciences**. The Foundation's interests include, but are not limited to, Chinese cultural heritage, classical studies, the Republic of China (Taiwan), and China-related comparative studies. The Senior Scholar Awards Program is a new line of grants designed to allow full professors at academic institutions to complete research and writing while on sabbatical.

Typical grant size: Up to $40,000. Senior Scholar Awards are intended to supplement one year of sabbatical pay.

Requirements: No allowance is made for capital equipment, administrative costs, or overhead. Individual scholars may accept only one grant from the Senior Scholar Awards program, American Council of Learned Societies Fellowship, or Chiang Ching-kuo Foundation/Joint Committee on Chinese Studies Fellowship in a single annual cycle.

CIES/Fulbright Scholar Program
Council for International Exchange of Scholars
Suite 5M
3007 Tilden Street, NW
Washington, DC 20008-3009
Telephone: 202-686-4000 or -7866

Description: The Council for International Exchange of Scholars (CIES) was established in 1947 to administer the Fulbright Scholar Program in cooperation with the U.S. government. The purpose of the Fulbright Program is "to enable the government of the United States to increase mutual understanding between the people of the United States and the people of other countries" by supporting university teaching, advanced research, graduate study, and teaching in elementary and secondary schools.

Fulbright Scholar Program. CIES publishes an awards book that describes over 1,000 teaching and research opportunities for American faculty and professionals in about 135 countries. For the PRC, grants are available in the categories of **distinguished lecturer and lecturer.**

Typical grant size: Varies according to program and location.

Requirements: All applicants must be U.S. citizens. Most categories require a Ph.D. and appropriate professional experience. Some awards require fluency in a foreign language.

CSCC/National Program for Advanced Study and Research in China
Committee on Scholarly Communication with China
1055 Thomas Jefferson Street, NW
Suite 2013
Washington, DC 20007
Telephone: 202-337-1250
FAX: 202-337-3109

Description: The Committee on Scholarly Communication with China (CSCC) offers support to scholars and advanced graduate students to visit the People's Republic of China. Under the National Program for Advanced Study and Research in China, the Graduate and Research Programs support American scholarly interests in the **social sciences and humanities** through sponsorship of long-term study and research in China.

Research Program: The Research Program supports individuals in the social sciences and humanities to conduct China studies research in the PRC. Members of joint research projects must submit separate applications. In-depth research on China, the Chinese portion of a comparative study, or exploratory research on an aspect of contemporary China is supported. This program may allow limited research in Hong Kong or elsewhere in East Asia to supplement primary research in the PRC. Tenure of two months to one year is required. The Committee gives preference to those who have not previously participated in the program, but encourages former participants to apply on the basis of publications resulting from research done during an earlier visit.

Typical grant size: Awards are determined by academic rank and duration of the project.

Requirements: Applicants must be U.S. citizens or permanent residents who hold a Ph.D. at the time of application.

Graduate Program: The Graduate Program supports individuals enrolled in a U.S. graduate program in the social sciences or humanities to carry out research or fieldwork at a Chinese institution. Chinese language proficiency is required; candidates must undergo an oral interview and written language exam as part of the selection process.

Typical grant size: $17,000

Requirements: Applicants must be U.S. citizens or permanent residents who hold a B.A. at the time of application. Chinese language proficiency acquired through at least three years of college-level study or its equivalent, preferably including time in a Chinese language environment, is required. Successful applicants must agree to complete 11 consecutive months in the PRC.

Fogarty International Center
Senior International Fellowship Program
Bldg. 31, Room B2C39
National Institutes of Health
Bethesda, MD 20892
Telephone: 301-496-1653

Description: The Senior International Fellowship Program supports foreign study or research by established **biomedical, behavioral, or health scientists**.

The program is intended to enhance the exchange of ideas and information about the latest advances in health sciences, including the basic, clinical, and public health sciences; to permit U.S. scientists to participate abroad in ongoing study or research in the health sciences; and to improve the research, education, and clinical potential of the fellow's institution.

Senior International Fellowships are awarded for a total of three to twelve months. The award may be divided into as many as three terms, used over a three-year period, with a three-month minimum for any term.

Typical grant size: Awards include a stipend based on current salary level, foreign living allowance, round-trip airfare, and an institutional allowance of up to $500/month.

Requirements: Applicants must (1) hold a doctoral degree in one of the biomedical, behavioral, or health sciences; (2) have at least five years of postdoctoral experience; (3) have professional experience in one of the biomedical, behavioral, or health sciences for at least two of the last four years; (4) hold a full-time appointment on the staff of an institution, which must be a non-federal public or private not-for-profit research, clinical, or educational institution; and (5) be invited by a non-profit foreign institution. Federal government employees are not eligible. Applicants must be U.S. citizens or permanent residents and may not have received more than one previous Senior International Fellowship.

The Fogarty International Center will not accept any proposal that has as its major feature brief observational visits; attendance at formal training courses; or full-time clinical, technical, or teaching services.

Samuel H. Kress Foundation
Kress Travel and Dissertation Fellowships
174 East 80th Street
New York, NY 10021
Telephone: 212-861-4993

Description: The Kress Foundation supports advanced graduate work in the **history of art and advanced training in fine art conservation.** Kress Travel Fellowships facilitate the viewing of materials essential for completing dissertation research. Kress Dissertation Fellowships support final preparation of the doctoral dissertation.

Typical grant size: Travel Fellowships programs of three to six months average $3,000 to $5,000. Dissertation Fellowships average $10,000.

Requirements: Applicants must be active doctoral candidates matriculated at an institution in the U.S. at the time of application. Applicants must be nominated by their affiliated department. Departments may nominate no more than three candidates to the Travel Fellowships program and one candidate to the Dissertation Fellowship program per cycle. No fellowships will be awarded to foreign students matriculated at non-U.S. institutions.

The Charles A. Lindbergh Fund, Inc.
Lindbergh Grants Program
708 South 3rd Street, Suite 110
Minneapolis, MN 55415
Telephone: 612-338-1703
FAX: 612-338-6826

Description: The Lindbergh Grants Program supports research and educational projects that focus on a balance between the **advancement of technology and preservation of the human/natural environment** in the following categories: aviation/aerospace, agriculture, arts and humanities, biomedical research, conservation of natural resources, exploration, health and population sciences, intercultural communication, oceanography, waste disposal management, water resource management, and wildlife preservation. The Fund gives priority to research and educational projects that best address the issue of balance and are technically superior, regardless of category.

Typical grant size: Up to $10,580

Requirements: Citizens of all countries are eligible but related application materials must be submitted in the English language. The Fund welcomes candidates affiliated with academic or non-profit institutions.

The Henry Luce Foundation, Inc.
U.S.-China Cooperative Research Program
111 West 50th Street
New York, NY 10020
Telephone: 212-489-7700

Description: The United States-China Cooperative Research Program encourages sustained, multi-year interaction among Chinese and

American scholars working on topics in the **humanities and social sciences.** The program supports projects involving specialists from all parts of China—the People's Republic, Taiwan, and Hong Kong. Interaction among scholars from different institutions is encouraged. Proposals will be reviewed on the basis of intellectual merit and potential contribution to China studies, feasibility, mutual benefit, and level of institutional support.

Typical grant size: Awards range in size from $60,000 to $180,000 per project, over a three-year period.

Requirements: Luce welcomes proposals submitted by both Chinese and American scholars.

National Endowment for the Humanities
Division of Fellowships and Seminars, Room 316
1100 Pennsylvania Avenue, NW
Washington, DC 20506
Telephone: 202-606-8466

Description: National Endowment for the Humanities (NEH) Fellowships support work that will make a significant contribution to thought and knowledge in the **humanities.** The term "humanities" includes, but is not limited to, the following disciplines: history; philosophy; languages; linguistics; literature; archaeology; the history, theory, and criticism of the arts; ethics; comparative religion; and those aspects of the social sciences that employ historical or philosophical approaches. NEH fellowships are awarded through two programs: Fellowships for University Teachers, and Fellowships for College Teachers and Independent Scholars. The program to which a scholar applies is determined by the individual's institutional affiliation or circumstance. Projects proposed for support may address broad topics or consist of research in a single field.

These fellowships are designed to support scholars with a range of experience in a variety of circumstances: school, college, and university faculty and staff; scholars and writers affiliated with institutions with research or educational connections; scholars and writers affiliated with institutions with no connection to the humanities; and unaffiliated scholars and writers.

Typical grant size: Up to $30,000 for six to twelve months of full-time, uninterrupted study or research.

Requirements: Scholars currently enrolled in degree-granting programs and those seeking support for work toward a degree are not eligible.

National Geographic Society
Grants-in-Aid
Committee for Research and Exploration
17th and M Streets, NW
Washington, DC 20036-4688
Attn: Steven S. Stettes, Secretary
Telephone: 202-857-7439

Description: The National Geographic Society, through its Committee for Research and Exploration, provides grants-in-aid for basic, original **scientific field research and exploration** covering a broad spectrum of disciplines from anthropology to zoology. Particular emphasis is placed on multi-disciplinary projects of an environmental nature.

Typical grant size: $15,000 and $20,000 per annum. Overhead, indirect expenses, or fringe benefits to an individual or institution will not be covered. Salaries and stipends are paid only in unusual and extreme circumstances and must be justified by the principal investigator (PI). The Society does not provide fellowships or scholarships, or pay tuition at any level.

Anticipated travel expenses will be verified through the Society's travel office and should be based on economy airfare rates. The Society does not provide funds for publication of research results (including page charges or reprints) and will not provide funds for travel to scientific meetings or conferences.

Research proposals will be considered for projects up to three years in length. Applications are accepted at any time and must be submitted on the official "green" application form. Each investigator, when requesting an application packet, must briefly describe in writing the research project for which funding is being requested. This preliminary statement should outline the significance of the research and list the project location and the intended dates of the research. This action will help candidates avoid completing an application for a project that is outside the scope of the Society. A current copy of the PI's curriculum vitae must accompany this descriptive preliminary statement. Projects for which the PI is a graduate student should so note and be submitted in the name of the student.

Requirements: PIs with advanced degrees (Ph.D. or equivalent) who are associated with institutions of higher learning or other scientific and educational nonprofit organizations or museums are eligible to apply. Grants have occasionally been awarded to exceptionally qualified graduate students with established publication records and to scientific researchers without advanced degrees. Ph.D. candidates must submit reprints of their recent publications. Citizens of any country may apply.

National Science Foundation
U.S.-China Program
Office of International Programs
4201 Wilson Boulevard
Arlington, VA 22230
Telephone: 703-306-1704

Description: The National Science Foundation (NSF) encourages U.S. participation in international science and engineering activities that promise significant benefit to U.S. research and education. Through the Division of International Programs (INT), the Foundation supports programs to initiate and develop **international scientific cooperative activities** and to foster U.S. knowledge of science and engineering developments in foreign countries.

INT supports the following activities: initial phases of cooperative research projects, postdoctoral research fellowships abroad, seminars and workshops, and short-term scientific visits for planning cooperative research activities. Proposals may be submitted at any time.

For proposed research in the People's Republic of China, counterpart agency approval is usually required. Counterpart agencies include the Chinese Academy of Sciences, the Chinese Academy of Social Sciences, the National Science Foundation of China, and the State Education Commission. Other Chinese institutions may qualify. Call the East Asia and Pacific Program coordinator for information.

Typical grant size: The average grant is between $30,000 and $45,000 for two years. Grants are available for up to three years; the amount of the award depends on the duration of the proposed research.

Requirements: Standard NSF eligibility criteria apply. Note that proposals from any NSF-supported field are eligible; this excludes the humanities and biomedical and clinical sciences. INT strongly encourages the involvement of U.S. graduate and postdoctoral students in proposals submitted to the division. Proposals involving research in China may also be submitted to the relevant disciplinary program at NSF. Applicants should contact those programs directly.

U.S. Department of Education
Center for International Education
400 Maryland Avenue, SW
Washington, DC 20202-5331
Attn: Karla Ver Bryck Block
Telephone: 202-708-8763

Description: The Center for International Education (CIE) administers fellowships for pre- and postdoctoral scholarship in China and other countries.

Faculty Research Abroad Fellowship Program: This program offers opportunities to faculty members of institutions of higher education for research and study abroad to contribute to the development and improvement of the study of modern foreign languages and area studies.

Typical grant size: $6,000 to $960,000 for three to twelve months

Requirements: Candidates must be U.S. citizens or permanent residents. Candidates must be employed at an institution of higher learning and have been engaged in teaching relevant to their foreign language or area studies specialization for the two years immediately preceding the date of the award. Proposed research must be relevant to the modern foreign language or area studies specialization. The project must contribute to the development or improvement of the study of modern foreign languages or area studies in those fields essential to full understanding of the areas, regions, or countries in which those languages are commonly used. The project cannot be dissertation research for a Ph.D. Applicants must possess adequate skills in the language(s) necessary to carry out the project.

Doctoral Dissertation Research Abroad Fellowship Program: This program provides opportunities for graduate students to conduct full-time dissertation research abroad that contributes to the development and improvement of modern foreign languages and area studies.

Typical grant size: $3,000 to $60,000 for six to twelve months.

Requirements: Candidates must be U.S. citizens or permanent residents. Candidates must be graduate students in good standing at an institution of higher education and, when the fellowship period begins, have been admitted to candidacy in a doctoral degree program in modern foreign languages and area studies at that institution; they must be planning a teaching career in the United States upon graduation and possess adequate skills in the language(s) necessary to carry out the dissertation research project.

The World Bank
The Robert S. McNamara Fellowships Program
Room M-4029
World Bank Headquarters
1818 H Street, NW
Washington, DC 20433
Telephone: 202-473-6441

Description: Each year, the program awards approximately ten fellowships to support innovative and imaginative postgraduate research in areas of **economic development.** It does not support work toward an advanced degree (this includes field work for a Ph.D.). Fellowships are awarded for periods of 12 months, normally beginning July 1 and ending June 30 the following year. They cannot be extended or renewed.

Typical grant size: $25,000. Applicants may submit budgets up to $35,000; all budgets over the standard award are subject to negotiation.

Budgets may be supplemented by a flat $5,000 family allowance if family members accompany the fellow to the host country for six months or longer.

Requirements: Candidates must be nationals of World Bank member countries. Awards are not usually given to applicants over the age of 35. Applicants must hold an M.A. or equivalent at the time of application. Candidates for a Ph.D. at the time of application must have completed the degree by the program's initiation date in order to receive a fellowship.

Fellows must carry out their research under the auspices of an adviser in a host institution in a World Bank member country other than his/her own. Candidates are expected to make their own arrangements in connection with the project. Fellows are expected to have at least a working knowledge of the language spoken in the country in which they will carry out the research.

APPENDIX B

Language Study Programs in the People's Republic of China

The institutions listed below offer Chinese language study programs to individuals wanting to spend a summer, semester, or full year in the PRC. Some programs include cultural study and tours. Students are usually housed in dormitories and receive meals on campus. Fees, program dates, and eligibility requirements vary among programs. Students are advised to confirm with their home insitutions that program credit is transferable.

Inclusion in this list does not imply endorsement by the CSCC.

U.S. Institution	Chinese Institution(s)/Location
American Institute for Foreign Study 102 Greenwich Ave. Greenwich, CT 06830 Telephone: 800-727-AIFS 203-869-9090 FAX: 203-869-9615	Beijing Language Institute (BLI), Beijing
Boston University Division of International Programs 232 Bay State Rd. Boston, MA 02215 Telephone: 617-353-9888 FAX: 617-353-5402	Capital Normal University, Foreign Language Institute, Beijing

U.S. Institution	Chinese Institution(s)/Location
Brethren Colleges Abroad Manchester College Box 183 N. Manchester, IN 46962 Telephone: 219-982-5238 219-982-5025 FAX: 219-982-7755	Dalian University of Foreign Languages, Dalian
China Advocates 1635 Irving St. San Francisco, CA 94122 Telephone: 800-333-6474 415-665-4505 FAX: 415-753-0412	Peking University, Beijing Beijing Language Institute, Beijing
China Educational Tours 1110 Washington St. Lower Mills Boston, MA 02124 Telephone: 800-225-4262 617-296-0270 FAX: 617-296-6830	Capital Normal University, Foreign Language Institute, Beijing Harbin Institute of Technology, Harbin
Chinese Universities Exchange Program China Center University of Minnesota 50 Nicholson Hall 216 Pillsbury Drive, SE Minneapolis, MN 55455 Telephone: 612-624-1002 FAX: 612-625-0045	Fudan University, Shanghai Nankai University, Tianjin Peking University, Beijing
Chinese in Tianjin The Global Campus University of Minnesota 106 Nicholson Hall 216 Pillsbury Drive, SE Minneapolis, MN 55455 Telephone: 612-625-3379	Nankai University, Tianjin

U.S. Institution	Chinese Institution(s)/Location
The College of Staten Island/City University of New York (CUNY) Attn: Nanjing University Study Abroad Program Center for International Service North Admin. Bldg. #206 2800 Victory Blvd. Staten Island, NY 10314 Telephone: 718-982-2100 FAX: 718-982-2108	Nanjing University, Nanjing
Council on International Educational Exchange 205 E. 42nd St. New York, NY 10017 Telephone: 212-661-1414 FAX: 212-972-3231	Nanjing University, Nanjing Fudan University, Shanghai Peking University, Beijing
Duke Study in China Asian/Pacific Studies Institute Duke University 2111 Campus Drive Box 90411 Durham, NC 27708-0411 Telephone: 919-684-2604 FAX: 919-681-6247	Capital Normal University, Beijing Nanjing University, Nanjing
Hofstra University Summer Program in China 313 Calkins Hall Hempstead, NY 11550 Telephone: 516-463-5651	East China University, Shanghai
Institute of Asian Studies 223 West Ohio St. Chicago, IL 60610-4196 Telephone: 312-944-1750 FAX: 312-944-1448	Chinese Academy of Social Sciences, Beijing
NEH Fellowship Program Teachers K-12 Connecticut College 270 Mohegan Ave. New London, CT 06320 Telephone: 203-439-2282 FAX: 203-439-2700	Provides summer stipends to teachers with three years' experience to spend six weeks abroad studying foreign languages and cultures

U.S. Institution	Chinese Institution(s)/Location
Princeton in Beijing 211 Jones Hall Princeton University Princeton, NJ 08544-1008 Telephone: 609-258-4269 FAX: 609-258-6984	Beijing Normal University, Beijing
School for International Training College Semester Abroad Kipling Rd. P.O. Box 676 Brattleboro, VT 05302 Telephone: 800-336-1616 802-257-7751 FAX: 802-258-3296	Kunming Minorities Institute, Kunming Yunnan Teachers' University, Kunming
State University of New York (SUNY) at Albany Office of International Programs LI 84 Albany, NY 12222 Telephone: 518-442-3525 FAX: 518-442-3338	Fudan University, Shanghai Nankai University, Tianjin Nanjing University, Nanjing Peking University, Beijing

APPENDIX C

Colleges and Universities Accepting Direct Application from Foreign Students

INSTITUTIONS	TELEPHONE NUMBER	FAX NUMBER	CITY	POSTAL CODE
Beijing Language Institute	(1)2017585	(1)2017249	Beijing	100083
Peking U.	(1)2501230	(1)2564095	Beijing	100871
Renmin U. of China	(1)2566454	(1)2566152	Beijing	100872
Beijing Normal U.	(1)2016863	(1)2013929	Beijing	100875
Beijing Foreign Studies U.	(1)8422587	(1)8423144	Beijing	100081
Tsinghua U.	(1)2562504	(1)2568116	Beijing	100084
Beijing U. of Science & Technology	(1)2015565	(1)2017283	Beijing	100083
Northern Jiaotong U.	(1)3240341	(1)2255671	Beijing	100044
Beijing Institute of Posts & Telecommunications	(1)2013388	(1)2028643	Beijing	100088
Beijing Medical U.	(1)2017192	(1)2015681	Beijing	100083
Beijing College of Traditional Chinese Medicine	(1)4213458	(1)4220858	Beijing	100029
Central Institute of Fine Arts	(1)5134140	(1)5134140	Beijing	100730
Central Academy of Arts & Design	(1)5067964	(1)5022093	Beijing	100020
Central Academy of Drama	(1)4035626	(1)4035626	Beijing	100710
Central Conservatory of Music	(1)652585		Beijing	100031
Beijing Institute of Physical Education	(1)2562233	(1)2562363	Beijing	100084
Capital Normal U.	(1)8420845	(1)8416837	Beijing	100037
Beijing College of Economy	(1)5006091	(1)5001706	Beijing	100026
Beijing Institute of Commerce	(1)8417834	(1)8417834	Beijing	100037
Beijing Agricultural U.	(1)2582244	(1)2582332	Beijing	100094
U. of International Business & Economics	(1)4212022	(1)4212022	Beijing	100029

177

INSTITUTIONS	TELEPHONE NUMBER	FAX NUMBER	CITY	POSTAL CODE
China U. of Politics & Law	(1)2012096	(1)9746023	Beijing	100088
Beijing Second Foreign Languages Institute	(1)5762520	(1)5762520	Beijing	100024
Beijing Film Academy	(1)2013876	(1)2012132	Beijing	100088
Beijing Teachers College of Foreign Languages	(1)8328166	(1)8328166	Beijing	100037
Central Institute for Nationalities	(1)8327349	(1)8327352	Beijing	100081
Beijing U. of Technology	(1)7714088	(1)7714088	Beijing	100022
Beijing U. of Agricultural Engineering	(1)2017260	(1)2016320	Beijing	100083
Beijing College of Acupuncture and Orthopedics	(1)4361227	(1)5006782	Beijing	100015
China Academy of Traditional Medicine	(1)4016387	(1)4016387	Beijing	100700
Nankai U.	(22)344200	(22)344853	Tianjin	300071
Tianjin U.	(22)358744	(22)358706	Tianjin	300072
Tianjin Foreign Languages Institute	(22)312410	(22)312410	Tianjin	300204
Tianjin College of Traditional Chinese Medicine	(22)716845	(22)716842	Tianjin	300193
Tianjin Institute of Light Industry	(22)841803	(22)841536	Tianjin	300222
Tianjin Normal U.	(22)351206	(22)358494	Tianjin	300074
Tianjin U. of Commerce	(22)673169	(22)673169	Tianjin	300400
Fudan U.	(21)5483962	(21)5491669	Shanghai	200433
East China Normal U.	(21)2570590	(21)2570590	Shanghai	200062
Tongji U.	(21)5458933	(21)5458965	Shanghai	200092
Shanghai U. of Technology	(21)6626286	(21)6635364	Shanghai	200072
East China U. of Science & Technology	(21)4394280	(21)4703678	Shanghai	200237
China Textile U.	(21)2594553	(21)2518971	Shanghai	200051
Shanghai U. of Science & Technology	(21)9528926	(21)9529932	Shanghai	201800
Shanghai Medical U.	(21)4372396	(21)4330543	Shanghai	200032
Shanghai Second Medical U.	(21)3287078	(21)3202916	Shanghai	200025
Shanghai College of Traditional Chinese Medicine	(21)4398290	(21)4398290	Shanghai	200032
Shanghai Conservatory of Music	(21)4330536	(21)4330866	Shanghai	200031
Shanghai International Studies U.	(21)5318882	(21)5313756	Shanghai	200083
Shanghai Normal U.	(21)4700700	(21)4339150	Shanghai	200234
East China Institute of Politics & Law	(21)2512190		Shanghai	200042

INSTITUTIONS	TELEPHONE NUMBER	FAX NUMBER	CITY	POSTAL CODE
College of Liberal Arts of Shanghai U.	(21)5428133	(21)5428133	Shanghai	200434
Shanghai Academy of Drama	(21)2512920	(21)2512646	Shanghai	200040
Shanghai Institute of Physical Education	(21)5485546	(21)5490649	Shanghai	200433
Shanghai Second Institute of Education	(21)5483915		Shanghai	200433
Shanghai Jiaotong U.	(21)4310310	(21)4731562	Shanghai	200030
Shanghai U. of Engineering & Technology	(21)2759779	(21)2518511	Shanghai	200335
Shanghai Institute of Mechanical Engineering	(21)5433040	(21)5431258	Shanghai	200093
Shanghai Institute of Education	(21)4330179		Shanghai	200031
Nanjing U.	(25)300550	(25)316747	Nanjing	210008
Nanjing Normal U.	(25)303666	(25)307448	Nanjing	210024
Southeast U.	(25)714233	(25)714212	Nanjing	210018
Wuxi Institute of Light Industry	(510)606751	(510)607976	Wuxi	214036
China Pharmaceutical U.	(25)636020	(25)302827	Nanjing	210009
Nanjing College of Traditional Chinese Medicine	(25)649121	(25)741323	Nanjing	210029
Hohai U.	(25)631000	(25)315375	Nanjing	210024
Jiangnan U.	(510)668761	(510)601668	Wuxi	214063
Yangzhou Teachers College	(514)430011		Yangzhou	225002
Nanjing U. of Science & Technology	(25)432727	(25)431622	Nanjing	210014
China Institute of Mining & Technology	(516)880922	(516)888640	Xuzhou	221008
Jiangsu Junior College of Commerce	(514)348499		Yangzhou	225001
Jiangsu Institute of Technology	(511)424071	(511)421739	Zhenjiang	212013
Xuzhou Teachers College	(516)335547	(516)335547	Xuzhou	221009
Suzhou U.	(512)221028	(512)771918	Suzhou	215006
Zhejiang U.	(571)572244	(571)523315	Hangzhou	310027
Zhejiang Agricultural U.	(571)641053	(571)774636	Hangzhou	310029
Zhejiang Academy of Fine Arts	(571)779585	(571)770039	Hangzhou	310062
Hangzhou U.	(571)871224	(571)870107	Hangzhou	310028
Zhejiang College of Traditional Chinese Medicine	(571)746914		Hangzhou	310009
Zhejiang Medical U.	(571)722700	(571)771571	Hangzhou	310006
Wuhan U.	(27)722712	(27)712661	Wuhan	430072

INSTITUTIONS	TELEPHONE NUMBER	FAX NUMBER	CITY	POSTAL CODE
Huazhong U. of Science and Technology	(27)701541	(27)700063	Wuhan	430074
Wuhan Institute of Water Transportation Engineering	(27)611694	(27)614406	Wuhan	430063
China U. of Geosciences (Wuhan)	(27)702136	(27)701763	Wuhan	430074
Tongji Medical U.	(27)558920	(27)558920	Wuhan	430030
Hubei Medical College	(27)721495	(27)716966	Wuhan	430077
Central China Normal U.	(27)715696	(27)716070	Wuhan	430070
Central China Agricultural U.	(27)715057	(27)715057	Wuhan	430070
Hubei College of Traditional Chinese Medicine	(27)741051	(27)874738	Wuhan	430061
Central South Institute for Nationalities	(27)701741	(27)701223	Wuhan	430074
Hubei U.	(27)611903	(27)614263	Wuhan	430062
Jianghan U.	(27)271208	(27)271533	Wuhan	430010
Wuhan Institute of Physical Education	(27)703496	(27)702806	Wuhan	430070
Zhongshan U.	(20)4425465	(20)4429173	Guangzhou	510275
Sun Yat-sen U. of Medical Sciences	(20)7778223	(20)7765679	Guangzhou	510089
Guangzhou College of Traditional Chinese Medicine	(20)6661233	(20)6664735	Guangzhou	510407
South China Agricultural U.	(20)5511299	(20)5511393	Guangzhou	510642
Wuyi U.	(750)352112	(750)354323	Wuyi	529042
Shenzhen U.	(755)6661940	(755)6660642	Shenzhen	518060
South China Normal U.	(20)7501131	(20)5516011	Guangzhou	510631
Guangzhou Academy of Fine Arts	(20)4429572	(20)4428460	Guangzhou	510261
Guangzhou Institute of Foreign Languages	(20)6627595	(20)6627367	Guangzhou	510421
Shantou U.	(754)221123	(754)221120	Shantou	515063
Jinan U.	(20)5516395	(20)5516941	Guangzhou	510632
South China U. of Science & Technology	(20)5516862	(20)5516386	Guangzhou	510641
Shandong U.	(531)803860	(531)802167	Jinan	250100
Shandong Teachers U.	(531)267711	(531)266954	Jinan	250014
Shandong College of Traditional Chinese Medicine	(531)266901	(531)658823	Jinan	250014
Qingdao U.	(532)515944		Qingdao	266071
Qingdao U. of Oceanography	(532)283461	(532)268735	Qingdao	266003
Yantai U.	(535)248995		Yantai	264005
Yantai Normal U.	(535)246451		Yantai	264000
Xiamen U.	(592)286211	(592)286402	Xiamen	361005

INSTITUTIONS	TELEPHONE NUMBER	FAX NUMBER	CITY	POSTAL CODE
Fuzhou U.	(591)713229	(591)713866	Fuzhou	350002
Huaqiao U.	(595)226991	(595)226969	Quanzhou	362001
Fujian College of Traditional Medicine	(591)572528	(591)572524	Fuzhou	350003
Fujian Normal U.	(591)442840	(591)442840	Fuzhou	350007
Sichuan U.	(28)582844	(28)582844	Chengdu	610064
Chengdu U. of Science and Technology	(28)581554	(28)582670	Chengdu	610065
Chengdu Geological College	(28)334712	(28)334963	Chengdu	610059
Chengdu College of Traditional Chinese Medicine	(28)784542	(28)763471	Chengdu	610075
Southwest Institute for Nationalities	(28)583730	(28)589294	Chengdu	610041
Sichuan Normal U.	(28)442612		Chengdu	610066
Sichuan International Studies U.	(811)811875	(811)811875	Chongqing	630031
Sichuan Agricultural U.	(835)2278		Ya'an	625041
Chongqing U.	(811)964893	(811)966656	Chongqing	630044
Southwest Normal U.	(811)863805	(811)863805	Chongqing	630715
Guangxi Medical College	(771)201477	(771)204553	Nanning	530027
Guangxi Agricultural College	(771)333381	(771)204177	Nanning	530005
Guangxi Normal U.	(773)225850	(773)442383	Guilin	541001
Guilin Medical College	(773)222914		Guilin	541001
Guangxi U.	(771)332391	(771)332391	Nanning	530001
Guangxi College of Traditional Chinese Medicine	(771)335812		Nanning	530001
Guangxi Institute for Nationalities	(771)334141	(771)229052	Nanning	530006
Guangxi Teachers College	(771)332288 ext. 343		Nanning	530001
Liaoning U.	(24)643356	(24)652421	Shenyang	110036
Northeast Institute of Technology	(24)391829	(24)391829	Shenyang	110006
Dalian Maritime Institute	(411)4671611	(411)4671395	Dalian	116024
China Medical U.	(24)365197	(24)375539	Shenyang	110001
Liaoning Normal U.	(411)4601181	(411)4606394	Dalian	116022
Dalian Institute of Foreign Languages	(411)2803121	(411)2639958	Dalian	116601
Liaoning College of Traditional Chinese Medicine	(24)661407		Shenyang	110032
Shenyang Teachers College	(24)647147		Shenyang	110031
Shenyang Institute of Civil Engineering & Architecture	(24)383215		Shenyang	110015
Fuxin Mining Institute	(418)223977		Fuxin	123000
Northeast U. of Finance & Economics	(411)4691811	(411)4691862	Dalian	116023

INSTITUTIONS	TELEPHONE NUMBER	FAX NUMBER	CITY	POSTAL CODE
Dalian U. of Science				
& Technology	(411)4671616	(411)4671009	Dalian	116024
Jilin U.	(431)825787	(431)823907	Changchun	130021
Jilin U. of Technology	(431)682351	(431)688902	Changchun	130025
Changchun College of				
Geology	(431)828327	(431)824087	Changchun	130026
Changchun U.	(431)687435		Changchun	130022
Yanbian U.	(433)515921	(433)519618	Yanbian	133002
Changchun College of Traditional				
Chinese Medicine	(431)58760	(431)683463	Changchun	130021
Northeast Normal U.	(431)685722	(431)684009	Changchun	130024
Norman Bethune U. of				
Medical Science	(431)644739	(431)644739	Changchun	130021
Heilongjiang U.	(451)62786	(451)65470	Harbin	150080
Heilongjiang Institute				
of Commerce	(451)403227	(451)401086	Harbin	150076
Heilongjiang College of Traditional				
Chinese Medicine	(451)232786	(451)232786	Harbin	150040
Harbin Institute of Shipbuilding				
Engineering	(451)340010	(451)340010	Harbin	150001
Harbin Normal U.	(451)65015	(451)65382	Harbin	150080
Harbin Inst. of Technology	(451)343436	(451)321048	Harbin	150006
Harbin U. of Science				
and Technology	(451)61080	(451)61849	Harbin	150080
Daqing Petroleum Institute	(453)881741		Harbin	151400
Xi'an Institute of Highway				
Transportation	(29)754024	(29)751532	Xi'an	710061
Xi'an Jiaotong U.	(29)335011	(29)334716	Xi'an	710049
Northwest U.	(29)712323	(29)712323	Xi'an	710069
Shanxi Normal U	(29)751391	(29)751391	Xi'an	710062
Xi'an United U. Xi'an				
Teachers College	(29)751308		Xi'an	710061
Xi'an Foreign				
Languages Institute	(29)751133	(29)751350	Xi'an	710062
Xi'an Conservatory of				
Music	(29)752340		Xi'an	710062
Hebei Normal U.	(311)649759		Shijiazhuang	050016
Henan U.	(378)551029	(378)551029	Zhengzhou	475001
Zhengzhou U.	(371)773895	(371)773895	Zhengzhou	450052
Luoyang U.	(379)338966		Luoyang	471000
Luoyang Institute				
of Technology	(379)413632	(379)413632	Luoyang	471039
Shanxi U.	(351)740908	(351)740981	Taiyuan	030006
Lanzhou U.	(931)413355	(931)485096	Lanzhou	730000
Anhui Normal U.	(553)335966	(553)339452	Wuhu	241000

INSTITUTIONS	TELEPHONE NUMBER	FAX NUMBER	CITY	POSTAL CODE
Anhui U.	(551)337832		Hefei	230039
U. of Science and Technology of China	(551)331134	(551)332579	Hefei	230026
Qinghai Institute of Education	(971)53291		Xining	810008
Jiangxi College of Traditional Chinese Medicine	(791)223131	(791)216708	Nanchang	330006
Jiangxi Institute of Education	(791)331833		Nanchang	330029
Inner Mongolia U.	(471)43141		Huhehot	010022
Inner Mongolia Normal U.	(471)41291		Huhehot	010022
Inner Mongolia College of Agriculture & Animal Husbandry	(471)44746		Huhehot	010018
Ningxia U.	(951)76301 ext. 519		Yinchuan	750021
Xinjiang U.	(991)265202		Urumchi	830046
Xinjiang Institute of Technology	(991)441369		Urumchi	830008
Xinjiang Normal U.	(991)412513		Urumchi	830053
Xinjiang August First Agricultural College	(991)247150		Urumchi	830000
Xinjiang Academy of Arts	(991)266464		Urumchi	830001
Kashi Teachers College	(998)22302		Kashi	844000
Yunnan U.	(871)5151187	(871)5153832	Kunming	650091
Yunnan Institute for Nationalities	(871)5154308	(871)5154308	Kunming	650031
Yunnan Normal U.	(871)5152910	(871)5153804	Kunming	650092
Yunnan Institute of Education	(871)5153987	(871)5151503	Kunming	650031
Kunming Medical College	(871)8182571	(871)8182571	Kunming	653301
Hainan Teachers College	(898)884241		Haikou	571158
Guizhou U.	(851)551187	(851)551381	Guiyang	550025

APPENDIX D

General Guidelines for Direct Application to a Chinese College or University as a Self-Sponsored Student and Excerpts from "Regulations Concerning the Admission of Foreign Students in Chinese Schools (1986)"

GENERAL GUIDELINES FOR DIRECT APPLICATION TO A CHINESE COLLEGE OR UNIVERSITY AS A SELF-SPONSORED STUDENT

Adapted from *Study in China*, The Chinese National Society of Universities and Colleges for Foreign Student Affairs, Beijing Language and Culture University Press, March 1993.

Categories of Foreign Students Eligible for Admission

A. Undergraduates: The applicant should be at least equivalent of a graduate of senior middle school (high school) in China. He/she should be 25 years of age or younger. The program lasts from four to six years.

B. Candidates for a Master's Degree: The applicant must come to China and pass the entrance exam for the master's program at the institution to which he/she is assigned. If the applicant has been graduated with honors from a Chinese institution of higher education and wishes to work for an advanced degree at the same school, he/she may, upon recommendation by his/her department, be approved for the degree program without examinations. The applicant should be 35 years of age or younger. The program lasts from two to three years.

C. Candidates for a Doctorate Degree: The applicant must be recommended by two of his/her professors and approved for the doctoral program by the institution to which he/she has been assigned. The

184

applicant should be 40 years of age or younger. The program lasts from two to three years.

D. General advanced students: The applicant should have completed at least two years of undergraduate studies in China or abroad, and should intend to continue studying in China a subject in which he/she already has some background (except for those wishing to study elementary Chinese). The applicant should be 35 years of age or younger. The program lasts from one to two years.

E. Senior advanced students: The applicant should have at least the equivalent of the Chinese master's degree or be a candidate for a doctorate degree in another country. The student pursues advanced study independently under the direction of Chinese tutors. He/she should be 45 years of age or younger. The program generally lasts one year.

Application Procedures

Self-sponsored students who are not applying under an institution-to-institution agreement may send their applications directly to the university to which they are applying. Applicants should submit the following materials:

(1) Completed "Application Form for Foreigners Wishing to Study in China."

(2) Health Certificate, completed by a medical doctor after a physical examination of the applicant. The form should bear a seal of a clinic or a hospital. Those who fail to meet the health requirements will not be admitted to study in China. Anyone who fails to meet the requirements come to China will be asked to leave the country within a month at his/her own expense.

(3) Duplicated copies of notarized diploma or certificate and school-certified transcript of complete academic records, in English or Chinese, or with a translation in English or Chinese.

(4) Master's and doctoral degree candidates must submit recommendation letters from at least two professors or associate professors (or people holding equivalent titles). Advanced students intending to pursue studies in the fine arts may be required to submit the following additional materials (check with institution):

Art history: copy of an original term paper or other substantial piece of work on some aspect of art history;

Graphic arts: three original pieces, or color photographs of six samples of the applicant's work;

Music (performance): 30-minute tape recording of vocal or instrumental performance;

Music (composition): copy of an original composition.

(5) Undergraduates in fine arts may be required to submit the same material as above except that:
— no letter of recommendation from teachers is required;
— students of art history may submit a shorter criticism or commentary on some aspect of art history.

Application Deadlines

These may vary among institutions. In general, applications for fall term admission should be submitted between March 1 and May 31; applications for spring term admission should be submitted between October 1 and November 30.

Entrance Examinations

A. Undergraduates in liberal arts and general advanced students need not take entrance examinations. The admission decision will be based on the applicant's academic record. Undergraduates in the sciences, engineering, agriculture, and medicine are typically required to take standard examinations in basic mathematics, physics, and chemistry. Those intending to study management are required to take an examination in basic mathematics.

B. Candidates for graduate degrees must first come to China as advanced students. Candidates for master's degrees must take written examinations in subjects required by the school in question (except for foreign languages and political studies). Candidates for doctoral degrees will be examined orally by faculty members. Those who fail such examinations may nevertheless be permitted to stay on as advanced students at a level suited to their academic background. If they are recipients of Chinese government scholarships, the amount of their allowances will be reduced accordingly.

C. After enrollment, senior advanced students will be evaluated by their tutors on their subject knowledge. Those who do not meet the requirements must change their status to that of general advanced students. If they are recipients of Chinese government scholarships, the amount of their allowances will be reduced accordingly.

Elementary Chinese and Preparatory Courses

A. Students without adequate knowledge of Chinese are required to study the language and pass an examination in it before taking up their specialties. Undergraduates in Chinese language and literature, Chinese history, Chinese philosophy, history of Chinese art and Chinese medicine are required to take a two-year course in elementary Chinese. Undergraduates and advanced students in the sciences, engineering, or other specialties are required to take a one-year course in elementary Chinese.

General advanced students studying liberal arts who have attained an adequate level of competence in Chinese may enter their schools directly. Supplementary language courses will be organized for them by their schools as necessary.

Senior advanced students studying liberal arts and candidates for advanced degrees should have attained a higher level of competence in Chinese and be able to use it in pursuing study and research in their special fields.

B. Students in mathematics, physics, and chemistry whose examination scores fall below the minimum requirements for admission may apply for a one year preparatory course in those subjects. Those who pass the final course examinations will be promoted to undergraduate classes; those who fail will be asked to withdraw.

The time spent in preparatory courses does not count toward the length of specialized studies.

Expenses Borne by Self-Supporting Students

A. Before coming to China, foreign students providing their own financial support must have a financial guarantor and must make sure that they have adequate resources to pay all expenses during the period of their studies here. All expenses must be paid in cash. School fees for tuition and housing are calculated in U.S. dollars and are to be paid after conversion into Foreign Exchange Certificates (FEC), according to the exchange rates of February 1 and September 1 of the year in which payments are made.*

(1) Tuition fees for one academic year are as follows:

Students in the liberal arts
— Undergraduates and general advanced
students: US$1,500-3,000
— Master's degree candidates: US$2,000-3,500
— Senior advanced students: US$2,500-4,000
— Doctoral degree candidates: US$2,500-4,000

Students in the sciences, engineering,
agriculture, medicine, sport, and fine arts
— Undergraduates: US$2,000-3,500
— General advanced students: US$2,000-3,500
— Master's degree candidates: US$2,500-4,000
— Senior advanced students: US$2,500-4,500
— Doctoral degree candidates: US$4,000-6,000

---

*Since the Chinese government stopped issuing FEC, many schools have requested payment in U.S. dollars.—Ed.

(2) Expenses for housing, teaching materials, and food are as follows. Housing expenses are US$2-3 per bed per day for a double room in the school dormitory, with two students sharing one room and using a common lavatory and bath. Teaching materials cost between US$30 and $50 per year for schools of liberal arts and are a bit higher for schools of science, engineering, agriculture, medicine, sport, and art. Food costs between US$40 and $60 per month in the foreign students' cafeteria, and between US$20 and $30 per month in the Chinese students' cafeteria.

(3) Students are responsible for the costs of board, medical care, textbooks, and class handouts. They are also responsible for expenses for additional laboratory work, field work, and field trips which are not related to the teaching program, as well as the other expenses for transfer from one school to another.

(4) Students who fall ill during their studies in China may consult doctors in the school clinics who will refer them to outside hospitals for treatment, if necessary.

C. Tuition is payable in two parts, half at the beginning of each term. Students who fail to pay tuition at the specified time will not be allowed to register. In special cases, a student may apply to the school authorities for permission to delay payment. However, payment may not be delayed beyond one month after the beginning of the term, and a penalty will be charged for late payment in the amount of five percent of the total tuition for one term.

Students who stay at school for more than one term but less than a full academic year pay tuition for the entire academic year.

If, before the end of the term, a student transfers to another school for reasons not the responsibility of the Chinese, he/she will receive no refund of tuition, and no payments may be transferred to the new school. The student must pay tuition to the new school.

Housing expenses are also to be paid at the beginning of each term. However, if this creates a hardship for a student, with the approval of the school authorities, he/she may make monthly payments instead.

Students who terminate or suspend their studies, or who withdraw from school before the end of a term, must pay housing expenses only for the number of days they have actually lived in the dormitory.

The following sections are excerpted from "Regulations Concerning the Admission of Foreign Students in Chinese Schools (1986)," issued by the Bureau of Foreign Affairs of the State Education Commission of the PRC.

Academic Programs and Evaluations (Article VI)

A. All foreign students are expected to study hard, observe discipline and complete course work prescribed for them by their schools and teachers.

B. In principle, students are not permitted to transfer from one school to another, or to change either the subject or the duration of study that was agreed upon at the time of admission. In special cases, however, such changes may be approved by the Commission. For a change of subject, an application should be filed with the Commission before November 1 of the year in which the student is first enrolled, through the diplomatic mission or representative of the sponsoring organization in China of his/her country or through the sponsor in his/her home country. For extension of duration of study, an application should be filed with the Commission before March 1 of the year when the student is due to leave.

C. Undergraduates should, in principle, follow the regular academic program established by the school. If necessary, the school authorities will make adjustments in the student's program. Candidates for advanced degrees should, in principle, follow the same program as the Chinese students. General advanced students should follow the program originally agreed to; no tutors are allocated to them. Senior advanced students mainly study independently, with periodic guidance from the tutors assigned to them.

D. Schools are responsible for arranging field trips, field work and laboratory work in accordance with the needs of the academic programs. Students must observe the relevant regulations when they need to use reference books, archives and other materials.

E. With the exception of senior advanced students, who will receive written evaluations of their work from their tutors, all other students will be evaluated on the basis of their class work and of examinations taken at the end of each term. The schools will commend or reward those who excel in their studies and so notify their sponsors, if any. The sponsors may ask the school authorities for academic records of the students they are sponsoring.

F. Undergraduates who, in one academic year, fail a total of three subjects or two major subjects after taking make-up examinations are required to repeat the grade in question. They are allowed to repeat a grade no more than twice and to repeat the same grade only once.

Candidates for advanced degrees who fail in their examinations or thesis defense are allowed to extend the period of their studies in accordance with regulations formulated by the Chinese government.

General advanced students who fail in their final examinations for the academic year will be asked to withdraw from school. Schools using credit systems should follow relevant regulations.

Academic Degrees and Certificates (Article XI)

A. Undergraduates and candidates for a Master's degree who pass the examinations at the end of their studies will receive certificates and, in accordance with the *Regulations of the People's Republic of China for Conferring Academic Degrees*, the Bachelor's and Master's degrees respectively. Candidates for a Doctoral degree who pass the final examinations and the thesis defense will be awarded Doctoral degrees. Those who fail such examinations will receive certificates of completion of studies.

General advanced students and senior advanced students who have completed the required work will receive certificates of advanced study. No degrees will be conferred upon them.

B. Students who withdraw from school before completing their programs will be issued certificates indicating the period of time during which they have studied.

C. Foreign students should leave China within 15 days after their graduation or conclusion of studies.

Class Attendance, Suspension of Studies, Withdrawal from Studies, Disciplinary Action (Article VII)

A. Foreign students are expected to attend classes regularly and are not allowed to be absent without valid reasons. If they are ill or have a special need to be absent, they should ask for leave in accordance with the school regulations.

B. Foreign students should abide by the academic calendar of the school in which they are enrolled. Chinese schools do not observe the national holidays or other festivals of foreign countries. However, on such occasions a foreign student concerned may, on request, be granted a leave of absence. Foreign students must not ask for leave to travel as tourists while school is in session.

C. A student who takes a leave of absence for more than two months at a time and cannot catch up with classes upon his/her return will be asked to suspend studies or to repeat the term. This must be done no later than the next academic year.

A student who is absent from class too often without valid reason will be subject to disciplinary action in accordance with the regulations of the school. In serious cases, he/she may be asked to withdraw from school.

A student who has an extended illness, or who is absent too often, or whose academic record is not satisfactory will be asked by the school authority to suspend study or to withdraw. The diplomatic mission and representative of the sponsoring organization in China of the student's country, or his/her sponsor at home, if any, will be notified of the action in writing.

If, for any reason, a foreign student wishes to suspend studies or to withdraw, or if the government or organizational sponsor decided to recall its students from China, the diplomatic mission in China of the student's country, or his/her organizational sponsor should submit a formal request to the Commission or to the school authorities.

D. A student who breaches the discipline of his/her school, damages public property, fights with others or behaves in other unacceptable ways will be subject to disciplinary action by the school authorities. According to the circumstances and gravity of the offense, the student will be given a warning, a serious warning, or a demerit recording, be placed on probation, asked to withdraw or be expelled from school.

If a student on one year probation has clearly improved his/her conduct during the probation period, the disciplinary action against him/her may be rescinded. If a student fails to improve his/her conduct while on probation, he/she will be asked to withdraw from school.

When the school authorities take disciplinary action against a student, they will inform the student and also send written notification of the action to the diplomatic mission or representative of the sponsoring organization of the student's country in China, or to the student's sponsor at home.

Observance of Chinese Laws (Article VIII)

A. Foreign students must obey the laws and decrees of the Chinese government, abide by the rules and regulations of their schools and respect Chinese ways and customs.

B. Foreign students coming to study in China should have ordinary passports. Before starting school, bearers of diplomatic, service or special passports should go through certain special procedures at Chinese public security departments and submit to them necessary documents issued by their countries' diplomatic missions or representatives of their sponsoring organization in China. Such students will not enjoy diplomatic or other privileges during their studies in China.

C. Within a short period of time after their arrival in China, foreign students must obtain residence permits from their local public security departments.

When a foreign student wishes to travel to other countries, tour the Hong Kong and Macao regions, or return home for any reason, the diplomatic mission or representative of the sponsoring organization of his/her country in China should give written notification to the school ten days in advance, if possible. With the approval of the school, the student should go to the local public security department to apply for the necessary exit and reentry visas.

When a foreign student wishes to visit an area of China to which foreigners may gain access only with permission, he/she must apply to the local public security department for a travel permit.

D. Foreign students must observe the Chinese customs regulations concerning materials to be taken out of China or mailed abroad. The following items are allowable: textbooks, class handouts and related materials issued to them by the school, study notes, photographs and audiovisual materials related to study. Any materials issued by the school which are not intended for outside circulation must be approved for exit by the school authorities, who will provide the student with an itemized certificate of authorization to present to the customs officer.

E. Foreign students who have violated Chinese laws and regulations, endangered China's national security, disturbed public order or harmed the interests of others will be punished by the Chinese public security and judicial departments according to law.

Extracurricular and Holiday Activities (Article X)

A. Foreign students may take part in the activities organized by the student association of their schools, as well as in the athletic and recreational activities of the Chinese students. They may join the various athletic and performing arts groups of their schools. They may also, if they wish, take part in activities organized by the Chinese to mark major holidays. Normal and friendly contacts between foreign students and Chinese teachers, students and people in general are encouraged.

B. If foreign students wish to organize activities in their school to celebrate their national days and major national festivals, they must obtain the approval of the school authorities. They must observe the rules and regulations of their schools in this connection.

C. Foreign students on Chinese government scholarships may join trips organized by schools during winter and summer vacations; every other year, the school will bear a portion of the expense for their travel and lodging. The schools will likewise pay parts of the expense for those scholarship students who are pursuing advanced studies for at least one academic year but less than two.

All self-supporting students and scholarship students who are pursuing advanced studies for less than one academic year may join these tours at their own expense.

APPENDIX E

Visa Application for Foreigners Wishing to Study in China

外国留学人员来华签证申请表
Visa Application for Foreigners Wishing to Study in China

中华人民共和国国家教育委员会印制/Printed by State Education Commission (SEDC) of PRC   JW201

No.	接受院校/Sponsored Institution:	

	姓名: 姓/Family Name 名/Given Names Name:		
由 接 受 留 学 人 员 院 校 填 写	国籍/Nationality:	护照号码/Passport No.:	婚否/Marital Status:
	出生日期: 年 月 日 Date of Birth: year month day		出生地点/Place of Birth:
	通讯地址/Mailing Address:		
	最后学历/Highest Academic Degree Obtained:		职业/Occupation:
	工作或学习单位/Employer or School Affiliated:		
	来华学习专业/Field of Study in China:	学习专业期限:自 年 月至 年 月 Duration: from yr. mo. to yr. mo.	
	汉语预备院校/School for Supplementary Chinese:	汉语预备期限:自 年 月至 年 月 Duration: from yr. mo. to yr. mo.	
	学生类别/Student Status:	注册截止日期/Deadline for Registration:	
	经费办法/Financial Support: 全额奖学金/Full Scholarship ☐; 部分奖学金/Partial Scholarship (学费/Tuition ☐, 住宿费/Lodging ☐, 医疗费/Medical Care ☐ 教材费/Learning Material ☐); 其他/Other Source of Funding:		

国
家
教
委
签
证
审
核
盖
章
	Authorized by SEDC for X Visa
	
	(印章/Seal)
	
	199 年 月 日
	       yr. mo. day
		申请人签字:
		Signature of Applicant:
		
		199 年 月 日
		       yr. mo. day

备 注	1、此表用于办理国家计划内接受外国留学人员来华签证使用. 2、被中国高等院校录取的外国留学人员持本表前往中国使（领）馆申请来华学习签证. 3、来华入学者凭此表到校注册。超过注册日期，无校方延长允许，此表失效. Notes: 1. This form is to be used by SEDC sponsored foreign students only. 2. Foreign student who has been admitted by a Chinese university can use this form to apply for student entry visa (X visa) at the Chinese embassy or consulate. 3. Foreign student must present this form to the Chinese university at the time of registration. Those forms which exceed the time limit without the permission of the university, will be invalid.

第一联: 寄外国来华留学人员

194

APPENDIX F

The People's Republic of China Visa Application Form

中 華 人 民 共 和 國
THE PEOPLE'S REPUBLIC OF CHINA

簽 證 申 請 表
VISA APPLICATION FORM

1. 姓 _____ 名 _____ 中文姓名 _____
   Surname (Last name)   Given name   In Chinese (if any)

   請貼照片
   Stick Photo Here

2. 國籍 _____ 出生日期 _____ 年 ___ 月 ___ 日   性別 ___
   Nationality   Date of Birth   Yr   mth   day   Sex

3. 出生地點 _____ 職業 _____
   Place of birth   Occupation

4. 護照種類 _____ 號碼 _____ 有效期至 _____ 年 ___ 月 ___ 日
   Passport Type   No.   Valid until   Yr   mth   day

5. 工作處所 _____ 電話號碼 _____
   Place of work   Tel. No.

6. 家庭住所 _____ 電話號碼 _____
   Home address   Tel. No.

7. 來中國事由 _____ 邀請單位 _____
   Purpose of Journey   Host unit in China (for business only)

8. 離美日期 _____ 擬入境日期 _____
   Date of departure from U.S.A.   Intended date of entry

9. 擬在中國停留期限 _____ 入境後前往地點 _____
   Duration of stay in China   Places to visit in China

10. 在華親友(此項只需探親者填寫) _____
    Relatives or friends in China, if any

    與申請人
    的關系
    Relationship
    to applicant

姓名 Name	國籍 Nationality	職業及住址 Occupation and address	

我保證以上填寫的全部內容屬實.
I guarantee that the statement given above is true and correct.

申請人簽字 _____ 填寫日期 _____
Applicant's signature   Date of application

備註 _____
Remarks

195

APPENDIX G

Physical Examination Record for Foreigners

外 国 人 体 格 检 查 记 录

PHYSICAL EXAMINATION RECORD FOR FOREIGNER

姓 名 Name		性别 Sex	□男 Male □女 Female	出 生 日 期 Birth Day-Month-Year		照 片 （加盖检查 单位印章） Photo stamped Offical Stamp）
现在通讯地址 Present mailing address					血 型 Blood type	
国 籍 Nationality		出生地址 Birth Place				

过去是否患有下列疾病：（每项后面请回答"否"或"是"）
Have you ever had any of the following diseases?
(Each item must be answered "Yes"or"No")

斑 疹 伤 寒 Typhus fever	□No□Yes	菌 痢 Bacillary dysentery	□No□Yes
小儿麻痹症 Poliomyelitis	□No□Yes	布氏杆菌病 Brucellosis	□No□Yes
白 喉 Diphtheria	□No□Yes	病毒性肝炎 Viral hepatitis	□No□Yes
猩 红 热 Scarlet fever	□No□Yes	产褥期链球 Puerperal streptococcus infection	
回 归 热 Relapsing fever	□No□Yes	菌 感 染	□No□Yes
伤寒和付伤寒 Typhoid and paratyphoid fever		□No□Yes	
流行性脑脊髓膜炎 Epidemic cerebrospinal meningitis		□No□Yes	

是否患有下列危及公共秩序和安全的病症：（每项后面请回答"否"或"是"）
Do you have any of the following diseases or disorders endangering the pubic order and security?(Each item must be answered "Yes"or"No")

毒物瘾 Toxicomania·· □No□Yes
精神错乱 Mental confusion·· □No□Yes
精神病 Psychosis：躁狂型 Manic Psychosis ························· □No□Yes
　　　　妄想型 Paranoid psychosis ································· □No□Yes
　　　　幻觉型 Hallucinatory psychosis ····························· □No□Yes

身高 Height	厘米 cm	体重 Weight	公斤 kg	血压 Blood pressure	毫米汞柱 mmHg
发育情况 Development		营养情况 Nourishment		颈部 Neck	
视 力 左 L——————— Vision 右 R		矫正视力 左 L——————— Corrected vision 右 R		眼 Eyes	
辨色力 Colour sense		皮肤 Skin		淋巴结 Lymph nodes	
耳 Ears		鼻 Nose		扁桃体 Tonsils	
心 Heart		肺 Lungs		腹部 Abdomen	

绢号：42(19×27cm)

脊 柱 Spine		四 肢 Extremities		神经系统 Nervous system	
其它所见 Other abnormal findings					
胸 部 X 线 检 查 结 果 （附检查报告单） Chest X-ray exam (attached chest X-ray report)		心电图 ECG			
化 验 室 检 查 （包括艾滋病、梅 毒等血清学检查） Laboratory exam (Attached test report of AIDS, Syphilis etc)					

未发现患有下列检疫传染病和危害公共健康的疾病：
None of the following diseases or disorders found during the present examination.

霍　乱　Cholera	性　病　Venereal Disease
黄热病　Yellow fever	肺结核　lung tuberculosis
鼠　疫　Plague	艾滋病　AIDS
麻　风　Leprosy	精神病　Psychosis

意　　　见 Suggestion	检查单位盖章 Official Stamp
医师签字 Signature of physician	日期 Date

APPENDIX H

Organizations Sponsoring English Teachers in China

The programs listed below are open to all applicants, although, in most cases, an undergraduate degree is required. Prerequisites, fees, and compensation vary widely among programs. Chinese language capability is not necessarily required. Contact program offices for current information.

Several schools, including Grinnell, Oberlin, Wellesley, and Williams Colleges, and Yale University, offer programs for teaching in China that are open exclusively to their alumni. Prospective teachers are encouraged to inquire about such opportunities.

The inclusion of programs on this list does not imply endorsement by the CSCC.

China Advocates
1635 Irving Street
San Francisco, CA 94122
Telephone: 1-800-333-6474
FAX: 415-753-0412

China Educational Exchange
1251 Virginia Avenue
Harrisonburg, VA 22801
Telephone: 703-432-6983

Colorado China Council
932 Marine Street
Boulder, CO 80302
Telephone: 303-443-1107
FAX: 303-443-1107

International Schools Services
P.O. Box 5910
Princeton, NJ 08543
Telephone: 609-452-0990
FAX: 609-452-2690
Facilitates placement of certified teachers in schools teaching primarily expatriate children, grades K-12.

International Scientific & Information Services, Inc.
49 Thompson Hay Path
Setauket, NY 11733
Telephone: 516-751-6437
FAX: 516-751-6437

National Council of Churches of Christ, USA
China Program Office
475 Riverside Drive
Room 616
New York, NY 10115
Telephone: 212-870-2630
FAX: 212-870-2055

Princeton-in-Asia
224 Palmer Hall
Princeton, NJ 08544
Telephone: 609-258-3657
FAX: 609-258-5300

Volunteers in Asia
P.O. Box 4543
Stanford, CA 94309
Telephone: 723-3228
FAX: 415-725-1805

United Board for Christian Higher Education in Asia
475 Riverside Drive
New York, NY 10115
Telephone: 212-870-2608
FAX: 212-870-2322
Provides support for experienced professors only.

Western Washington University
China Teaching Program
Old Main 530A
Bellingham, WA 98225-9047
Telephone: 206-650-3753
FAX: 206-650-2847

WorldTeach
Harvard Institute for International Development
One Eliot Street
Cambridge, MA 02138-5705
Telephone: 617-495-5527
FAX: 617-495-1239

APPENDIX I

Application for Teaching Positions in China

Chinese Education Association
for
International Exchanges
(CEAIE)

APPLICATION FOR TEACHING POSITIONS IN CHINA

1. Name: Miss □   Mrs. □   Mr. □   Dr. □   Prof. □   Others □

   ....

2. Address: Present

   ....

   ....

   ....

   Permanent (if different)

   ....

   ....

   ....

   Telephone: (area code) ....

   Recent or most recent employing unit or employer

       Address: ....

       ....

       ....

       Reference (attach letter or recommandation)

       ....

       ....

3. Date of Birth: ....

4. Sex and Marriage Status:

       Male □   Female □

       Single □   Married □   Divorced □   Seperated □

5. Citizenship: ....

Photo

6. Academic Qualifications:

    A. Course ....

       Degree or Certificate ....

       Name of University ....

       Year of Graduation ....

    B. Course ....

       Degree or Certificate ....

       Name of University ....

       Year of Graduation ....

    C. Course ....

       Degree or Certificate ....

       Name of University ....

       Year of Graduation ....

7. Major University Subjects (undergraduate)

       ....

       ....

       ....

    Major University Subjects (graduate)

       ....

       ....

       ....

8. Other Academic Qualifications:

       ....

       ....

       ....

9. Teacher Training:

    A. Name of Certificate ....

       University or Other Institution

       ....

       Length of Course ....

       Description of Course Content ....

       ....

       ....

B. Name of Certificate ....
   University or Other Institution ....
   Length of Course...............................
   Description of Course Content ....
   ....
   ....

10. Teaching Experience (subjects, length of time, full or part time, school or university, etc.)
   ....
   ....
   ....
   ....

11. Description of Professional Titles, Academic Ranks, Assignments of Added Reponsibility, Awards, etc.
   ....
   ....
   ....
   ....

12. Publications (if any), List of Published Materials, Dates of Publication and Descriptions:
   ....
   ....
   ....
   ....

13. Other Skills and Qualifications:
   ....
   ....

14. Travel and Living Experiences In Other Countries (dates, duration and description):
   ....
   ....

15. Reasons for Coming to Teach in China:
   ....
   ....
   ....
   ....

16. Health (general health and disabilities, if any)
   ....

17. Accompanying Family Members (if any):

    A. Name of Accompanying Spouse ....

       Date of Birth .... Citizenship...

       State of Health ....

       Education..

    NOTE: If spouse also wishes to teach, attach a separate completed application form.

    B. Accompanying Children (if any):

       Name .... Sex ....

       Date of Birth ....

       Name .... Sex ....

       Date of Birth...

18. Contract Period:

    A. Preferred Time for Beginning Work in China (September or February of any year) ....

    B. Preferred Length of Stay in China ....

    C. Preferred Place(s) of stay in China (if any) ....

19. Other Information (if any):

    ....

    ....

    ....

    ....

    ....

    ....

20. List of Attached Documents:

    1. ....

    2. ....

    3. ....

    4. ....

    5. ....

    6. ....

    ....

    ....

Signature of Applicant ....

Date of Application ....

NOTE: Use the extra page(s) to supply information (if any) that cannot be filled in the space provided.

APPENDIX J

Sample Contract for Teachers

A sample contract for Foreign Experts and Foreign Teachers is reprinted below. An American teaching in China, who sent this contract to the National Association for Foreign Student Affairs, indicated that particular items to be noted in the Annex, "Regulations Concerning the Living Conditions of Foreign Experts Working in Cultural and Educational Institutions," include:

Section II.A: "Only tickets from the Civil Aviation Administration of China (CAAC) shall be provided if its international flights are available ..."

Section II.C: The items to be provided in the housing facilities are specified, but individuals should be aware that these sometimes do not function properly and that electricity and water supplies are very erratic.

Section II.D: Americans teaching in China should not expect to teach and be able to do a great deal of traveling. The only long vacation is Spring Festival, which is about four weeks in late January, February, or early March, depending on the date of the Chinese New Year, which is determined by the lunar calendar. At that time, trains are terribly crowded, and it is very cold. Since indoor heating is rare, travel can be quite uncomfortable at that time. In the summer, at the end of the academic year, it is quite hot. So individuals whose objective is to travel should consider teaching only in the fall semester and traveling in the months of March, April, and May.

CONTRACT (FORM)

PREFACE   The form of the Contract and the Annex, "Regulations Concerning the Living Conditions of Foreign Experts Working in Cultural and Educational Institutions," are sample copies. Subsequently, Party A and Party B can, before signing the contract, submit amendments and supplements to the sample copies according to their specific conditions. (Wages and benefits will be more generous for Foreign Experts.) The contract will come into force only after both sides have, through consultation, established in written form and confirmed through signature the content and the living conditions therein.

Party A _____ wishes to engage the service of Party B _____ as (teacher, compiler, translator, etc.). The two parties, in a spirit of friendly cooperation, agree to observe this contract.

I. The period of service will be from _____ to _____.

II. The duties of Party B are as follows:

III. Requirements for Party B to fulfill.

A. Party B shall observe the laws, decrees, and relevant regulations enacted by the Chinese government and Party A's work system.

B. Party B shall cooperate with Party A and make every effort to complete the tasks agreed on.

C. Party B shall accept Party A's arrangement and direction in regard to his/her work. Without Party A's consent, Party B shall not render service elsewhere or hold concurrently any post unrelated to the work agreed on with Party A.

D. Party A shall pay Party B a salary of _____ yuan (renminbi) each month and provide him/her the benefits stipulated in the "Regulations Concerning the Living Conditions of Foreign Experts Working in Cultural and Educational Institutions."

E. Neither of the two parties shall terminate the contract ahead of time or alter it without mutual consent.

If Party A wants to terminate the contract before it expires, Party B must be given thirty (30) days' notice and reasons for breaking the contract. During Party B's term of service, his/her salary shall be paid as agreed on for the term of the contract. Party A shall also pay for the return air tickets of Party B and his/her family [i.e., Party B's spouse and child(ren) under twelve (12) who have been permitted to come and remain with Party B in China for the whole duration of the contract; they will hereafter be referred to as Party B's family] and for the transportation of their luggage.

If Party B wants to terminate the contract before it expires, he/she should hand in a written request with his/her reasons for breaking the contract thirty (30) days in advance. Party A shall stop paying Party B's salary and providing any benefits for Party B starting from the day when Party A consents to the request. Party B shall bear all the expenses involved in traveling back home together with that of his/her family. Party A is entitled to claim compensation for any loss brought about by Party B's termination of the contract.

Both parties shall continue to execute this contract until the request for termination has been agreed upon.

F. Party A has the right to cancel the contract in any of the following cases:

1. If Party B violates either Regulation II or Regulation III of the contract and fails to correct the error after Party A's mentioning it to him/her, Party A has the right to terminate the contract and arrange for him/her and his/her family's air ticket(s) and the cost of the transportation of their luggage.

2. If Party B cannot resume work after a doctor's certified sick leave of two months (60 days), Party A may arrange, in consideration of Party B's health, for Party B and his/her family to return home within a month (30 days). Party A shall pay for the air ticket(s) of Party B and his/her family and the transportation of their luggage.

G. The contract takes effect when Party B reports for work and becomes void automatically upon the expiration of the contract. Either party that makes a proposal for the extension of the contract should put forward his/her request three months (90 days) prior to the expiration of the contract. A new contract on an extension of the period of service shall be signed by both parties if they agree to it after consultation.

All stay expenses incurred after the contract expires shall be borne by Party B.

H. The contract is written in both Chinese and English, both texts being equally valid.

Signed on the _____ day of _____, 19 ___.

Party A   Party B
(Signature)   (Signature)

ANNEX: Regulations Concerning the Living Conditions of Foreign Experts in Cultural and Educational Institutions

I. Salary

A. Party A shall fix Party B's salary according to his/her professional abilities, the work assigned, his/her educational and professional background. Party A shall inform Party B of the amount of salary before he/she consents to accept the position.

B. Party B's salary shall be paid regularly by the month. It shall begin from the day of Party B's commencement of his/her work in China until the expiration of the contract. If the work to be done will take less than a month, the payment shall be made by the day, each being one-thirtieth of the monthly salary.

C. Party B's salary shall be paid in renminbi, which can be changed into foreign currency under the following conditions:

If Party B comes to China alone, he/she may change fifty percent (50%) of his/her monthly salary into foreign currency.

If Party B comes with his/her family [spouse and child(ren) under twelve (12) who come and remain in China with Party B at Party A's consent; hereafter referred to as Party B's family], he/she may change thirty percent (30%) of his/her monthly salary.

If Party B's spouse is invited as a foreign expert at the same time and they have no children living in China, each may have fifty percent (50%) of his/her salary changed into foreign currency.

Party B may change his/her foreign currency allowance either every month or all at once at the expiration of the contract.

II. Traveling Expenses

A. If Party B's period of service is over one year, he/she may bring with him/her, at Party A's consent in advance, his/her spouse and child(ren) under twelve (12) to come and remain in China. Party A shall provide Party B and his/her family with economy-class air return tickets from the airport nearest to the city where Party B is when he/she accepts the invitation from Party A (of Party B's permanent residence) when coming to the place of work in China and when returning home upon the expiration of the term of Party B's service. Only tickets from the Civil Aviation Administration of China (CAAC) shall be provided if its international flights are available in Party B's country.

Party B shall bear all expenses of his/her family on temporary visits to China.

B. Party A shall pay for the cost of transportation of twenty-four (24) kilograms (kg) per person [no more than a total of seventy-two (72) kg for a family of more than three] of luggage by nonaccompanied air freight incurred by Party B and his/her family for the same distance as mentioned above, both when coming and on their return after the expiration of the period of service. Expenses for packing and delivering the luggage between Party B's temporary residence at the time of his/her application for the post (or his/her permanent residence) and the airport when coming to China or on his/her return home shall be borne by Party B.

At the request of Party B, for sending his/her luggage by sea instead of by air, Party A shall pay for the cost of one cubic meter of unaccompanied luggage per person (but no more than two cubic meters for a family of over two people) by sea, including the expenses charged for delivering the luggage to and from Party B's place of work and the seaport in China. Expenses incurred for packing and delivering luggage outside of China between the temporary residence at the time of Party B's application for the post (or his/her permanent residence) and the seaport on coming to China and on returning home shall be borne by Party B.

The cost of transportation of incoming luggage within the stipulated limits can be reimbursed only on presentation of receipts.

C. During Party B's period of work in China, Party A shall bear the following expenses on behalf of Party B.

1. Housing (with furniture, bedding, a bathroom, a television set, a refrigerator, and the facilities for heating and air conditioning).

2. Transportation to and from work.

3. Medical care to be subsidized in accordance with China's medical system except for expenses incurred in registration, doctors' home visits, fitting false teeth, cleaning teeth, undergoing cosmetic surgery, buying spectacles, boarding in hospital, and nonmedical tonics.

D. Vacations

1. In addition to China's national holidays, such as New Year's Day, the Spring Festival (three days), May 1, and National Day (two days), Party B is entitled to 30 days' vacation in China every year. The vacation time of those working in colleges and universities shall correspond to the summer and winter vacations. Those working in institutions of information and publication shall not be entitled to a vacation until after they have worked for half a year. After Party B has worked for a year, he/she shall be given an additional _____ yuan renminbi vacation allowance. If the term of service is over half a year but less than a year, Party B shall enjoy a vacation of two weeks and be given an additional _____ yuan vacation allowance.

The vacation allowance cannot be changed into foreign currency.

Party B shall receive his/her salary as usual for the vacation period.

2. If Party B comes to China alone and is on a contract for two years, he/she may spend the vacation visiting his/her home country once at the end of one year's work. Party A shall pay for an economy-class return air ticket. Only tickets of CAAC shall be provided if its international flights are available. In such cases, Party B shall no longer be

given a vacation allowance that year, but his/her salary for the month when he/she is on vacation at home can all be changed into foreign currency.

If Party B gives up such opportunity to go for a vacation in his/her home country, he/she shall be given a sum in renminbi* equivalent to a one-way economy-class air ticket instead of the vacation allowance for that year. If the price of the ticket is less than _____ yuan, Party B shall be given the difference.*

E. Sick Leave or Absence from Work

1. If he/she is ill, Party B shall ask for sick leave and produce a doctor's certificate. His/her salary shall be paid as usual if the sick leave is up to sixty (60) days in succession. If Party A does not exercise the right stipulated in Item F.2. in the Annex (i.e., if Party A does not propose termination of the contract), Party B shall receive seventy percent (70%) of his/her regular salary from the sixty-first day until the day he/she resumes regular work or to the expiration of the contract.

2. If Party B asks for leave of absence and obtains Party A's consent, a deduction in salary shall be made according to the number of days Party B is absent.

F. Severance Pay

Severance pay shall be granted to Party B when Party B leaves China at the end of his/her service, namely an additional half a month's salary for each full year's service. No severance pay shall be granted if Party B has worked less than one year.

Severance pay may be changed into foreign currency.

---

*Nonconvertible

APPENDIX K

American Express Emergency Check Cashing Locations

In the following cities, you can cash your personal check with your American Express card at designated branches of Bank of China, CITIC Industrial Bank, or Bank of Communications. Call the American Express office in Beijing at (01) 505-2639 for more information.

Anhui:	Hefei, Wuhu
Beijing	
Fujian:	Fuqing, Fuzhou, Putian, Quanzhou, Xiamen, Zhangzhou
Gansu:	Lanzhou
Guangdong:	Chaozhou, Guangzhou, Huizhou, Jiangmen, Maoming, Meixian, Panyu, Shantou, Shaoguan, Shenzhen, Taishan, Xingning, Zhanjiang, Zhaoqing, Zhongshan, Zhuhai
Guangxi:	Beihai, Guilin, Liuzhou, Nanning
Guizhou:	Guiyang
Hainan:	Haikou, Sanya, Wenchang
Hebei:	Baoding, Chengde, Qinhuangdao, Shijiazhuang, Tangshan
Heilongjiang:	Harbin
Henan:	Kaifeng, Luoyang, Zhengzhou
Hubei:	Shashi, Wuhan, Yichang
Hunan:	Changsha
Jiangsu:	Huaiyin, Jiangyin, Lianyungang, Nanjing, Nantong, Suzhou, Wuxi, Yancheng, Xuzhou, Yangzhou, Zhangjiagang, Zhenjiang
Jiangxi:	Jingdezhen, Jiujiang, Nanchang

Jilin:	Changchun, Jilin
Liaoning:	Dalian, Dandong, Shenyang, Yingkou
Neimonggu:	Baotou, Huhehaote
Ningxia:	Yinchuan
Qinghai:	Xining
Shaanxi:	Xi'an
Shandong:	Jinan, Qingdao, Taian, Yantai
Shanghai	
Shanxi:	Datong, Pingshuo, Shuxian, Taiyuan
Sichuan:	Chengdu, Chongqing Tianjin
Xinjiang:	Kashi, Shihezi, Turfan, Wulumuqi, Yili
Xizang:	Lhasa
Yunnan:	Dali, Dehong, Kunming, Luliang, Qujing, Ruili, Wandingzhen, Xishuangbanna, Yuxi
Zhejiang:	Hangzhou, Ningbo, Shaoxing, Wenzhou

AMERICAN EXPRESS WORLDWIDE CUSTOMER CARE SERVICE LOCATIONS, PRC

American Express Beijing Office   Tel: 01-505-2639
L115D Shopping Arcade
China World Trade Center
1 Jianguomenwai Dajie
Beijing

China International Travel Services   Tel: 021-321-7200
Shanghai Branch
66 Nanjing Dong Lu
Shanghai

China International Travel Services   Tel: 029-21749
Xi'an Branch
Bell Tower Hotel
South West Corner of Bell Tower
Xi'an, Shaanxi

China International Travel Services   Tel: 0773-225-588
Guilin Branch
Lobby, Sheraton Guilin Hotel
Binjiang Nan Lu
Guilin, Guangxi

China International Travel Services   Tel: 028-679-186
Chengdu Branch
19 Renmin Nan Lu 2nd Section
610021 Chengdu, Sichuan

White Swan Hotel Travel Service Dept.   Tel: 020-888-6968
White Swan Hotel, Shamian
Guangzhou

APPENDIX L

*Approximate Costs of Hotel Rooms, Food, Internal Travel,
Services, Clothing, and Medical Care, Fall 1993**

HOTEL RATES AND FOOD COSTS

Beijing

Landmark Hotel	US$40/night
21st Century Hotel	US$30/night

Changsha

Rong Yuan Hotel	US$35/night
Food	US$10/day

Hangzhou

Provincial hotels	US$40-50/night

Shanghai

Yangtze Hotel	single: Y100/night
	double: Y150/night

DORMITORIES AND FOREIGN EXPERT BUILDINGS

Beijing

Beijing University, Shaoyuan Lou
(twin beds, TV, refrigerator,
telephone, bathroom)   Y81/night

---

*Prices are rising rapidly in China. Costs noted in this section are intended to
provide a point of reference but are likely to have increased since publication.

Beijing University, Building #6
(single bedroom, shared living area, bathroom,
carpet, TV, telephone)   Y1,025/month

People's University, Foreign Experts' Building
(single room with bathroom, refrigerator,
desk, AC, telephone, TV)   Y100/night
   Food   Y10-15/day

Western buffets (in hotels)   Y30-90

Changchun

Jilin University Guest House
(with bathroom and TV)
   Foreign visiting scholars   US$16/night
   Students   US$8/night

Fuzhou

Fuzhou Normal University,
Foreign Experts' Building
   Single room, two beds   Y90/night

Guangxi

Guangxi Normal University
Foreign Students' Building
   Double room   US$12/night

Hangzhou

Hangzhou University, Old Foreign Experts'
Building
   Single room   Y45/night

Shanghai

Shanghai Academy of Social Sciences Guesthouse
   Room with bathroom, TV, AC, refrigerator,
   phone, twin beds)   Y74/night

Shanghai Conservatory of Music
   Single room with twin beds   Y53/night
   Double room   Y28/night
   Food   Y50/day

Shashi

Shashi Hospital Staff Housing
   Shared 3-room apartment   Y2,000/month

Tianjin

Nankai University, Foreign Student Dormitory
  Room with private bath, AC, maid service)   US$8/night
  Food   Y3/meal

Xiamen

Xiamen University, Foreign Experts' Guesthouse
  Apartment   Y1,500 month

TRANSPORTATION COSTS

Airfares (one-way)

Beijing-Shanghai	Y590
Chengdu-HongKong	Y2,220
Hangzhou-Beijing	Y600
Shanghai-Guangzhou	Y620

Taxis
Calculated by distance and
quality of car Y1-Y2/km   Y10 (minimum)

Beijing:
  People's University to airport   Y8

Shanghai:
  City center to outlying
  factory area   Y50-Y70 (one way)

Buses
Y0.1-Y0.2/km
  Qinghai-Gansu   Y300

Vans/Jeeps
Beijing   Y20-30/day
Chengdu   Y150-250/day

Bicycles
Beijing   Y180-200 used
                                                    Y340-800 new

SERVICES

Banking
Beijing: charge US$ on credit card (Visa) for 4% fee

Dental Care
Shanghai: US$15

Medical Care
Beijing: medical testing/blood drawing: Y17.50, plus Y20 processing fee

Shipping
Shanghai: Y15-30/kilo

MISCELLANEOUS ITEMS AVAILABLE

teflon frying pan	Y40
coffee maker	Y60
Sino-French wine	Y25
fountain pen	Y4
airmail envelopes	Y1 (10-pack)
3"×5" index cards	Y2.5 (100-pack)
notebooks	
Chinese	Y0.8
Japanese	Y6.80
paperclips	Y0.5 (100-pack)
9"×12" clipboard	Y10
desk lamp	Y17
correction fluid	Y8.2
post-it notes	Y8.5
voltage transformer/stabilizer	Y350
power strip	Y50
3.5" diskettes (1MB)	Y85/10
small crescent wrench	Y7.2
screwdriver	Y1
4'×6' straw mat	Y25
toilet paper	Y0.3-Y0.8
map of Beijing bus routes	Y1.2
500g oranges (1 *jin*)	Y1-2
International Herald Tribune	Y15
bath towel	Y10
rabbit fur-lined gloves	Y17

RESEARCH COSTS

Beijing

Peking University	
photocopying	Y0.2-Y0.8/page
microfilm	Y1.4/page (11"×18")
transcribing	Y8-Y12/hour
user fee	
microfilms	Y2
rare books	Y1-Y3/box

Number One Historical Archive
  microfilm   Y2.50–3.60/sheet

Chengdu

Chengdu University of Technology
  photography   Y3-10

Sichuan Provincial Archives
  copying   Y0.5 (8.5"×11")
                                                          Y0.8 (11"×16")
  microfilming
    color   Y10/frame
    black and white   Y2/frame
  preservation
    microfilm   Y5/reel/day
    PRC founding documents   Y0.5/*juan*
    Qing documents   Y2/*juan*
    Republican documents   Y0.8/*juan*
    Revolution documents   Y1/*juan*
  storage
    ordinary documents   Y2/*juan*
    special documents   Y10/*juan*

Nanjing

Number Two Historical Archive
  looking fee
    pre-1937   Y3/*juan*
    post-1937   Y1.5/*juan*
  hand copying   Y0.3/page
  xeroxing
    (large)   Y1.5/page
    (small)   Y1/page
  add Y0.3/page surcharge for "protection"

Shanghai

Fudan University
  copying
    (small)   Y0.5/page
    (large)   Y1/page

Shanghai Academy of Social Sciences
  library card   Y40
  copying   Y0.4/page

Shanghai Municipal Archives
  ID card   Y4/month

Shanghai Municipal Library
  photocopying
    (8"×11")   Y0.3/page
    (12"×16.5")   Y1.3/page
  photographing   Y5/photo

Tianjin

Tianjin Municipal Archives
  copy fees, foreign scholars
    fuyin fee   Y0.5/page
    baohu fee   Y1/file
    liyong fee   Y20-30/file

Xiamen

Xiamen University
  copying   Y0.2-0.3/page

APPENDIX M

Selected Reading List and References

ESPECIALLY RECOMMENDED

Bruun, Ole et al., eds. *Modern China Research: Danish Experiences.* Copenhagen Discussion Papers Special Issue. Copenhagen: University of Copenhagen Center for East and Southeast Asian Studies, 1991.

Chang, Jung. *Wild Swans: Three Daughters of China.* New York: Simon and Schuster, 1991.

Fairbank, John K. *China: A New History.* Cambridge: Harvard University Press, 1992.

Harding, Harry. *A Fragile Relationship: The United States and China Since 1972.* Washington, D.C.: The Brookings Institution, 1992.

Joseph, William A., ed. *China Briefing, 1992.* Boulder: Westview Press, in cooperation with the Asia Society, 1993.

Link, Perry. *Evening Chats in Beijing.* New York: W.W. Norton & Co., 1992.

Spence, Jonathan D. *The Search for Modern China.* New York: W.W. Norton & Co., 1990.

SUPPLEMENTARY READING

General

Mahoney, Rosemary. *The Early Arrival of Dreams: A Year in China.* New York: Fawcett Publishers, 1992.

Rittenberg, Sidney and Amanda Bennett. *The Man Who Stayed Behind.* New York: Simon and Schuster, 1993.

Salzman, Mark. *Iron and Silk.* New York: Random House, 1986.

Shambaugh, David, ed. *American Studies of Contemporary China.* Armonk, NY and Washington, D.C.: M.E. Sharpe and the Woodrow Wilson Center Press, 1993.

History

Cheng, Nien. *Life and Death in Shanghai.* New York: Viking Penguin, 1988.

Gao Yuan. *Born Red: A Chronicle of the Cultural Revolution.* Stanford: Stanford University Press, 1987.

Gray, Jack. *Rebellions and Revolutions: China from the 1800s to the 1980s.* New York and Oxford: Oxford University Press, 1990.

Hinton, W. *Fanshen: A Documentary of Revolution in a Chinese Village.* New York: Random House, 1968.

Snow, Edgar. *Red Star Over China.* New York: Grove Press, 1989.

Thurston, Anne F. *Enemies of the People: The Ordeal of the Intellectuals in China's Great Cultural Revolution.* New York: Alfred A. Knopf, 1987.

Yue, Daiyun and Carolyn Wakeman. *To the Storm: The Odyssey of a Revolutionary Chinese Woman.* Berkeley: University of California Press, 1985.

Society

Chin, Anne-Ping. *Children of China: Voices from Recent Years.* New York: Alfred A. Knopf, 1988.

Honig, Emily and Gail Hershatter. *Personal Voices: Chinese Women in the 1980s.* Stanford: Stanford University Press, 1988.

Link, Perry, Richard Madsen, and Paul G. Pickowicz, eds. *Unofficial China: Popular Culture and Thought in the People's Republic.* Boulder: Westview Press, 1989.

Politics and Economics

Byron, John and Robert Pack. *The Claws of the Dragon.* New York: Simon and Schuster, 1992.

Hsu, Immanuel C.Y. *China Without Mao: The Search for a New Order.* New York and Oxford: Oxford University Press, 1990.

Lardy, Nick. *Foreign Trade and Economic Reform in China, 1978-1990.* New York: Cambridge University Press, 1992.

Mann, Jim. *Beijing Jeep: The Short, Unhappy Romance of American Business in China.* New York: Simon and Schuster Trade, Inc. 1990.

Nathan, Andrew J. *China's Crisis: Dilemmas of Reform and Prospects for Democracy.* New York: Columbia University Press, 1990.

Pye, Lucian. *The Spirit of Chinese Politics.* Cambridge: Harvard University Press, 1992.

Rosenbaum, Arthur Lewis, ed. *State and Society in China: The Consequences of Reform.* Boulder: Westview Press, 1992.

Saich, Tony, ed. *The Chinese People's Movement: Perspectives on Spring 1989.* Armonk, NY: M.E. Sharpe, Inc. 1990.

Shambaugh, David. *Beautiful Imperialist: China Perceives America, 1972-1990.* Princeton: Princeton University Press. 1991.

Tidrick, G. and C. Jiyuan, eds. *China's Industrial Reform.* New York: Oxford University Press for the World Bank, 1987.

Vogel, Ezra. *One Step Ahead in China: Guangdong Under Reform.* Cambridge: Harvard University Press, 1989.

White, Gordon. *Riding the Tiger: The Politics of Economic Reform in Post-Mao China.* Stanford: Stanford University Press, 1993.

Education

Epstein, I. ed. *Chinese Education: Problems, Policies, and Projects.* New York: Garland Publishing, Inc., 1991.

Kallgren, J.K. and Simon, D.F., eds. *Educational Exchanges: Essays on the Sino-American Experience.* Berkeley: Institute of East Asian Studies, 1987.

Hayhoe, Ruth. *Education and Modernization: The Chinese Experience.* Oxford: Pergamon Press, 1992.

Lampton, David M., with Joyce A. Madancy and Kristen M. Williams for the Committee on Scholarly Communication with the People's Republic of China. *A Relationship Restored: Trends in U.S.-China Educational Exchanges, 1978-1984.* Washington, D.C.: National Academy Press, 1986.

Muehl, Lois, and Siegmar Muehl. *Trading Cultures in the Classroom: Two American Teachers in China.* Honolulu: University of Hawaii Press, 1993.

Reed, Linda A. *Education in the People's Republic of China and U.S.-China Educational Exchanges.* Washington, D.C.: National Association for Foreign Student Affairs, 1988.

Unger, Jonathan. *Education Under Mao: Class and Competition in Canton Schools, 1960-1980.* New York: Columbia University Press, 1982.

Science

Baark, Eric. "Fragmented Innovation: China's Science and Technology Policy Reforms in Retrospect." Pp. 531-545 in *China's Economic Dilemmas in the 1990s: The Problems of Reforms, Modernization, and Interdependence.* Joint Economic Committee, Congress of the United States. Armonk, NY: M.E. Sharpe, 1992.

Committee on Scholarly Communication with China. *Grasslands and Grassland Sciences in Northern China.* Washington, D.C.: National Academy Press, 1992.

Panel on Global Climate Change Sciences in China. *China and Global Change: Opportunities for Collaboration.* Washington, D.C.: National Academy Press, 1992.

Simon, Denis Fred and Merle Goldman, eds. *Science and Technology in Post-Mao China.* Harvard Contemporary China Series 5. Cambridge: Council on East Asian Studies and Harvard University, 1989.

Smil, Vaclav. *China's Environmental Crisis: An Inquiry into the Limits of National Development.* Armonk, NY: M.E. Sharpe, Inc., 1993.

REFERENCES

The following books and articles, noted or cited in *China Bound*, are listed below for easy reference.

Arlington, L.C. and W. Lewisohn. *In Search of Old Beijing*. New York: Oxford University Press, 1988.

Barlow, T.E. and Lowe, D.M. *Teaching China's Lost Generation: Foreign Experts in the People's Republic of China*. San Francisco: China Books and Periodicals, Inc., 1987.

Bartlett, Beatrice. "Archive Materials in China on United States History." Pp. 504-506 in Lewis Hanke, ed., *Guide to the Study of United States History outside the U.S., 1945-1980, vol. 1*. White Plains: Kraus International Publications.

_____. *Monarchs and Ministers: The Grand Council in Mid-Ch'ing China, 1723-1820*. Berkeley: University of California Press, 1991.

_____. "The Number Three Archives of China: The Liaoning Provincial Archives." *China Exchange News*, Fall-Winter 1991, pp. 2-6. Washington, D.C.: Committee on Scholarly Communication with the PRC.

Bock, Norman. "The Ultimate Power Trip: Setting up and Operating a PC in China." *China Exchange News*, Fall-Winter 1991, pp. 27-30. Washington, D.C.: Committee on Scholarly Communication with the PRC.

Bredon, Juliet. *Peking*. Hong Kong: Oxford University Press, 1982.

China Phone Book and Business Directory. Hong Kong: The China Phone Book Co., 1993.

Colfax, David and Micki. *Homeschooling for Excellence*. A Warner Communications Company, 1988.

Customs Hints for Returning U.S. Citizens: Know Before You Go. Washington, D.C.: U.S. Government Printing Office, 1986.

Directory of Chinese Libraries. Beijing: China Academic Publishers, 1982.

Friedman, Edward, et al. *Chinese Village, Socialist State*. New Haven: Yale University Press, 1991.

Health Information for International Travel. Washington, D.C.: U.S. Government Printing Office (#017-023-00192-2), 1993.

Henderson, Gail. "Survival Guide to Survey Research in the China." *China Exchange News*, Spring 1993, pp. 23-25;33. Washington, D.C.: Committee on Scholarly Communication with China.

Hook, Brian, and Denis Twitchett eds. *The Cambridge Encyclopedia of China, 2nd ed.* Cambridge, New York, and Melbourne: Cambridge University Press, 1991.

Isaacs, Harold R. *Images of Asia: American Views of India and China*. New York: Capricorn Books, 1962. (Out of print; may be available through your local library.)

Kaplan, Frederick M., J. Sobin, and Arne J. de Keijzer. *The China Guidebook*. New York: Eurasia Press, 1993. (Updated yearly)

Kapstein, Matthew. "New Sources for Tibetan Buddhist History." *China Exchange News*, Fall-Winter 1991, pp. 15-19. Washington, D.C.: Committee on Scholarly Communication with the PRC.

Moore, Raymond and Dorothy. *Home Style Teaching: A Handbook for Parents and Teachers*. Dallas, Sydney, and Singapore: World Publishing, 1984.

Moss, William. *Archives in the People's Republic of China: A Brief Introduction for American Scholars and Archivists.* Washington, D.C.: Smithsonian Archives, 1993.

Nagel's Encyclopedic Guide to China. Geneva: Nagel Publishers, 1986.

Paver, William and Yiping Wan. *Postsecondary Institutions of the People's Republic of China: A Comprehensive Guide to Institutions of Higher Education in China.* Washington, D.C.: American Association of Collegiate Registrars and Admissions Officers and NAFSA: Association of International Educators, 1992.

Schnepp, Otto. "Fieldwork in China." *China Exchange News,* March 1994, pp. 1-3. Washington, D.C.: Committee on Scholarly Communication with the PRC.

Seligman, Scott. "A Shirtsleeves Guide to Corporate Etiquette." *The China Business Review,* January-February 1983, p. 13. Washington, D.C.: The China Business Forum.

Storey, R., et al. *China: A Travel Survival Kit.* Berkeley: Lonely Planet, 1994.

Thurston, Anne F. and B. Pasternak. *The Social Sciences and Fieldwork in China: Views from the Field.* Boulder: Westview Press, Inc. for the American Association for the Advancement of Science, 1983.

Werner, David. *Where There is No Doctor.* Palo Alto: The Hesperian Foundation, 1977.

Wood, Frances. *Blue Guide to China.* New York: W.W. Norton & Co., 1992.

Yale-China Association. *The Yale-China Guide to Living, Studying and Working in the PRC, Hong Kong, and Taiwan.* New Haven: Yale-China Association, Inc., 1993.

APPENDIX N

Trial Procedures for Foreign Organizations
and Individuals to Use Chinese Archives*

STATE ARCHIVES BUREAU ORDER #3

"Trial Procedures for Foreign Organizations and Individuals to Use Chinese Archives" is hereby published, and it is effective from 1 July 1992.

Feng Zizhi, Director-General, 26 December 1991

TRIAL PROCEDURES FOR FOREIGN ORGANIZATIONS AND INDIVIDUALS TO USE CHINESE ARCHIVES

1. These procedures are established in accordance with the provision of "Implementation Procedures for the Archives Law of the People's Republic of China" that pertains to use of archives by foreign organizations and individuals.

2. Foreign organizations and individuals may go in person, write, or telephone to archives at any level to read, copy, or excerpt from archives that are already opened to society.

3. In accordance with relevant cultural exchange agreements concluded at each level of government or government departments in China for use of archives in archival repositories at each level, foreign organizations and individuals may, through introductions from the relevant Chinese authorities that have signed [such] agreements, submit an application to the pertinent archival repository. Using another approach, to use archives in state archival repositories at the central level

---

*Translated by W.W. Moss from *Archives Science Bulletin [Danganxue Tongxun]* Number 2 of 1992, 18 April 1992, page 3.

225

or provincial (autonomous region or special municipality) level, submit an application to the State Archives Bureau or to the relevant archival repository; to use archives in state archival repositories at the district (municipal, prefectural, or league) level or at the county (town, district, or banner) level, submit an application to the State Archives Bureau or to the pertinent government administrative authorities at the provincial (autonomous district, or directly subordinate city) level. Applicants must clearly identify themselves, the subject and range of use [of the archives], and other relevant circumstances. Except for those seeking certificates of their own relatives, all applications must be delivered thirty days in advance.

4. Only after considering the opinion of the depositor will a decision be made on whether or not to provide archives that have been deposited in an archival repository to be used by foreign organizations and individuals.

5. Copying and letter or telephone use of archives by foreign organizations and individuals must be according to the regulations of the archival repository and payment according to its fee schedule.

6. Foreign organizations and individuals [who wish to] copy archives must fill out a copying applications form, [have their request] approved by the archives repository director, and [the copying] must be carried out by responsible archival staff. The content and quantity of copying of archives is decided at the discretion of the archival repository.

7. Foreign organizations and individuals [who wish to] extract from or copy archives, provided they do not violate our State regulations, may quote them in research work, but they may not publish them in any form without obtaining permission. All contents of archives cited in works should clearly indicate the unit of custody and the archives number. Archival repositories encourage users to favor [the repositories] with a gift of their writings or other research results that use the archives.

8. When foreign organizations and individuals go to State archival repositories at any level to use archives, they must submit to the arrangements made by that repository, [must] abide by every item of pertinent regulations, and must not engage in any activity that is not already permitted.

9. The State Archives Bureau is the interpreter of these procedures.

10. These procedures are implemented beginning 1 July 1992.

APPENDIX O

Packing it in: Preparing for Fieldwork in the PRC*

John Olsen

Preparation is the better part of success when planning research in China. Scholars who have conducted field research in remote areas are perhaps most keenly aware that being prepared means knowing what to pack. It is not only one's health, but the achievement of one's work that may well depend on the contents of a few duffle bags. Although basic necessities for fieldwork in China may be much the same as those required anywhere, availability of goods, peculiarities of transportation, and standards of sanitation vary significantly among—and often within—countries. Here, I offer advice on preparing for fieldwork in China: not only what to pack, but also how to handle in-country logistics of food, housing, and transportation.

WATER, FOOD AND SHELTER

WATER Fortunately, the pervasiveness of tea-drinking in China and its borderlands means that adequate supplies of boiled water are generally available. On the other hand, fieldwork conducted in areas where local supplies of water are scarce, heavily laced with minerals, or rendered unpotable because of proximity to settled populations requires special considerations. By far, the best way to make all but the most chemically polluted water potable (although not necessarily palatable) is to pass the raw water through a porous (less than 0.4 micron) ceramic and/or activated charcoal filter. The microfiltration systems manufactured by the Katadyn Corporation enjoy World Health Organization and International Red Cross approval but are relatively expensive (individual units cost about $250 and larger filters for base camps

*Reprinted from *China Exchange News*, Spring 1992

are available). The MSR Waterworks, First Need, and Basic Designs systems, though not as efficient or durable as the Katadyn, cost far less and are sensible alternatives. No simple filtration system, including those referenced, can render salty or otherwise mineralized water potable.

Fieldworkers should be aware that simply boiling water makes it relatively safe and potable, but only if it is kept at a full, rolling boil for at least 20 minutes. Limited fuel often makes this water-purification method impossible, especially at high altitudes. Boiling also does not remove the particulate matter, herbicides, pesticides, and some of the smaller microbial agents (such as *Giardia* and other protozoa and bacteria) as do the Katadyn, MSR Water works, and General Ecology Trav-L-Pure microfiltration systems.

Treatment of water with iodine or other chemicals is not recommended since these techniques are inefficient water purifiers and some individuals suffer nausea and stomach cramps as a side effect.

FOOD   The quality and quantity of locally available foodstuffs vary greatly across China, but in general, acquiring fresh meats, vegetables, and fruits is more problematic in the north than in the south, regardless of season. Individual researchers should decide in advance the extent to which the demands of particular field activities will require them to bring quantities of packaged "backpacking food" from the West. In such cases, primary considerations include whether or not base camps can be established near main transportation arteries, the number of people participating in the fieldwork, and cost, because such "convenience foods" are vastly more expensive than locally available supplies.

While small camp stoves that burn bottled butane are convenient, they should be avoided in China since they cannot be transported by air (intrepid but uninformed mountaineering expeditions regularly have their bottled fuel confiscated by Chinese airport authorities, much to their chagrin) and replacement canisters are not yet available in China.

The new multi-fuel stoves, such as MSR's International and X-GK II or Coleman's Peak 1, are good alternatives to those that burn butane. Multi-fuel stoves have the advantage of being able to burn nearly any combustible liquid, from leaded or unleaded gasoline and diesel fuel to kerosene. One field researcher working in Xinjiang reports he successfully ran an MSR X-GK II stove for an entire field season on low-octane gasoline siphoned from a jeep supplemented with aviation fuel purchased at a local airport! Such stoves are extremely compact, efficient, user-friendly, and relatively inexpensive (about $75).

For base camp applications (not including demanding high-altitude work), another option is to purchase a Chinese-made kerosene (paraffin) stove locally. A wide range of models is available, from Primustype single-burner stoves to larger models capable of handling several pots at once. Kerosene (*shilayou* or *meiyou*) is readily available in most areas of China and the low cost of these stoves may offset their relatively large size and weight. Those unfamiliar with the joys of cooking on a paraffin stove should remember that regular cleaning, maintenance, and general tinkering are part of the regime.

SHELTER   Foreign fieldworkers should expect to negotiate long and hard over the issue of appropriate housing. Chinese are often less willing than their Western counterparts to "rough it" for weeks on end, preferring a proper roof over their heads and a real bed at night. However, the daily 50 to 100 km round-trip commute from a county government guest house will significantly reduce time in the field.

Self-contained base camps notwithstanding, county-level government rest houses in China (called *xian zhengfu zhaodaisuo*) often are the best alternative for short-term stays in China's back-of-beyond. Most offer reasonably clean rooms and edible food for just a few *yuan* per day. Given the enormous variability in local conditions, however, it is always advisable to look over the accommodations (and kitchen facilities) before "checking in."

FIELD VEHICLES

Since most foreigners are technically not permitted to drive in China outside of major metropolitan areas, each field vehicle will necessarily be accompanied by a driver. Driving is considered a highly specialized male skill in China, a fact that occasionally leads to friction under otherwise amiable circumstances. Unfortunately, drivers are often the weak link in the most rigorously planned field enterprises. Even highly respected senior Chinese scientists must be properly deferential to drivers, especially in the field. Among the highest paid of Chinese workers, drivers are accustomed to working relatively short hours. Many drivers are not qualified mechanics (though they may be billed as such), thus the foreign fieldworker should check that assigned drivers possess at least rudimentary auto-repair skills. To be sure, many, if not most, Chinese drivers are competent, cooperative people; however, the choice of who will drive should not be taken lightly and Western researchers should always reserve the right to demand a substitute driver in the event of "irreconcilable differences."

Since there are no car and truck rental agencies per se in China, most foreign fieldworkers will enter into a contractual arrangement for the use of vehicles with a local governmental organ (generally the Foreign Affairs Office of the county or district-level People's Government) or branch of the Chinese Academy of Sciences.

Charges for the use of field vehicles are highly negotiable in China and subject to rapid inflation; thus, foreign researchers are advised to pay particular attention to the following points:

1. Are vehicle use charges set according to a daily fee (regardless of the number of kilometers driven) or is there a strict per-kilometer charge? The usual practice is to charge a flat daily fee (say, Y240) that includes a set number of kilometers (often 100). Additional mileage is charged per kilometer (say, Y1.00) beyond whatever maximum is established in advance.

2. If a "per-kilometer fee" is charged, is the rate the same for on-road versus off-road use? Be certain that the definitions of "on-" and "off-road" are explicitly understood and agreed to in advance. Who will be responsible for keeping track of mileage—each driver, an expedition team member, or some other designated authority?

3. Is the cost of gasoline/diesel and insurance included in the vehicle charges? What about the drivers' food and lodging expenses? How many days per week or month will the drivers expect to have off? Who pays for spare parts and repairs? Always arrange for a substitute vehicle and driver to be made available in case of illness or vehicle repairs requiring more than one day.

There is an increasingly wide range of mostly Japanese 4x4 field vehicles available in China (Toyota Land Cruiser, Nissan Patrol, Mitsubishi Pajero/Montero, Isuzu Trooper). Most are gasoline powered, although a small number of diesel Land Cruisers seem to have been imported in the early 1980s.

The short wheel-base Beijing Jeep (especially the 212 and its re-engineered successor, the 2020N, both unabashed copies of the somewhat superior Russian GAZ Jeep) is generally a cheaper alternative to the Japanese vehicles that might be available. This machine, which rides like a buckboard and is invariably too hot or too cold because of improper ventilation, is also extremely reliable and simple to prepare. Many fieldworkers find that a Toyota Land Cruiser and a Beijing Jeep are a winning combination for field parties of six to eight people since the Land Cruiser's relative comfort and superior visibility make it a natural for transporting people while the smaller jeep can be used to haul luggage and equipment and carry out reconnaissance, often at a lower per-kilometer charge.

Some Chinese work units, concerned about their foreign colleagues' physical comfort, will offer the notorious Beijing Jeep Cherokee (BJ 2021) for use. This pretty, gentrified vehicle is of no more value in off-road conditions than the family station wagon. It is admirably well-suited for surviving China's pot-holed paved roads, but its very low clearance and underpowered engine prevent it from being a serious field vehicle. In addition, the Cherokee's "black box" electrical, ignition, and fuel pump systems make in-field repairs nearly impossible. Remember, the Cherokee is not an Everyman's Range Rover—the BJ 2021 will extract a very high price in terms of reliability for a dubious increase in comfort.

Chinese gasoline (*qiyou*; called benzene in the Turkic-speaking Northwest) is generally of very low octane; frequently, it is degraded locally to 75 or less and is often quite dirty when dispensed out of corroded drums. As a result, it is wise to bring a large number of high-quality replacement fuel filters (the simple, universal in-line variety). One advantage of both the Beijing 212/2020N Jeep and Toyota Land Cruiser is that their float-bowls are readily accessible and can be cleaned with minimal difficulty in the field.

MAPS

Maps pose special problems for fieldwork in China. The general rule, passed down from the 1970s, is that foreigners are not allowed access to maps with a scale of 1:400,000 or less. Obviously, maps of such coarse scale are of only limited use to most field projects.

Topographic maps (defined by Chinese agencies as maps of any scale with contour lines indicated, *regardless* of interval) are considered *neibu*: for internal (i.e., limited Chinese) use only. Foreign researchers often find that, once in the field, they are given relatively free access to maps that were off-limits back in someone's office or library. This access is accompanied by the responsibility, on the part of the foreign researcher, not to abuse the privilege by publishing such maps or even discussing their existence widely.

Chinese authors themselves must have maps approved by the National Bureau of Surveying and Mapping (Guojia Cehuiju) before they can be published, indicating that maps are very special, closely controlled items in China.

Basically, three characteristics are evaluated in deciding whether or not particular maps can be made accessible to foreigners:

1. the map's scale,
2. the presence of topographic features (contours), and
3. the geographic location depicted by the map (border area, military zone, etc.)

Satellite imagery, derived mostly from the American Landsat and Space Shuttle, the French SPOT, and assorted Russian systems, continues to be a sensible solution to most field cartographic needs.* Obvi-

---

*Satellite imagery should not be displayed, let alone declared, at Chinese customs on entering and leaving the country.

ously, the cost of satellite imagery generally precludes optimal detailed coverage, but in many cases, one or two scenes are superior to even the most detailed of available Chinese maps.

In the past five years, Global Positioning Systems (GPS) have begun to augment, if not replace, more traditional compass-based orienteering techniques in the field. While GPS continues to be a relatively expensive technology, prices are rapidly dropping; some systems (such as the AccuNav by Eagle) sell for under $900. In areas such as China, where high-quality maps are largely unavailable, the combined application of satellite imagery and GPS technology may ultimately prove superior for nearly all cartographic needs.

APPENDIX P

Student Advisory Resource Centers and General Reference Holdings

The United States Information Service (USIS) office at the U.S. Embassy provides student advisory materials to advisory centers and libraries throughout China. The following list gives names, addresses, and telephone numbers of centers and libraries that house materials provided by USIS. "Advisory centers" have trained academic advisors on staff to assist students in their search for suitable universities and financial aid. "Libraries" make the advisory materials available to visitors but do not have trained advisors to assist students.

Beijing Consular District

Advisory center:
Chinese Service Center for Scholarly Exchange (CSCSE)
Beijing Language Institute
No. 15 Xueyuan Lu   TEL: 01-202-7149
Beijing 100083   FAX: 01-202-7147

Libraries:
Beijing National Library
39 Baishiqiao Lu   TEL: 01-841-5566
Beijing 100081   x2022/5252
                                     FAX: 01-841-9291

Tianjin Municipal Library
Fukang Lu   TEL: 022-36-1478 x262
Tianjin 300071

Study Abroad Training Department
Xi'an Foreign Languages Institute
Wujiafen
Xi'an, Shaanxi 710061

TEL: 029-71-1133

Shaanxi Provincial Library
146 Xi Dajie
Xi'an, Shaanxi 710002

TEL: 029-22-420

Hubei Provincial Library
Wuluo Lu, No. 45
Wuchang, Hubei 430060

TEL: 027-87-1284

Hebei Provincial Library
Shijiazhuang, Hebei 050011

TEL: 0311-64-3828

Henan Provincial Library
150 Songshan Nan Lu
Zhengzhou, Henan 450052

TEL: 0371-77-1425
or 77-1366

Shandong Provincial Library
275 Daming Hu Lu
Jinan, Shandong 250011

TEL: 0531-61-2338 x34

Shanxi Provincial Library
Taiyuan, Shanxi 030001

TEL: 0351-22-2353

Gansu Provincial Library
Lanzhou, Gansu 730000

TEL: 0931-28-982

Hunan Provincial Library
38 Shaoshan Lu
Changsha, Hunan 410011

TEL: 0731-42-9384

Jiangxi Provincial Library
Nanchang, Jiangxi 330008

TEL: 0791-65-093

Shanghai Consular District

Advisory center:
Shanghai Educational Information Center
 for International Exchanges
Shanghai International Studies
 University
410 Tiyuhui Dong Lu
Shanghai 200083

TEL: 021-544-2187
FAX: 021-544-2187

Libraries:
Reference Room of Foreign Universities
Shanghai Municipal Library
Nanjing Xi Lu, No. 325
Shanghai 200003   TEL: 021-327-3176

Shanghai Jiaotong University Library
1594 Huashan Lu
Shanghai 200030   TEL: 021-431-0310

East China Normal University Library
3663 Zhongshan Bei Lu
Shanghai 200062   TEL: 021-257-7577

Shanghai Bureau of Higher Education
202 Shaanxi Nan Lu
Shanghai 200031   TEL: 021-473-7605

Nanjing Library
66 Chengxian Jie
Nanjing, Jiangsu 210018   TEL: 025-63-4165

Zhejiang Provincial Library
102 Daxue Lu
Hangzhou, Zhejiang 310009   TEL: 0571-77-3414

Anhui Provincial Library
14 Wuhu Lu
Hefei, Anhui 230001   TEL: 0551-25-7602

Chengdu Consular District

Advisory centers:
Intensive Languages Training
   Center for Scientists Going Abroad
Chengdu University of
Science and Technology
Xingnanmenwai Moziqiao   TEL: 028-58-1851
Chengdu, Sichuan 610065   028-58-1554 x2540
                                                   TELEX: 60166 CUST CN

Study Abroad Training Department
Sichuan Foreign Languages Institute
Shapingba
Chongqing, Sichuan 630031 TEL: 0811-66-4940

Libraries:
Sichuan Provincial Library
Dongfeng Lu, No. 222 `
Chengdu, Sichuan 610016 TEL: 028-29-219

Guizhou Provincial Library
Guiyang, Guizhou 550001 TEL: 0851-62-6938

Guizhou Normal University Library
Huancheng Dong Lu
Guiyang, Guizhou 550003 TEL: 0851-62-7546

Yunnan Provincial Library
2 Cuihu Nan Lu
Kunming, Yunnan 650031 TEL: 0871-62-7546

Lhasa Kungshan Language School
5 Baguo Jie
Lhasa, Xizang 850001 TEL: 26-907

Guangzhou Consular District

Advisory center:
Guangzhou Advisory Office
of the Chinese Education Association
for International Exchanges (GAOCEAIE)
Guangdong Higher Education Bureau
225 Dongfeng Dong Lu TEL: 020-777-8110 x60
Guangzhou, Guangdong 510080 FAX: 020-776-6239

Libraries:
Guangzhou Municipal Library
Zhongshan Si Lu, No. 42
Guangzhou, Guangdong 510055 TEL: 020-333-3885

Fujian Provincial Library
39 Dong Jie
Fuzhou, Fujian 350001 TEL: 0591-55-1204

Guangxi Provincial Library
Minzu Dadao No. 22
Nanning, Guangxi 530022 TEL: 0771-27-441

Hainan University Library
Haikou
Hainan 570009   TEL: 0898-25-8112 x2419

Shenyang Consular District

Advisory center:
TOEFL Office and Educational
  Advisory Center
Dalian Foreign Languages Institute
110 Nanshan Lu, Zhongshan District   TEL: 0411-80-3121 x355
Dalian, Liaoning   FAX: 0411-23-9958

Libraries:
Liaoning Provincial Library
48 Shaoshuaifu Dong Hutong
Chaoyang Jie
Shenyang, Liaoning 110011   TEL: 024-44-5717

Jilin Provincial Library
10 Xinmin Dajie
Changchun, Jilin 130021   TEL: 0431-88-3796

Heilongjiang Provincial Library
Fendou Lu
Harbin, Heilongjiang 150001   TEL: 0451-22-4581

GENERAL REFERENCE WORKS CONTAINED IN THE COLLECTIONS

Accredited Institutions of Postsecondary Education 1992
Accredited Programs Leading to Degrees in Engineering, 1988
Accredited Programs Leading to Degrees in Engineering Technology
  1988
Adviser's Manual of Federal Regulations Affecting Foreign Students
  and Scholars 1992
Allied Health Education Directory 1992
American Art Directory
Arco's The Right College
Barron's Profiles of American Colleges
Cassidy The International Scholarship Book
Cassidy The Graduate Scholarship Book
Cassidy Alves The Scholarship Book
The College Handbook and Index of Majors (two volumes)

Comparative Guide to American Colleges 15th edition
1992 Directory of Engineering and Engineering Technology
  (undergraduate programs)
1992 Directory of Engineering Graduate Studies and Research
Directory of Graduate Programs: 15th Edition
  Volume A: Natural Sciences
  Volume B: Engineering and Business
  Volume C: Social Sciences and Education
  Volume D: Art, Humanities and Other Fields
Directory of Overseas Educational Advisory Centers 1992-93
English Language and Orientation Programs in the United States
Foundation Grants to Individuals
Funding for U.S. Studies
Higher Education Directory 1993
Lovejoy's College Guide, 21st edition
The National Guide for Training Programs to Educational Credit
Occupational Outlook Handbook 1992-93
The Official Guide to MBA Programs
Open Doors: 1991-92 Report on International Educational Exchange
Peterson's Annual Guides to Graduate Study, 1993 (six volumes)
  Graduate and Professional Programs: An Overview (Book 1)
  Graduate Programs in the Humanities and Social Sciences (Book 2)
  Graduate Programs in the Biological, Agricultural Sciences (Book 3)
  Graduate Programs in the Physical Sciences and Mathematics (Book 4)
  Graduate Programs in Engineering and Applied Sciences (Book 5)
  Graduate Programs in Business, Education, Health, and Law (Book 6)
Peterson's Guide to Four-Year Colleges 1993
Peterson's Guide to Two-Year Colleges 1993
Peterson's National College Databank
Profiles: Detailed Analyses of the Foreign Student Population 1989/90
World Directory of Medical Schools: 6th Edition

APPENDIX Q

Protocol Between the Government of the United States of
America and the Government of the People's Republic of
China for Cooperation in Educational Exchanges

The Government of the United States of America and the Government of the People's Republic of China [represented by the United States Information Agency and the State Education Commission of the People's Republic of China], hereinafter referred to as "the Parties," recognizing the role of education in furthering progress in both nations and in building understanding between the people of the two countries, subject to the "Agreement on Cooperation in Science and Technology between the Government of the United States of America and the Government of the People's Republic of China" and in accordance with the principles of the "Cultural Agreement between the Government of the United States of America and the Government of the People's Republic of China," have, with a view to promoting educational exchanges, agreed on activities of educational exchanges described in this accord.

ARTICLE I—GUIDING PRINCIPLES

The Parties agree and affirm that the principal objective of this accord is to provide opportunities for cooperation and exchange in educational fields based on equality, reciprocity and mutual benefit. Recognizing differences in the societies and systems of the two countries, both Parties will initiate educational exchange activities based on their own as well as mutual interests. The receiving side will facilitate and assist in implementing those educational exchange projects to every extent possible to assure that the requests of the sending side for study and research opportunities are met to the extent required in each case in accordance with each country's laws and regulations.

Both Parties will undertake measures to enhance educational exchange objectives. Scholarly data and information derived from activities under this accord may be made available to the world scholarly community through customary channels in accordance with the normal procedures the participating institutions and individuals would follow in their own countries.

Receiving institutions of each country will have final approval of students and scholars applying from the other country. Both Parties will, however, use their best efforts to assure the fulfillment of the principles of this accord.

The Parties further agree that the principles of this accord will be the basis of all official educational exchanges. While recognizing the independence of non-official arrangements, the Parties agree these principles should also be extended, to the degree applicable, to the full range of educational exchanges between the two countries.

The Parties will reach detailed agreement on specific programs through regular exchanges of letters or other instruments on at least an annual basis.

ARTICLE II—OFFICIAL EXCHANGES OF INDIVIDUALS

The Parties agree on the following categories of official exchanges of individuals:

(A) RESEARCH SCHOLARS   Each Party may select and sponsor scholars from its own country to engage in research in the other country. Each Party may select and sponsor scholars from the other country to engage in research in its own country. Scholars may be placed in association with educational research or other institutions relevant to the accomplishment of research objectives or may, with the approval of the host government, engage in independent research. Research fields will include the humanities, the social sciences, the natural sciences and the technological sciences.

(B) GRADUATE STUDENTS   Each Party may select and sponsor qualified graduates of institutions of higher learning or equivalent of its own country to pursue degree or non-degree graduate programs of study and research in the other country. Each Party may select and sponsor qualified graduates of institutions of higher learning or equivalent from the other country to pursue degree or non-degree graduate programs of study and research in its own country. Fields of study will include the humanities, the social sciences, the natural sciences and the technological sciences.

(C) TEACHERS AND LECTURERS   The Parties agree to encourage and sponsor teachers, lecturers, professors and other qualified people of the institutions of higher learning of their respective countries to teach or to give a series of lectures in the other country. Fields of teaching and lecturing will include the humanities, the social sciences, the natural sciences and the technological sciences.

ARTICLE III—OFFICIAL DELEGATIONS AND GROUP PROJECTS

The Parties agree to exchange delegations and groups in various educational fields which may include participation in joint meetings such as conferences and symposia in the areas of mutual interest as agreed.

ARTICLE IV—EXCHANGE OF MATERIALS

The Parties agree to encourage and facilitate the exchange of scholarly and other educational materials between educational and research institutions of both countries and individuals. Materials may include books, periodicals, monographs and audio-visual materials.

ARTICLE V—NON-OFFICIAL EXCHANGES

The Parties agree to continue to encourage and promote direct educational exchanges and cooperation between educational organizations, universities, colleges, schools, research institutions and individuals of their respective countries. The assistance to these exchanges should be facilitated in accordance with each country's laws and regulations.

ARTICLE VI—FINANCIAL PROVISIONS

(A) The Parties agree that the expenses of official delegations and groups under the auspices of Article III of this accord will be as follows: The sending side shall bear the two-way international travel expenses of the delegation or group. The receiving side shall bear the expenses of board and lodging, transportation, and medical care or health and accident insurance when the delegation or group is in its territory; any exception to these provisions shall be determined by written agreement of the Parties.

(B) The Parties agree that the necessary expenses for the official exchange of individuals under the auspices of Article II of this accord shall be based on the principle that the sending side pays the costs associated with its participants. Exceptions to this principle will be by agreement of the Parties.

(C) The Fulbright and university-to-university affiliations programs, and other designated programs shall share certain costs mutually agreed by the Parties and the participating institutions.

(D) The financial provisions for non-official exchanges shall be determined by the participating institutions, the Parties recognizing that public and private institutions of both countries have limited capacity to support educational exchange activities.

(E) The Parties agree that activities under this accord shall be carried out subject to the availability of funds.

ARTICLE VII - EXECUTIVE AGENTS

(A) The Executive Agent of this accord on the United States side shall be the United States Information Agency. The Executive Agent of this accord on the People's Republic of China side shall be the State Education Commission of the People's Republic of China.

(B) Upon signature, this accord will become a part of the official agreements concluded under Article 5 of the Agreement between the Government of the United States of America and the Government of the People's Republic of China on Cooperation in Science and Technology signed January 31, 1979, extended January 12, 1984.

(C) As agreed by the Executive Agents of the Parties, the representatives of agencies or organizations concerned in both countries will exchange visits for the working out of plans and programs of educational exchange and for discussing progress, problems and matters related to educational exchange projects. These meetings may be held in the United States of America or in the People's Republic of China as agreed.

(D) This accord will supersede "The Understanding on Exchange of Students between the United States of America and the People's Republic of China" reached in October 1978, and be the guiding document for educational exchange of the two countries.

This accord shall enter into force upon signature and remain in force for a five-year period. It may be amended or extended by the written agreement of the two parties; it may be terminated by either Party by giving six months' written notice to the other Party of its intention to terminate.

Done at Washington, this 23rd day of July 1985, in duplicate in the English and Chinese languages, both equally authentic.

RONALD REAGAN

LI XIANNIAN

For the Government of the
United States of America

For the Government of the
People's Republic of China

Index

A

Academic calendar, 81-82
AIDS, 15, 16
Air China, 23
Airline travel, 46-47
  within China, 150, 216
  departure arrangements, 153, 154
Alcoholic beverages, 21, 61, 63, 106
Allergies, 17, 62
American Council of Learned
  Societies, 2, 159-161
American Express, 212-213
  emergency check cashing locations,
  211-212
Anhui Province, 21
Anthropological research, 102, 107
Appliances, electric, 27, 30-31, 40, 41-
  42
Archeology, 84
Archival research, 92-97
  procedures, 225-226
Arrival in China, 46-48
  customs regulations, 20-23
  registration with U.S. embassy, 138
Asian Cultural Council, 161-162
Association of International
  Educators, 4
Ayi, 27, 75, 78

B

Baggage
  allowances, 23
  customs procedures, 21-22
  train travel, 151
Banking, 18-20, 142-143
  emergency check cashing locations,
  211-212
Banquets, 61-64, 104-105, 106, 118
Batteries, 31, 33
BBC, 35
Beijing
  availability of reading matter in,
  37-38, 41
  banking in, 142
  computer supplies/repairs in, 33-
  34
  cost of research services in, 217-218
  exercise clubs in, 148
  guidebooks, 40
  health care in, 13, 14, 16-18, 146
  hotels, 214
  public transportation, 147
  restaurants, 149
  schools for children of visitors, 79,
  81
  sightseeing, 149
  student advisory resource centers
  in, 233-234
  U.S. government services in, 139
  weather, 17, 26

243

Beijing Language Institute, 81
Beijing Review, 7
Beijing University, Princeton-in-Asia
program, 130-131
Bicycles, 37, 148, 216
Black market, 65
Blue Shield International, 16
Books. *See* Reading material
Buses, 147
Business cards, 39

C

Calculators, 41
Cameras. *See* Film equipment
Center for Field Research, 162-163
Center for International Education,
170-171
Centers for Disease Control and
Prevention, 13
Changchun, 8, 215
Changsha, 214
Chengdu, 9, 139, 218
student advisory resource centers
in, 235-236
Chiang Ching-kuo Foundation, 160-
161, 163-164
Children. *See* Spouses and children
China Advocates, 198
China Daily, 35, 38, 40
China Educational Exchange, 198
China Educational Tours, 4
China Exchange News, 32, 107, 109
China Health and Nutrition Survey,
100
China National Tourist Office, 46
China Reconstructs, 7
China Travel Service, 11, 12, 47, 150
Chinese Academy of Sciences (CAS),
87-88, 90, 110, 460
Chinese Academy of Traditional
Medicine, 146
Chinese government
banking, 142-143
control of printed matter, 21
currency, 142
customs regulations, 20-23
educational exchange agreement
with U.S., 239-242
foreign affairs office in, 51-53
health examination requirements, 15

offices in U.S., 9, 10
photography restrictions, 36
postal services, 140-142
regulations, 65-68
research bureaucracy, 86-89
surveillance of visitors, 55-56
tax policy, 24, 66
travel permits, 150
work unit and, 48-59
Chinese language instruction
in China, 35, 128, 173-176
in Chinese-language institutes, 132-
133
in Taiwan, 130
in U.S., 130
U.S.-sponsored programs for, 3-4,
131-132
Christmas, 69, 82
Cigarettes, 21, 38
Civil Aviation Administration, 150
Classified information, 66
Clothing
availability in China, 25
cleaning, 27
mailing restrictions, 23
purchasing, in China, 28
repairs, 27-28
tailors in China, 27
wardrobe planning, 26-27, 28
Coffee, 24, 30
Collaborative research, 84, 86-87, 98,
100, 103
copublishing and, 111
laboratory work and, 111
model for, 99
reciprocity in, 111
survey research, 109
Colleges and universities, Chinese
academic regulations in, 189-193
archival resources of, 93
commercial activities in, 49, 53, 84,
95-96, 100-101
decision-making in, 87
eligibility for enrollment in, 184-
185
enrollment procedure, 4, 18, 133-
134, 185-186
list of, 177-183
political considerations in, 50
research environment in, 83-84, 94
student preparation for, 186-187

teaching opportunities sponsored by, 6-7
work units in, 49-50
Colleges and universities, U.S.
study programs sponsored by, 4, 130-132
teaching opportunities sponsored by, 5
Colorado China Council, 198
Committee on Advanced Study in China, 91-92
Committee on Scholarly Communication with China, 2, 3, 98-99, 164-165
CompuServe, 143-144
Computers, 32-34, 41, 68
Condoms, 17
Conferences, 114
Contraceptives, 17
Contracts
researcher, 89
teacher, 7, 117-118, 205-210
Copying machines/services, 41-42, 43
in libraries, 96-97
Costs
of banquets, 62-63
bicycle, 37, 216
in Chinese hospitals, 147
of Chinese-made goods, 25
of computers, 33
currency type and, 65
customs deposits, 108
of domestic air travel in China, 150
of fax services, 143
of field research, 100-102
of film supplies, 35-36
food, 29, 30
foreign expert buildings, 214-216
health certification, 15
of hired cook, 75
hotel, 75-76, 214
housing, 69-71
laundry, 27
of library services, 95-96
motor vehicle, 230
of passports and visas, 9
of postal services in China, 140-142
of research, 90-91, 217-219
of schools for children of visitors, 79, 80, 81
taxi, 48, 147, 216

train travel, 151, 152
of tuition in Chinese colleges/ universities, 187-188
of typewriters, 31
of Western goods in China, 25
Council for International Exchange of Scholars. See Fulbright awards
Council on International Educational Exchange, 4
Credit cards, 19, 20, 216
Cultural relics, 66
Cultural revolution, 50
Currency. See Banking; Money
Customs regulations, 20-22, 34, 47
bonds, 108
departure from China, 154
educational equipment, 44
film equipment, 36
research equipment, 108
U.S., 22-23

D

Danwei. See Work unit
Dental care, 18, 216
Departure for China, preparations for
assessment of current conditions, 8, 9
baggage and shipping, 23
customs regulations, 20-23
for field researchers, 97-98
health considerations, 12-18
individual considerations, 8
negotiating research fees, 101-102
passports and visas, 9-12
personal needs, 24-39
planning for arrival, 46-48
professional considerations, 39-45
for short-term academic visit, 113-114
for students, 136
suggested reading, 24
supplies, 17-18
tax considerations, 24
for teachers, 115-116
Departure from China
customs regulations, 20-21
goodbyes, 153-154
possession of classified material, 66
shipping arrangements, 153
taking cultural artifacts, 66

travel arrangements, 153, 154
U.S. customs, 22-23
via Hong Kong, 153
Detention, 67
Dictionary, 42
Dissertation research, 3
Dry cleaning, 27

E

E-mail, 143-144
Earthwatch, 3
Electricity in China, 29-33, 40, 124
Embassies, U.S., 138-140, 146
Embassy/consular offices, Chinese, in
U.S., 9, 10
Emergencies
check cashing, 211-212
medical, 146, 147
U.S. embassy services, 138
visa authorization, 11
English language teachers in China
credentials, 6-7
opportunities for, 7, 116
resources for, 43-44
workload, 119
Entertainment, 148-149
Ethical issues, possession of classified
information, 66
Exercise, 148
Eye care, 17-18

F

Family. *See* Spouses and children
Fax machines/services, 34, 143
Fellowships and grants
for book purchases, 43
for research, 1-3
sources of, 159-172
Field research
Chinese collaborators in, 103
costs, 100-102
drivers and vehicles for, 105, 229-
231
electrical power considerations, 30-
31
in ethnic minority areas, 107
evolution of Chinese policy on, 98-
99
foreign affairs office and, 102-103

funding sources, 162-163
health considerations in, 106
interpreters in, 104
laboratory conditions, 110
local officials and, 104-105
maps for, 231-232
opportunities for, 98
personal supplies for, 24-25
placement in field, 102
preparations, 97-98, 99
research assistants in, 103-104
research proposal for, 89
site considerations, 105-107
supplies, 107-108, 227-232
Film equipment, 35-36
brought into China, 21, 22
Film processing, 36
First-aid kit, 17
Fogarty International Center, 165-166
Food/dining, 25, 29
field conditions, 106-107, 228-229
home preparation, 29, 30, 73, 75
in hotels, 76
in restaurants, 29, 39, 62-63, 73, 75
at ritual banquets, 61-62
on trains, 151
Western, in China, 30, 149
Footwear, 26, 28
Ford Foundation, 98
Foreign affairs office, 51-53, 84
field research and, 102-103
teacher's relations with, 117-118
Foreign community, 68-69
Foreign exchange currency, 142
Foreign Experts Bureau, 7, 11
Foreign experts in China
buildings for, 214-216
contract for, 205-210
housing for, 70
recruitment of, 6
salary and compensation, 6
visas, 11
vs. foreign teacher, 6
see also Teaching in China
Foreign Language Press, 7
Foreign teachers in China
application process, 7
attire, 26
contracts for, 7, 205-210
course content considerations, 66
English language teachers, 6-7, 43, 116

housing for, 70
opportunities for, 5-7
opportunities for spouses of, 7
preparations for departure to
China, 42-45
recruitment of, 6-7
salary and compensation, 7
special amenities for, 56-57
visas, 11
vs. foreign expert, 6
see also Teaching in China
Free-lance work, 24
Friendship Stores, 25, 30, 35, 37, 39,
40, 76, 153
Fudan University, 147
Fulbright awards, 5, 43, 164
Fuzhou, 215

G

Games, 38
Gamma globulin, 13, 14
Geology, 99
Gifts
brought from China, 22
brought into China, 21
for Chinese colleagues/friends, 38-
39, 153-154
recorded music, 35
ritual observances in giving of, 64
Global Positioning Systems, 232
Graduate/postgraduate studies, 1-2, 91
funding sources, 159-172
Group travel, 23
Guangxi, 215
Guangzhou, 80
student advisory resource centers
in, 236-237
U.S. consulate in, 140
Guanxi, 58-60, 85, 88-89, 99-100
Guidebooks, 40

H

Hangzhou, 214, 215
Health
certification, 15, 196-197
cold weather preparations, 26-27
dining considerations, 29
field research and, 106
funding for science research in,
165-166

of hired help, 78
insurance, 16
pediatric care, 77, 79
preparations for departure to
China, 12-16
Rh-negative blood supply in China,
146
services in China, 145-147, 216-217
supplies, 17-18
water treatment and, 227-228
HIV/AIDS, 15, 16
Holidays, 81-82, 192-193
Hong Kong, 12, 36, 41, 46, 153
Hopkins-Nanjing Center, 4-5, 69
Hospitals, 146
Hotels, 71, 75-77, 112
costs, 214
food in, 29, 30, 149
laundry services in, 27
payment in, 20
shuttle buses, 48
telephone communications in, 145
traveling in China, 150
Housing
campus apartments, 74-75
cleanliness of, 25
costs, 69-71
dining facilities, 29, 70, 73
for families, 77-78
in field research, 106, 229
in foreign community, 68-69
for foreign experts, 6, 214-216
for foreign teachers, 7
for friends/relatives visiting
foreigners in China, 12
hotels, 75-77
management of, 55
quality of, 56-57
in rural areas, 71
storage space, 26
student dormitories, 72-74, 188
Humanities
research environment, 88
research funding, 2, 3, 159-162, 163-
165, 167-168

I

Identification
card, 49
medical, 146

photographs for, 37
see also Passports; Visas
Immunizations, 13
Insurance, 16
Intellectual property rights, 90
Internal Revenue Service, 24
International Medical Center, Beijing,
13, 14, 17, 146
International School of Beijing, 79
International Schools Service, 199
International Scientific and
Information Services, Inc., 199
Interpersonal relations
among professionals, 125-126, 127
appropriate behavior for visitors,
56
Chinese style, 54-55, 57, 118-119
concept of privacy in, 54
departure from China, 153-154
with foreign affairs office, 51-53
in foreign communities, 68-69
gift giving, 21, 35, 38-39
guanxi concept, 58-60
meeting fellow students,
opportunities for, 135-136
political issues in, 57-58
reciprocity in, 60
research process and, 85
with research team drivers, 105
role of ritual in, 60-61
romantic relationships, 67
student-teacher, 116, 124, 126-127,
137
taking of photographs and, 36
in work unit, 50-51
Interpreters
classroom instruction and, 121-122
for field research, 104
specialized dictionaries for, 42

J

Japan, 12
Japanese encephalitis, 14
Jiangsu Province, 21
Johns Hopkins University, 4-5, 69
Joint Committee on Chinese Studies, 2

K

Kress Foundation, 166-167

L

Laboratory research, 42, 110-112
Lanzhou, 41
Laundry, 27
Legal issues, 65-68
China-U.S. educational exchange
protocols, 239-242
for foreign students, 191-192
intellectual property rights, 90
see also Chinese government
Libraries, 92-97
general reference works in, 237-238
student advisory resource centers
in, 233-237
see also Archival research
Lindbergh Fund, 167
Liuban, 51
Luce Foundation, 2, 98, 167-168
Lunar New Year, 81

M

Malaria, 13-14
Maps, 231-232
May Day, 82
Medicines
brought into China, 13, 17, 21
Chinese, 146
mailing of, 142
syringes for, 14
Meetings, 64
Microfilm, 96, 97
Milk, 29
Minorities of China, 107
Money
banking in China, 18-20, 142-143
conversion, 6, 65, 142
currency and banking in China,
142-143
departure arrangements, 154
emergency check cashing, 211-212
transactions in remote areas, 105-
106
traveler's checks, 19-20
from U.S. sources, 18-19
see also Costs
Montessori School, 79, 80
Motor vehicles, 147, 229-231
Movie-theaters, 148
Music, Chinese, 35, 135, 148-149

N

NAFSA, 4
Nanjing, 218
Nanjing University, 4-5, 69, 94
National Council of Churches of
   Christ, 199
National Day, 82
National Endowment for the
   Humanities, 2, 168
National Geographic Society, 3, 169
National Program for Advanced
   Study in Research in China, 2, 3,
   164-165
National Science Foundation, 2-3, 90,
   98, 110, 170
Neibu material, 66
Newspapers and periodicals, 7
   Chinese, 38, 40, 41
   Western, availability of, 37-38

O

Office equipment, 31-32, 41-42
Opera, 148

P

Parks, 148
Passports, 138
   cost of, 9
   forms for, 194-197
   preparations for departure to
      China, 9-12
   renewing, 65
   types of, 9
Peace Corps, 5
Peking Union Medical College, 17,
   146, 147
Peking University, 50, 94, 97, 147
Pets, 22
Pinyin romanization, 141
Plagiarism, 124
Political context
   of academic institutions, 50
   of friendships, 57-58
   research in ethnic minority areas,
      107
   survey research and, 109
   visitor behavior, 55-56
   visitor's privacy and, 55

Postal services, 140-142
Princeton-in-Asia, 130-131, 199
Printed matter
   shipping, 23
Privacy, 54-55, 56
Proposal for research, 89-90
Public Security Bureau, 65-66, 150
Public transportation, 147

Q

Questionnaires, research, 109-110

R

Rabies, 106
Radios, 35
Reading material
   availability in China, 37-38, 42
   classified information, 66
   for classroom instruction, 121, 125
   confiscation of, 21
   as gift, 38
   needs of foreign teachers in China,
      42-44
   newspapers, Chinese/Western, 7,
      37-38, 40, 41
   professional/scholarly resources,
      40-41, 42-44
   resources about China, 24, 40, 220-
      224
   specialized dictionaries, 42
Religious practice, 67, 136
Researchers and scholars in China
   academic environment, 83-85
   affiliations of, 93-94
   archival research, 92-97
   costs of research for, 90-91, 95-96,
      217-219
   formal invitation to, 91-92
   funding sources for, 1-3, 159-172
   guidelines for research proposal,
      89-91
   housing for, 70-71
   laboratory considerations, 110-112
   preparations for departure, 40-42
   relations with host unit, 84, 85-89
   short-term visits, 112-114
   special amenities for, 56-57
   survey research, 109-110
   travel within China, 152

See also Field research
Restaurants, 29, 62-63, 107, 149
    treating colleagues and friends, 39
Rh-negative blood, 146
Ritual
    of banquets, 61-64, 118
    role of, 60-61
Rural areas
    banquets in, 106
    consumer goods in, 24-25
    health considerations, 13, 14
    housing in, 71
    monetary transactions in, 105-106
    social science fieldwork in, 98-100

S

Salary and compensation
    for foreign expert in China, 6
    for foreign teachers in China, 7
    for interviewers/interviewees, 110
    tax policies, 24
    from U.S. sources, 18-19
Sanitary napkins, 17
Schools for children of visitors, 77, 78-81
Scientific equipment
    in Chinese laboratories, 110-111
    customs regulations, 21-22, 108
    for field research, 107-108
    research needs, 41-42
Shandong Province, 99
Shandung University, 94
Shanghai, 80, 140, 147, 214, 215, 218-219
    customs officials, 21
    student advisory resource centers in, 234-235
Shashi, 215
Shenyang, 80, 140, 237
Shifu, 73
Shipping
    into China, 22, 23
    costs, 217
    of equipment, 108
    out of China, 22, 153
    postal services in China, 140-142
Shopping in China, 25
    for clothing, 28
    for food and cooking supplies, 29, 30

Short-term academic visits, 112-114
Shortwave radios, 35
Sister-city programs, 136
Smithsonian Institution, 3
Social life
    for foreign teachers in China, 126-127
    reciprocity in, 60
    recreation and entertainment, 148-149
    ritual in, 60-64
    student-teacher interaction, 116
Social Science Research Council, 2
Social sciences
    fieldwork, 98-108
    research, 86, 88
    research funding, 2, 3, 159-161, 163-165, 167-168
    survey research, 109-110
Software, 34
Sports, 135, 148
Spouses and children, 25, 38
    employment opportunities, 7
    of foreign expert in China, 6
    housing for, 77-78
    passport/visa considerations, 9
    regulations regarding, 77
    schooling for, 77, 78-81
Spring Festival, 81
Stamps, 39
Stanford University, 99
State Education Commission, 11, 86-87, 88, 109
Students, Chinese
    academic preparation of, 123, 124
    advisory/resource centers for, 233-237
    class participation by, 120, 122-123
    English language ability, 121-122
    observations from foreign teachers, 120-121
    organizations, 123
    student-teacher relations, 116, 123, 126-127, 137
    study habits, 43
    workload expectations, 123
Students, foreign
    in Chinese-language institutes, 132-133
    daily living for, 134-136

enrollment in Chinese university,
    133-134, 184-188
expenses for, 187-188
foreign affairs office for, 51, 52
housing for, 69-70, 72-74
library fees, 95-96
opportunities for, 3-5, 130-132
school regulations, 189-193
spouses and children of, 77
travel in China, 136, 152
tutors for, 136-137
visas, 11
visits from friends/relatives, 12
Summer, 112
Supplies
    camera/film, 35-36
    classroom, 124-125
    costs, 217
    for daily living, 24-39
    electrical, 30, 31-34
    for fieldwork, 107-108, 227-232
    food and cooking, 29-30
    health and hygiene, 17-18
    identification photographs, 37
    medical, 13, 14, 17, 21
    office, 34-35, 42
    for researchers going to China, 40-
        42
    roach killer, 75
    sewing, 27
    tape recorder, 35
    for teachers going to China, 42-45
    Western, in China, 18, 25
Surveillance, 55
Survey research, 109-110

T

Tape recorders, 30, 31, 35, 41, 44
Taxes, 24, 66
    departure, 154
Taxi service, 47-48, 147, 216
Teaching English as a Second
    Language, 116
Teaching in China
    adjustment process, 128-129
    application for, 201-204
    bureaucratic relations, 117-119
    contract for, 205-210
    establishing terms/conditions of,
        117-118

materials for, 116
non-academic responsibilities, 119
opportunities for, 116
professional relationships, 125-126,
    127
role of teacher in China, 116
size of classes, 119
sponsorship sources, 198-200
student-centered approach, 121
student-teacher relations, 123, 126-
    127
working conditions, 124-125
workloads, 119-120
see also Foreign experts in China;
    Foreign teachers in China;
    Students, Chinese
Telephone communications, 13, 73,
    144-145
E-mail, 143-144
fax machines/services, 34-35, 143
Television, 148
Test of English as a Foreign
    Language, 43
Textbooks, 42-43
Theft, 68, 151-152
    bicycle, 37
    precautions, 32
Tiananmen Square, 50, 58, 109
Tianjin, 80, 216, 219
Tibet, 107
Time zones, 145
Toiletries, 17-18
Tourist season, 12, 113, 153
Train travel, 70, 71-72, 150-152
Travel in China, 112, 149-152
    car rental, 147
    costs, 216
    domestic airlines, 150
    drivers and vehicles, 38, 105, 229-
        231
    off-limits areas, 65
    permits, 65-66
    permits for, 150
    preparations for, 12
    scheduling, 81, 82
    taxi service, 47-48
    urban transportation, 147-148
    via train, 70, 71-72, 150, 151-152
Traveler's checks, 19-20, 143
Tutors, 81, 136-137
Typewriters, 30, 31-32, 41

U

United Board for Christian Higher Education in Asia, 199
United States
  Department of Education fellowships, 170-171
  educational exchange agreement with China, 239-242
  embassies/consulates in China, 138-140
  opportunities for Chinese colleagues in, 103, 111
  preparations for return to, 22-23
  questions about, 44-45, 54
  schools in China, 80
United States-China Cooperative Research Program, 2
Universities. *See* Colleges and universities, Chinese; Colleges and universities, U.S.
U.S. Information Agency, 5

V

Vacations, 81-82
Vehicles, 105
Video equipment, 36, 40, 44, 125
Viral hepatitis A, 13, 14
Visas, 9-12, 194-195
Visual and performing arts, research funding for, 161-162
Voice of America, 35
Volunteers in Asia, 199

W

Waiban. See Foreign affairs office
Water, 30, 227-228
Western Washington University, 199
Winter, 8, 17, 26-27, 28, 29, 69
Work schedules, 89-90
Work units
  in academic settings, 49-50
  authority in, 86
  characteristics of, 48-51
  field research and, 100-101
  health services in, 145-146
  individual differences in, 53
  interpersonal relations in, 50-51
  mail distribution in, 141
  meals, 76
  research environment and, 84, 85-89
  teacher's relations with, 117
  welcoming banquet, 61
World Bank, 171-172
World Wildlife Fund, 3
WorldTeach, 200

X

Xiamen, 216, 219
Xi'an, 41
Xinhua News Agency, 7
Xinjiang, 107
Xitong, 86, 87, 88, 89

Z

Zhejiang Province, 21
Zouping County, 99